Cults, Martyrs and Good Samaritans

Religion in Contemporary English Political Discourse

James Crossley

First published 2018 by Pluto Press
345 Archway Road, London N6 5AA

www.plutobooks.com

Copyright © James Crossley 2018

The right of James Crossley to be identified as the author of this work
has been asserted by him in accordance with the Copyright, Designs
and Patents Act 1988.

British Library Cataloguing in Publication Data
A catalogue record for this book is available from the British Library

ISBN 978 0 7453 3829 3   Hardback
ISBN 978 0 7453 3828 6   Paperback
ISBN 978 1 7868 0309 2   PDF eBook
ISBN 978 1 7868 0311 5   Kindle eBook
ISBN 978 1 7868 0310 8   EPUB eBook

This book is printed on paper suitable for recycling and made from fully
managed and sustained forest sources. Logging, pulping and manufacturing
processes are expected to conform to the environmental standards of the
country of origin.

Typeset by Stanford DTP Services, Northampton, England

Simultaneously printed in the United Kingdom and United States of America

Contents

Introduction

At the time of writing, there is not yet a political position that has dominated English political discourse after the 2007/8 economic crisis. In other words, we do not know the settled, long-term successor to Thatcherite neoliberalism. We may still be in the midst of the chaos before the new settlement emerges. Or we might be at the beginning of a state of semi-permanent chaos and contradiction. Or we might be in for an intensified version of what came before. Or perhaps there is an impending catastrophe which will then open up a reordering of the world; as Slavoj Žižek put it, 'the light at the end of the tunnel is probably the headlight of another train approaching us from the opposite direction'.[1] Whatever might happen in the future, this book is a history, a retrospective look at the different options that emerged, and were vying for dominance, in the midst of the post-2008 crisis of capitalism. But more specifically still, this book is a look at how ideas and assumptions about 'religion' and commonly related language about, for instance, Christianity, the Bible and Islam, were tied up with, and typically provided an authority for, dominant ideological shifts in English political discourse with particular reference to changes since the financial crash. Before we move on to such ideas, there is the inevitable question of definitions. And definitions relating to 'religion' can be especially slippery.

What 'religion' means

If we want to know about how and why religion has been used in contemporary politics we could begin with the difficult, seemingly preliminary question of definition: 'What is religion?' This is, of course, a loaded question. Any attempt at defining 'religion' might immediately lead to debates or confusion over inclusion (are yoga and football 'religions' or are their participants behaving in a 'religious' manner?) or it might introduce concepts that are too broad to be analytically useful (is that which gives meaning to life somehow 'religious' or 'religion'?). What I want to do is to avoid coming at the question from such debatable angles. This is not to dismiss the importance of all issues associated with the critical study of religion (e.g., ritual, sacred, profane, symbolism, meaning) but rather

I want to select a particular focus of study, in this case one which looks at how and why language popularly assumed to be about, or related to, 'religion' has been used. In other words, the approach to the critical study of religion which suits my interests and purposes is that which works at the level of discourse and ideology, and with a materialist grounding.[2] Put yet another way, the initial question could now be reformulated: 'What do people mean when they talk, write or make assumptions about "religion" and terms commonly associated with such language (e.g., Christianity, Muslim, sect, cult, God, gods, martyr, Bible, etc.)?' This will mean that I will not be providing an external, fixed definition of 'religion' other than working with popularly assumed definitions, nor assessing truth claims by insiders, nor deciding whether a given tradition is 'really about' peace or violence, nor making judgements about what 'true' or 'false' Christianity, Judaism, Islam, or religion might be. Instead, I am looking at how such language popularly understood has been used to legitimate the development of, maintenance of, or opposition to various ideological positions or social formations in English political discourse. This does not necessarily mean that politicians, journalists or activists necessarily identified as 'religious' or 'Christian' when they (say) alluded to the Bible, or indeed that they necessarily knew that they were alluding to a biblical text. Whether people consciously used such language or not, and whether they consciously used language in a way identified as 'religious' or not, is in many ways irrelevant because we can still see how meanings changed over time irrespective of the intentions of speakers and authors. After all, we all use words and phrases that are sometimes uncritically and unthinkingly inherited from our cultural contexts, and language associated with 'religion' is but one example.

It may have been noticed that the examples of 'religious' language I chose above are popular examples associated with Christianity, Judaism and Islam. The main reason for this is because of my choice of 'English political discourse' as the area of focus. In parliamentary politics, Christianity has historically been the dominant reference point until the late 1980s (especially after the Salman Rushdie affair) and 9/11 when Islam and Muslims (typically understood in connection with an Oriental religiosity) became the object of even more intense scrutiny. Despite the recurrence of issues relating to antisemitism, Judaism constructed in terms of 'religion' has not been as prominent in English political discourse post-Thatcher, with the emphasis far more likely to be on more contentious racial issues and has thus been used in such a way in an attempt to critique the Labour Left on the issues of Palestine, Israel and Zionism. Non-Christian, non-Muslim and non-Jewish viewpoints have not been entirely absent in English political discourse either. Occasionally, they are present but part of my choice of subjects (alongside the limits of my expertise) involved covering language most associated with Christianity, Islam and to lesser extent Judaism because of the sort of language fore-grounded in parliamentary politics.

As this indicates, the reasons for the prominence of Islam and Muslims in English political discourse is obvious enough, and we will turn to further reasons behind such interests throughout this book. Reasons for Christianity being prominent may not be as well known, but they are relatively straightforward. While some explanations are as simple as Christianity being central in a politician's life (so, for example, Tony Blair) or upbringing (so, for example, Theresa May), there are broader historic reasons and inherited language, whether involving bishops in the House of Lords, vestiges of Conservative Anglicanism or Liberal Non-conformity, Thatcher's courting of a morally conservative Christianity, or the emotive role of Nonconformist, Catholic and Jewish traditions in the foundation and development of the Labour Party and trade union movement. While there is no serious Christian vote of the sort that might swing an election, politicians remain wary of isolating a denomi-national vote or pressure groups and so a well-placed allusion or even bill amendment could still potentially keep such people onside.[3] These are also the sorts of 'religious' traditions that might play well with the press, particularly the right-wing media, and earn a favourable headline. But the perception of *too much* Christianity (e.g., details of doctrine, practices deemed culturally odd, illiberal views) or inauthenticity means that, for a politician, much care needs to be exercised. We will see in Chapter 4 that there is some evidence that 'too much' religion was off-putting to certain voters in certain parts of the country. Nevertheless, the historic, political and cultural backgrounds and contexts means that Christian-ity and the Bible has functioned as (an often implicit) justification for any given political position on economics, foreign policy, social change, race, gender or sexuality, or parliamentary democracy more generally. What Erin Runions calls 'theodemocracy' with particular reference to American political discourse can be applied to English political discourse, even if it has been less overt.[4]

Similar points can be made about the choice of 'English political discourse'. Again, decisions always have to be made by a historian or interpreter and this often reflects areas of taste, interest and expertise. By 'English political discourse' I am primarily referring to the kinds of debates present in mainstream parliamentary politics, national media engagement, and their relationship with the electorate. Other ways of looking at notions of religion and politics might be to look at, for instance, pronouncements by the Church of England, a public theologian, a representative of a given tradition, or even the ways in which Christians pray or read the Bible in Parliament away from the public gaze. While these voices will not be ignored entirely (and they already receive much attention from theologians), and while I make no claims about what is a valid and invalid choice of study, I will keep the focus connected more with politicians, parties, newspapers, voter interests, pressure groups, and political or ideological histories, if only because this (in conjunction with the study of religion) is an under-investigated area, albeit one that seems to be growing.[5]

The choice of 'English', while doubtlessly reflecting my own biases and upbringing, is deliberate in the sense that 'British' (for instance) would require a bigger and different book. Religion in each of the non-English nations of the British Isles involves specific cultural and historical issues which are not significantly present in English-based politics (just think what 'religion' means in Belfast and Glasgow, for instance). Nevertheless, this is not to narrow down what should and should not be deemed 'English' for which I deliberately give no fixed definition beyond political discourses taking place in, or having connection with, England, Parliament and the home and primary audience of the English-based media. White voices in political discourses might be represented at the expense of others because of the demographics and interests of Parliament and journalism but in analysing English political discourse I hope to show how and why religion, ethnicity and nationalism are constructed, which in turn ought to show how stable, unstable, historically contingent and ideologically loaded such dominant constructions can be rather than merely replicating such discrimination.

Chronological starting points and subjects of study are also choices any historian has to make. My choices about the ways religion and related language have been understood are framed around major social, economic and ideological changes over the past 50 years, particularly the emergence, acceptance and crises of neoliberalism. More precisely, the bulk of this book will involve looking at the kinds of options that were available roughly between the two General Elections in 2015 and 2017, though generated by the crisis of 2007/8. While I focus on expected figures of recent years (e.g., party leaders), there is no reason why any other aspect of culture should not be brought in to illuminate historical changes, something I indeed do in this book (whether Monty Python, Barrovians, or fighters in northern Syria). Both the alien and the familiar, not to mention the unacknowledged, will always tell us something about a given time and context, no matter how we value them. No doubt other examples could have been chosen but those discussed in this book provide insight into some of the most notable shifts in the ways religion and related terms were constructed from the rise of Jeremy Corbyn, through the Brexit vote, and up to the 2017 General Election, though Chapter 1 will provide contextualisation in terms of post-1960s political discourse. To use an exaggerated analogy from the Bible or Christopher Hill (whichever you prefer), the post-2008 world is a world at least partially turned upside down and has thrown up a range of different ideological options, the long-term consequences of which we may not know for years, and the fate of some of these options may become long forgotten or morph into something quite different.

This book: from chaos to…?

In this book, I continue investigating my interests in the ways sustained social, political and economic upheaval can generate a range of contradictory ideas (including those relating to religion) from radical egalitarianism to reactionary nationalism, as well as their (often unintended) longer-term consequences. There is always subjective judgement involved in delineating what counts as such upheaval, but I think some relatively uncontroversial comments can be made. Changes in economic accumulation and social attitudes in the 1960s and 1970s generated a range of seemingly contradictory ideological reactions but, out of the chaos, the Thatcherite, neoliberal economic settlement in English political discourse (and, of course, beyond) emerged dominant and replaced the state-interventionist or Keynesian post-war settlement. Over the following decades, neoliberalism became accepted or assumed in mainstream English political discourse (e.g., Parliament, national media), though not without its challenges, differences, tweaks and qualifications. However, since the financial crash, the dominance of neoliberalism in English political discourse (and, of course, beyond) has been challenged like never before, with ideological reactions or political options ranging from intensification of neoliberalism (e.g., David Cameron's governments), through toying with nativism or ethnonationalism (e.g., EDL, UKIP, Theresa May), to bringing back socialism to mainstream politics (e.g., Jeremy Corbyn, Momentum).

What is particularly distinctive about this book is, of course, that I am looking at these changes through political assumptions about 'religion' and related terms. In one sense, the contemporary interest in Islam and Muslims shows how ideas relating to religion are common in English political discourse. But in another sense, a focus on religion might seem unusual. For a start, religion is not a regular feature of everyday political rhetoric. To some people based in, or familiar with, certain parts of England and English politics, this might seem a peculiar thing to do because we are not, to put it one way, dealing with American political discourse. Nevertheless, perspective is everything. When I have given papers on such topics at conferences, I am used to the surprise at the discovery of the amount of religious rhetoric in English political discourse. However, an Australian academic at one such conference, who had recently moved to the UK, said to me that he could not believe 'how religious' the UK is, and cited nativity plays and school hymns as evidence. Though this might have been obvious to someone coming from Australia, in some ways this was a surprise to me having been born and raised in the UK and, more specifically, in a town (Barrow-in-Furness) where I have never perceived religion to be foregrounded in public life. But I also grew up with nativity plays and school hymns and, like others, I could mime to hymns, deliberately insert the wrong words, try not to laugh at old-fashioned turns of phrase, and barely pay attention in moralistic assemblies illuminating biblical stories without remembering that something thoroughgoingly 'religious' had been happening in my life. On the other hand, it is hardly a stretch to think people might classify as 'religious' stories of angels, saviours and a virgin birth, or hymns about a lord of the dance, pilgrims and Christian soldiers, and that some might even have paid greater attention to the theological and ethical content. In this sense, we could reapply to notions of religion in state education from Matthew Engelke's argument (borrowing from notions of ambient music and ambient media) about the Bible Society's allusive, sensory and background promotional work which allows for engagement, ignoring or apathy, and works with a theology of choice.[6] Alternatively, given the cultural heritage of the UK, we think of Christianity at state schools (and even private and public schools) as having a ghostly presence, something that might once have struck fear, and may still do, but has now become an even paler imitation of its former self.

We can say similar things about Christianity and religion in English political discourse, an issue that will be taken up with a different emphasis in Chapter 4. Certainly, a political leader does not need to identify as Christian as every American president between Carter and Trump has done. Nevertheless, an observer or insider might see or hear in the Houses of Parliament inscribed quotations from the Bible, opening prayers, and a contingent of bishops in the Lords. Perhaps more significant for our purposes is that Thatcher explicitly and repeatedly used the Bible and her Methodist past to authorise Thatcherism-in-the-making and virtually all mainstream politicians since have likewise invoked notions of religion to support their agendas, or at least to try placating a certain type of voter or lobbyist, or even to satisfy their own conscience. Such invocations of Christianity have certainly been subtler than in America, but they have likewise been a constant feature of English political discourse.

In this sense, this book is part of an ongoing attempt to show why and how politicians construct the language associated with religion as part of the many ways the assumed meanings of language change, in this instance how they change in relation to the legitimation of different ideological positions and shifting social formations across Right, Left and Centre of English political discourse. To give a more precise summary, Chapter 1 provides a historical overview of the changing uses of such language since the 1970s, through the Thatcher-Blair settlement to the challenges to the parliamentary consensus thrown up by the 2007/8 crisis. This introductory summary will cover some old ground for those familiar with previously published work, but it is essential for setting the scene for the rest of the book, and particularly so for those unfamiliar with such research.

Picking up on the ideological options thrown up by the financial crash, Chapter 2 studies the political constructions of religion, the Bible, Christianity and Islam in English parliamentary political discourse by the time of the 2017 General Election, and compares them with their predecessors to see what impact issues like Brexit have had. The starting point will be their Christmas messages, which provide a convenient point of contrast with what came before, but then we will move out to broader constructions of religion. The most notable developments were a shift towards soft ethnonationalist understandings of Christmas, economically protectionist readings of religion, overtly socialist constructions of

Christianity and the Bible, and the ongoing influence of socially liberal assumptions about what religion should (and should not) be, particularly with reference to sexuality.

Chapter 3 delves deeper into ethnonationalist understandings of Christianity and Christians in relation to Islam and Muslims, particularly on the post-2008 far right (e.g., EDL) and their dismissal of the idea popular in mainstream political discourse that ISIS and al Qaeda are a 'perversion of Islam'. Having looked at thousands of comments among far-right groups online, it is overwhelmingly clear that Islam per se was deemed the problem and that, occasionally, Christianity and the Bible functioned as a kind of ethnic and 'liberal' marker over against Islam and Muslims (and 'Asians'). This was not the sort of thing that could be overtly embraced in mainstream politics. Nevertheless, certain far-right ideas were reflected in parts of mainstream political discourse by, seemingly paradoxically, professing disdain for the far right and qualifying statements by using the language of a 'perversion of Islam'. This was done partly to obfuscate complicity in problematic issues of class and foreign policy.

Chapter 4 investigates whether the different constructions of religion (and related terms) had wider traction among voters in light of the EU Referendum. This study involved a series of interviews in a so-called 'Brexit town', Barrow-in-Furness, in the aftermath of the Brexit result in the summer of 2016, along with reference to similar and dissimilar locations in England. As with reasoning for Leave and Remain in elite discourse, the answers were complex but there was an overwhelming puzzlement about, and rejection of, politicians referring to religion, Christianity or the Bible. There was no evidence of widespread dislike of religion, Christianity or the Bible, and there was a view that the Bible and Christianity represent basically good moral positions. However, there was constant disdain for politicians distorting or using religion and the Bible for their own ends and a common view that religion does not really have a place in political discourse. In this respect, it reflected an intense hatred of politicians in post-industrial contexts, with some exceptions (including, interestingly, Corbyn). Nevertheless, a minority of people repeated the cliches about Islam and Muslims, particularly found among the far right, despite Barrow having low levels of immigration and 0.2 per cent identifying as Muslim (and falling).

Developing notions of propaganda and mass media, Chapter 5 shifts to the crises of the liberal centre thrown up by Corbyn and Corbynism with particular reference to the reporting in the *Guardian*. The language of 'sect', 'cult', 'fundamentalism', 'puritanical', and so on was repeatedly employed to denote a deviation from the assumed notion of a pure 'church' or 'religion' representing the neoliberal settlement, while occasionally 'religion' or 'religious' could be used to denote the alleged irrationality of Corbynism. This was part of a long liberal tradition of constructing 'fanatical' anti-capitalist or illiberal Others. However, Corbyn's stronger showing in the election than (the *Guardian*) expected opened up space for some of the language of deviation to be dropped, modified, reapplied, or even embraced as the press struggled to come to terms with how to reconceptualise Corbynism.

Chapter 6 looks at developments relating to, and contextualising, younger extra-parliamentary leftists who have emerged with, and through social media have helped promote, the Corbynism and one revolutionary cause in particular which has risen to prominence in leftist political discourse in our period: Rojava. The focus in this chapter is on a Corbyn-supporting group largely from the British Isles who were (and some may still be) active in northern Syria and on English-based social media. They have gone by the name of the Bob Crow Brigade and they controversially brought notions of martyrdom (including gendered notions of martyrdom) relating to physical death for the socialist and feminist cause into English political discourse, as well as rethinking notions of political 'miracle' and revolutionary 'faith'.

Religion in English Political Discourse, 1979–2017: A Brief History

Before we look at the ways in which ideas relating to popular under-standings of religion were nuanced between 2015 and 2017, it is essential to know what assumptions were previously present in English political discourse. In other words, the ideas, understandings and figures discussed in this chapter will set the scene for the remaining chapters and help us understand from where the ideas distinctive to post-2008 English political discourse emerged. To do this we need to look to the emergence and acceptance of Thatcherite neoliberalism and accompa-nying constructions associated with religion from the 1960s onward. We will look at how such ideas and assumptions became embedded in mainstream politics and were then modified by Tony Blair and New Labour with socially liberal understandings of religion before the ideo-logical crises inaugurated by the 2007/8 financial crash. This chapter will also cover the ways in which socialist understandings of religion and the Bible were pushed out of parliamentary discourse with the ascendency of neoliberalism, only to return with the emergence of Jeremy Corbyn. Here, I will summarise work that I have carried out in detail elsewhere but now with additional material to reflect the years immediately before the 2017 General Election.[1] This is integral to understanding the rest of this book and it is necessary to do so at some length.

Religion and the rise of Thatcherism

In the late 1960s, the state-interventionist Keynesian consensus began to break down in Western political, economic and cultural discourses as neoliberalism began to emerge as the dominant ideological position from the 1970s onwards and only began to show signs of ideological and economic vulnerability with the 2007/8 crash. While it was understood that the role of the state would be diminished in areas such as welfare and industry, an accompanying neoconservative tendency meant that the state remained significant for military interventions to protect, support and promote neoliberal ideals (e.g., Falklands, Iraq). The Anglicised versions of these major global economic changes were starting to take shape in the 1970s. Thatcher and her circle took advantage of the anxieties of nostalgia, counterculture, radicalism, social liberalism, post-imperialism, consumerism, patriotism and conservatism generated or intensified in the 1960s. From this they moulded what would eventually become known as 'Thatcherism', with a stress on economic liberalism, deregulation, entrepreneurialism, the rhetoric of freedom, liberty and personal responsibility. The economic crises of the 1970s helped the Thatcherite Right into power and with a mandate to challenge unions and the role of the public sector, though not before she and her circle had effectively overthrown the Conservative establishment, which by the beginning of the 1970s was relatively settled in the post-war Keynesian consensus. This ideological revolution may have been incubated by the Conservative Party, but it would grow into the dominant (though not unchallenged) position across English parliamentary political discourse in differing forms.

Using her rediscovered Methodism, Thatcher saw the Bible as a key source for emerging Thatcherism, as well as representing the core values of Britain and the West. Her rhetoric involved a nostalgic vision of a Christian Britain lost which, through her radical economic changes, would become part of her rhetoric of a Christian Britain regained, and laid the template for what mainstream, English-based politicians would think that the Bible, Christianity and religion really meant. Thatcher's understanding of the Bible and Christianity was about authorising notions of individualism, freedom, tolerance, rule of law, and English or British heritage, but with an especially distinctive and influential emphasis on individual wealth creation and charitable giving as a partial alternative to state provision of welfare. Among her many memorable exegetical examples in the context of interviews or speeches connecting the free market with the Bible and Christianity were her claims that 'no-one would remember the Good Samaritan if he'd only had good intentions; he had money as well', 'Our Lord Jesus Christ, the Son of God, when faced with His terrible choice and lonely vigil *chose* to lay down His life' (italics in the original), and, using the additional example of 2 Thessalonians 3.10 ('If a man will not work he shall not eat'): 'we must work and use our talents to create wealth ... Indeed, abundance rather than poverty has a legitimacy which derives from the very nature of Creation.'[2]

Thatcher, in some ways unusually so for a Conservative of her time, was openly positive about Jews and Judaism. But this was not accidental and was partly pragmatic. For instance, her government were solid supporters of Israel and its role in the Middle East, and her Finchley constituency was around 20 per cent Jewish when she was elected in 1959.[3] She argued that Jews and Judaism were also advocates in their own right of Thatcherite economics and her critique of the welfare state. For Thatcher, Jews, Judaism and the Old Testament (as she labelled it) epitomised Thatcherite ideals of individualism, self-help, personal responsibility, entrepreneurism and community support. Judaism could also be incorporated into her political vision for Christianity. 'Judaeo-Christian tradition' was deemed to be a Western tradition which promoted creativity and individual uniqueness. Though not without some nuance, Thatcher's understanding of Jews and Christians was that they valued work and human dominance of their environment which she saw reflected in economic progress and living standards in the West.[4] Nevertheless, the myth of Christian superiority remained; she did not want to equate Judaism and Christianity and insisted that the Old Testament could only be fully understood with the New Testament.[5]

Even if Christianity took pride of place, Thatcher's understanding of religion was generally presented almost always as having a redeeming feature and in sharp contrast to Marxism and Soviet Communism. If religion and Christianity were about promoting individual creativity then, she argued, Marxism and Communism were all about crushing the individual.[6] It is worth noting how this distinction was implicitly employed. Terror in the name of religion was, she claimed, carried out only by people who *appear, profess, claim, or are not considered* to be religious whereas Marxist terrorists really *are* Marxist to the core:

> From the Assassins of the twelfth century through to their successors, the suicide bombers of Hamas, Hizbollah and Islamic Jihad in the twenty-first century, professed Muslims have certainly been involved. But the Tamil extremists ... claim to be Hindus. ETA ... and the murderous Shining Path guerrillas in Peru are both Marxist. Even where religion appears to be at the core of violence, appearances can deceive. Most Irish Republican terrorists long ago stopped consid-

ering themselves – and stopped being treated by the Church – as Catholics.[7]

This was an important distinction for Thatcher because of the philosophical incompatibility of her politics and her Christianity with Marxism and Communism and that in 'religion', no matter how it might manifest itself, there was always something which could still be salvaged in terms of individual rights and dignity because of its assumed emphasis on 'the concept of a unique and eternal human "soul"'.[8] Thatcher's logic was that, unlike the collectivist and ultimately violent essence of Marxism, religion is essentially concerned with the individual and is thus always potentially democratic.

What is crucial to understanding the success of Thatcher was the (often unconscious) Thatcherisation of culture which partly helped account for her electoral success. We can see this among groups and individuals who carried cultural, subcultural, and even countercultural capital, and could even be hostile to Thatcherism and Thatcher (and vice versa). To give one prominent example among many: the seemingly ever-popular film *Life of Brian* which had Brian as a cipher for what Monty Python believed to be the historical figure of Jesus reconstructed from behind the Gospel accounts. Monty Python stood in a long liberal and sometimes radical tradition of presenting a palatable Jesus in contrast to deluded or power-hungry followers or interpreters who were typically code for 'the church'. The Brian/Jesus who represented cultural values assumed to be normative, or at least decent, was the one who mouthed *the* serious claim of the film: you are all individuals. But, while this might have been a development of 1960s-style liberalism or even anarchism, this could be reappropriated in a different way and we should remember that this was also a film which lampooned trade unions in the form of different revolutionary groups as bureaucratic pedants who stop things getting done. We should also remember that Brian was not the only one in 1979 proclaiming the importance of individuals while criticising collectivist bureaucracy: this was, after all, the year Thatcher was elected as Prime Minister. *Life of Brian* entered the scene when Thatcherism was starting to take hold and the ongoing popularity of the film partly shows the popularity of a kind of rhetoric associated with Thatcherism, no matter how uncomfortable or unintentional such an association might be or have been for Monty Python.

Religion, a changing Left, and the rise of New Labour

Looking at the more unexpected carriers of cultural change is important because by the 1990s the Thatcher brand became toxic in electoral terms and John Major's premiership went from crisis to crisis while Thatcherism itself continued victorious. In parliamentary terms, neoliberalism's victory came through Tony Blair and New Labour, crucial in both the consolidation of Thatcherism and Thatcher's understanding of religion. Not only did Blair and the New Labour project accept the basic tenets of Thatcher's presentation of religion, there was a rethinking of Labour's connections with radical understandings of Christianity, which had once been prominent among Nonconformist churches and the Catholic Left with historic ties to the Labour movement. To this day, such a tradition has a romantic hold on the Left and has long been a constant point of reference. Repeated themes in this radical tradition included land and wealth redistribution, confronting power and wealth, egalitarianism, anti-clericalism and direct access to God, the importance of conscience, and prophetic critique of power. This often included 'apocalyptic' language, particularly with reference to a radical transformation of the social, economic and political order, or, in a darker manner, the idea that The End really is nigh, whether through nuclear war or environmental catastrophe. The more positive understanding of apocalyptic transformation was also part of the development of a particularly English or British tradition of radical and unorthodox interpreters of Christianity (e.g., among many others, Peasants' Revolt, Wyclif and the Lollards, Gerrard Winstanley, Diggers, William Blake, F.D. Maurice, Chartists, Socialist Sunday Schools) which was often invoked to keep Marx and English/British socialism free from perceived Stalinist contamination. While this was typically understood as a Christian-based tradition, it was sometimes applied to Judaism (e.g., Moses, Marx) and Islam (e.g., Muhammad), with the same pattern of pure radical origins corrupted by later interpreters but kept alive by 'heretics'. This rhetoric of such radical understandings of religion or religions could be seen in any number of figures from the Labour Party associated with the Left and leftist causes, such as Keir Hardie, Margaret and Rachel MacMillan, Will Crooks, R.H. Tawney, George Lansbury, Ellen Wilkinson, Nye Bevan, Stafford Cripps, Donald Soper, Eric Heffer and Tony Benn. Such understandings were also found among radical movements and figures close to, or well beyond, the Labour Party in the twentieth century, such as Rudolf

Rocker and East End Yiddish anarchism, Ethel Mannin, George Orwell, C.L.R. James, the British Marxist historians, Peggy Duff, Greenham Common Women's Peace Camp, various members of the Campaign for Nuclear Disarmament (CND) and the Green Party.[9]

As Thatcherism was in the ascendency, Tony Benn was the established standard bearer for this radical socialist tradition in parliamentary politics. From the early 1970s onwards, Benn was championing a number of major leftist (and, at the time, often unpopular) issues, such as post-1968 feminism, syndicalism, the Miners' Strike of 1984–85, Irish unification, anti-war(s), unilateral disarmament, and anti-hierarchical radical democratic equality (not least in the Labour Party), as well as continuing his long-standing opposition to racism and the treatment of migrants. For Benn, the Bible and its radical interpreters (particularly the Levellers) were also sources of, and indeed central to, what was deemed to be a particularly English or British form of democratic socialism and industrial workers' democracy.[10] But by the mid-1990s, Benn was forlornly defending the place of Clause 4 (a commitment to common/ public ownership) in the Labour Party Constitution by claiming that its sentiments went back to the Acts of the Apostles.[11] By now the Labour Party had shifted rightwards and, in terms of understandings of Christianity, a significant moment came in a Christian Socialist Movement publication (1993) edited by Christopher Bryant (who would go on to become a New Labour MP), *Reclaiming the Ground: Christianity and Socialism*. Blair wrote the foreword and, behind the anti-Thatcherite polemics, the then Labour leader, John Smith, tried to bring together ideas about the free market, individualism and the collective good that were not far removed from what Thatcher had been arguing.

By the time Blair became Prime Minister in 1997, the anti-Thatcherite polemics were disappearing as fast as socialist understandings of religion from parliamentary discourse. Crucial to the dislocation of socialist understandings of Christianity were attempts by New Labour to appropriate, rethink and reapply the language of radical Christianity to free-market economics and the War on Terror, even sneaking biblical allusions past the watchful eye of Alastair Campbell who was reluctant to bring God into political debate for pragmatic electoral purposes (i.e., voters do not want God near politics).

Probably the most thoroughgoing example is Blair's much-publicised Labour Party conference speech shortly after 9/11.[12] Socialist understandings of Christianity had previously been a notable presence in the founding of the National Health Service (NHS) and the development of the welfare state by its most celebrated government under Clement Attlee and featuring major figures of the British Left, most notably Nye Bevan. Rather than ridding Britain of the 'evil giants' of 'want', 'squalor', 'disease' and 'ignorance', as Labour (following the Beveridge Report) had promised in their 1945 Manifesto, Blair sought to reapply this and other 'apocalyptic' or biblical language (e.g., 'an act of evil', 'we were with you at the first. We will stay with you to the last', 'the shadow of this evil', 'lasting good', 'hope amongst all nations', 'a new beginning', 'justice and prosperity for the poor and dispossessed', 'the starving, the wretched, the dispossessed, the ignorant, those living in want and squalor'; cf. for example, Genesis 17; Isaiah 1.16–17; 42.5–7; 49.6–13; Micah 2.1; Psalms 5.4; 23; Proverbs 28.1–28; Mark 13.10; Matthew 5.1–16; 12.21; Luke 6.20–49; Romans 4.18; 2 Thessalonians 3.2; Colossians 1.27; 1 John 5.19; Revelation 6; 22.13). The object of benevolence was now areas that would define his foreign policy, 'from the deserts of Northern Africa to the slums of Gaza, to the mountain ranges of Afghanistan'. Such biblical allusions functioned as a dog whistle to a Labour Party familiar with such language but nervous about supporting the imminent War on Terror. Blair would again repeat related 'apocalyptic' language in his career-defining speech on the eve of the Iraq War to justify invasion, again with one eye on a jittery Labour Party.[13] Just as Labour had transformed Britain after the devastation of the Second World War, North Africa, the Middle East and Afghanistan could now expect their own transformations.

The New Labour appropriation of leftist traditions was used to support some obviously neoliberal positions. When he was explaining the financial crisis at St Paul's Cathedral, Gordon Brown bolstered the government's position with reference to different religious traditions and combined them with notions of individualism, personal morality, entrepreneurialism, the responsibilities of wealth, and the significance of capitalism, and with virtually no reference to the public sector or welfare, even its importance was broadly assumed. Brown argued that behind Adam Smith's arguments on the wealth of nations and globalisation 'runs a single powerful moral sense demanding responsibility from all and fairness to all' that belongs to 'each of our heritages, traditions and faiths'. Brown cited Christian, Jewish, Muslim, Buddhist, Sikh and Hindu sayings and, in this sense, was perpetuating standard (neo)liberal understandings of religion. But he singled out a particular authority from the Christian tradition, Gerrard Winstanley, a striking addition given that he was a central figure on the radical Left, at least when Christianity had been invoked. Instead of Winstanley-the-Digger who was the proponent of land occupations and radical egalitarianism, Brown's take on Winstanley was about 'the light in man' which involved duty, conscience and helping others. With an allusion to the Parable of the Good Samaritan so common in English political discourse, he further added that 'it means we cannot and will not pass by on the other side when people are suffering'.[14] Quite what all this entailed was not spelled out, but it was certainly clear that Winstanley was now invoked in support of the responsibility of markets and governments.

One of Blair's most influential qualifications of Thatcher's understanding of religion was to appropriate the rhetoric of egalitarianism by giving it a socially liberal spin, especially on issues relating to gender and sexuality, albeit in ways that were tolerable in liberal parliamentary democracy. Blair claimed that 'an abhorrence of prejudice based on race, class, gender or occupation is fundamental to the Gospels. It is what draws so many Christians into politics, across the political spectrum.'[15] It might be argued that even the Gospels contain passages not quite so liberal (e.g., Mark 7.26–28) but, in some ways, this would be an irrelevant counterargument for Blair. He would later explain that open-minded younger generations were crucial in helping the 'evolution' of the interpretation of the Bible, particularly in the case of homosexuality, and for bringing belief and communal worship in line with contemporary social liberalism. Without the constraints of party politics, his time after leaving office allowed him to explain his position in more detail. Blair read scriptures 'less literally' and 'more metaphorically' and (like Obama) he was flexible when it came to texts deemed illiberal on issues like sexuality and gender. Blair could attribute problematic texts to radically different ancient social contexts no longer readily endorsed by contemporary Christians in liberal democracies.[16]

The New Labour legacy in this respect was apparent in the parliamentary debates over same-sex marriage in 2013 where Jesus was invoked by the main parties as a supporter of same-sex marriage.[17] From Labour, Toby Perkins claimed that 'as a Christian' he had 'no worries about voting for this Bill' because 'what greater example of the equalities agenda could there be than Jesus Christ himself? ... Jesus Christ led the way on promoting equalities.' What was also notable was how this was an area where the radical language of the past could be brought firmly into the mainstream as homosexuality had become more normalised and less controversial beyond Parliament. As Perkins added, 'there are any number of stories in the Bible that make it absolutely clear that Jesus stuck up for groups that had been oppressed over the years'. A similar move was made by another Labour MP, David Lammy, where we can see a shift from Jesus the state criminal to Jesus defending victims of oppression: 'the Jesus I know was born a refugee, illegitimate, with a death warrant on his name, and in a barn among animals. He would stand up for minorities. That is why it is right for those of religious conviction to vote for this Bill.' What was also explicit was that Lammy's understanding of the Bible was shorn of Otherness, potentially malignant properties and illiberal elements (which, it might be noted, can also be found in the Bible) in his claim that 'those on the extremes of our faith have poisoned what is an important debate with references to polygamy and bestiality'. But this was a bill introduced by a Conservative-led government and to show how embedded such liberal assumptions about religion and the Bible had become we should add that the other main defence of same-sex marriage with reference to the Bible was from the Conservative MP Peter Bottomley who invoked the commandments about loving God and neighbour to argue that 'we are asking whether we can remove the barriers that stop same-sex couples enjoying the commitment – the "at one" meaning – of marriage. That is what the Bill comes down to. It does not redefine marriage; it just takes away barriers.' We will see in the next chapter that these were the kinds of liberal constraints on Tim Farron's understandings of homosexuality.

The Blair era was notable for another change in political use of the language of religion in that he brought discussions about Islam and Muslims firmly into the mainstream. As with his reading of the Bible, there were hermeneutical controls for Blair's understanding of the Qur'an, namely, general concepts which were compatible with liberal democratic values. In such liberal interpretations of the Bible this usually meant turning to the figure of Jesus and so it logically followed that Muhammad could be deemed to be the font of liberal values to trump any seemingly illiberal ones.[18] Indeed, for Blair, scriptural texts like the Qur'an and the Bible, or their first respectable interpreters, represented a purer form of tolerant, liberal, rational, principled, moralistic and democratic religion which were ultimately recoverable from what were assumed to be later corruptions. Blair even claimed to have read three versions of the Qur'an in order to find passages to counter extremist positions.[19] This idea of a 'distortion' or a 'perversion' of a purer 'religion' was something Blair stressed at key moments, for example, in response to the 7/7 attacks which infamously did not address the issue of the wars in Afghanistan and Iraq, and in the Prevent strategy targeting domestic terrorism (see Chapter 3). On the eve of the Iraq War, he targeted 'two begetters of chaos', namely, 'weapons of mass destruction and extreme terrorist groups who profess a perverted and false view of Islam'.[20] We will return to this issue in detail in Chapter 3 but for now we might note that Blair consistently used the tropes of 'false' or 'perverted' Islam as an ahistorical metaphysical aberration which must be attacked to prevent its growth and used to avoid any complicity of Western states in the emergence of 'rogue states' or groups like al Qaeda.

Christianity, Cameron and the Coalition

By the end of the New Labour era, economic and social liberalism, cultural heritage, civic responsibility, liberal democracy, as well as benign militarism and the state's monopoly on violence, made up the broadly agreed assumptions about 'religion' in mainstream, party-political discourse. It might be thought that the fallout from the contemporary crises of capitalism would have generated new ways of constructing religion as an authority for political beliefs. For a start, the 2007/8 crash effectively signalled the end of the New Labour project as the Conservatives and the right-wing press relentlessly focused on blaming the global financial crisis on Labour. Yet, for the first few years, it seemed that, if anything, the old assumptions were merely intensified. This was unsurprising given that the first post-crash election in 2010 saw the return of the Conservatives (in coalition with the Liberal Democrats) and an extreme austerity agenda and ushering in an era (though part of longer-term trends) marked by zero-hour contracts, precarious working life, weakened unions, crises in social housing, a lack of mortgage availability, indebtedness (including student debt), social cleansing and gentrification (particularly in London), social atomisation, loneliness, declining social mobility, a reversal of the pattern of children being more prosperous than their parents, growing inequality, and a high concentration of wealth among the financial elite who would become known as 'the one per cent'. By 2013, much was made (particularly in the *Guardian*) of those born between 1980 and 2000 (so-called 'Generation Y' or 'Millennials') in the British Social Attitudes report which appeared to show that alongside the increase of socially liberal values there were assumptions of decreasing respect for the welfare state and a broad acceptance of the idea that individual responsibility was crucial for economic advancement in life.[21] Were we really all liberal Thatcherites now?

In tackling the crash, the Conservative-led Coalition intensified neo-liberalism with a strict emphasis on cuts, austerity and deficit reduction, alongside social liberalism (e.g., same-sex marriage). Put another way, the Thatcher-Blair understanding of religion was being intensified, and this time enabled by the Liberal Democrats. Irrespective of the intentionality of the timing, Jo Latham and Claire Mathys published a collection of essays by prominent Liberal Democrat politicians in 2013 with the fairly self-explanatory title, *Liberal Democrats Do God*.[22] The book contained the usual liberal understandings of religion typically based on the idea that all human beings were thought to be created in the image of God and equally deserving of respect and thus there were concerns for immigrants, care for the environment, and equal rights irrespective of gender, sexuality or disability. The collection also drew on traditions picked up by Thatcher. Part of the suggestions by Steve Webb (then Minister of State for Pensions) that 'God is a liberal' involved the following claim: 'And God gave us the most extraordinary freedom – the freedom to reject and crucify his Son. There must be something very precious about freedom, a value dear to the heart of every liberal.'[23] While this was clearly compatible with the Liberal tradition, it was also strikingly close to one of Thatcher's more prominent assertions about Jesus in her justification for her take on the free market where, as Jonathan Raban remarked, 'Christ dying on the Cross joins those folk who have exercised their right to choose – to buy their own council houses, to send their children to private schools, to occupy "paybeds" in NHS-funded hospitals.'[24]

Indeed, hints of Liberal Democrat compatibility with Thatcher's critique of the state were also present in Webb's argument in his claim that 'the Almighty Creator of the universe does not impose his will on his creation' and so we 'should be deeply cautious about using the power of the state to impose our will on others'.[25] Economic liberalism was likewise a part of the Liberal tradition and it too was represented in the Liberal Democrats' invocation of the divine. John Pugh, for instance, claimed that 'all Liberals are passionate about free trade' and 'sceptical but supportive of state action'. Like Thatcher, Pugh stressed the dangers of the irresponsible use of wealth and unfair wealth distribution, adding that 'it doesn't necessarily follow that Christian Liberals would favour higher tax rates for the wealthy rather than the encouragement of philanthropy'.[26]

But if the Liberal Democrats were tentatively perpetuating positions compatible with Thatcherism then leading Conservatives were openly promoting them. It was just before, during and after the 400th anniversary of the King James Bible in 2011, that David Cameron publicly began to nuance his take on the neoliberal understanding of Christianity in detail. The 'Judeo-Christian roots of the Bible', he claimed in a development of Thatcher's use of such language, were the foundation for human rights, British language and culture, equality, parliamentary democracy, the abolition of slavery and the emancipation of women. Among his list were the expected host of 'social obligations' individuals have towards one another but, tellingly, the discussion of welfare (and even the formation of the welfare state) heavily stressed Christian intervention: 'from the role of the church in the first forms of welfare provision, to the many modern-day faith-led social action projects'.[27] This understanding of the ideal subject under neoliberal capitalism meant a de-emphasis of the state in welfare provision, and in this respect Cameron out-Thatchered Thatcher. He even went as far as to claim that Jesus founded the partial alternative to state provision of welfare, namely, the concept of Big Society, Cameron's one-time flagship project (see Chapter 2).[28]

In his 2014 Easter message, Cameron argued that the heart of Christianity was 'love thy neighbour' which made him think about 'the Alpha courses run in our prisons'. Of course, the specifics of the Alpha Course and its overt evangelical, charismatic and proselytising conversion programme were not mentioned explicitly, and there was certainly no mention of their interests in speaking in tongues or whether homosexuality could be cured. As ever, this would be far too alien to contemporary liberalism for a mainstream politician to discuss. Instead, Cameron saw the usefulness of citing Alpha in his speech to support his own views on charity overriding state provision. Alpha thus epitomised 'love thy neighbour' for its 'work with offenders to give them a new life inside and outside prison' just like 'the soup kitchens and homeless shelters run by churches'. Cameron added that the 'same spirit' was shown during the storms earlier in 2014: 'churches became refuges, offering shelter and food, congregations raised funds and rallied together, parish priests even canoed through their villages to rescue residents. They proved, yet again, that people's faith motivates them to do good deeds.'[29]

This emphasis on outsourcing the state came as Cameron's government had been criticised over its handling of flooding and after there had been sustained criticisms (not least by church leaders) over the rise of foodbank use and, later, after Corbyn's criticism of the increase in homelessness. In addition to these criticisms, there were allegations of complicity in creating war-torn countries and it was notable that Cameron (as we will see) developed assumptions about Christianity, the Bible and Islam to justify military intervention. From the logic of Cameron's version of Christianity, the rise in foodbank use (or those helping the homeless or those prepared to help the maimed) was actually to be deemed a Good Thing – Big Society in action. Beneath the vagueness, the consensual rhetoric, and the praise of canoeing priests, Cameron's understanding of Christianity provided a clear authority for his government's austerity agenda and outsourcing of state welfare while simultaneously promoting the benign militaristic state, as we will see in Chapter 2.

Corbynite Christianity

Cameron's tweaking of the neoliberal and neoconservative tendencies promoted by Thatcher and Blair and their accompanying understandings of Christianity and the Bible were part of the reactions to the financial crisis and were connected with a more rhetorically hostile discourse of blaming welfare, public sector workers or over-subsidised education for the financial state of the nation. The reaction from the Left, however, would eventually see the return of more socialist understandings of Christianity and the Bible, and it is striking that after Ed Miliband's failure in the 2015 General Election, Corbyn (then chair of Stop the War Coalition, a veteran socialist activist firmly on the Left of the Labour Party, and closely associated with, for example, anti-racism and anti-fascism campaigners, Marxists, left-wing trade unionists and nuclear disarmament, not to mention former trainee priest John McDonnell) was propelled forward by a Labour membership tired of compromising on issues tied in with neoliberalism.

But Corbynism hardly came out of the blue, even if it was surprising to virtually all commentators. There are numerous reasons which help explain the Corbyn phenomenon.[30] In broader terms, Corbynism represented an Anglicised version of reactions against social democratic parties in Europe and America, as well as part of the hostility towards 'the establishment' we will discuss further in Chapter 4. But there were more localised reasons. As a veteran left-wing campaigner and protester, Corbyn represented an ideological position more palatable to new leftist movements coming through Occupy, UK Uncut and student demonstrations, as well as influential strands in major unions (e.g., Unite, Unison, RMT). This involved a range of issues which were not typically part of the contemporary Labour Party with emphases such as environmental politics, student fees, irregular working patterns, and generational changes in living standards. This leftism was addressing different questions to those of the old industrial Left which was Labour's base for much of the twentieth century and which was now facing some of the worst humiliations in the era of neoliberal capitalism. As the traditional print media continued its long-term decline, social media provided a means to connect to supporters which could bypass the mainstream anti-Corbyn polemics (see Chapter 6). But Corbyn also represented an ideological position more palatable to an older Left. Since Blair's landslide victory in 1997, Labour haemorrhaged support, with the Iraq War and relative neglect of its working-class base being particularly damaging, and its managerial style, perceived metropolitanism, wealthy networks, and 'on message' media approach was never wholly embraced by the membership or its traditional voters. Labour, it seemed, had not only capitulated to neoliberal economics but also to neoconservative foreign policy. Against this backdrop, Corbyn represented the antithesis of Blair's New Labour and, as a leading backbench opponent and activist, he had radical credibility going back decades. With the harnessing of the new leftist support coming partly through the formation of Momentum, Corbyn was able to maintain the support of the Labour membership (now over 500,000 strong), see off leadership challenges, and increase Labour seats and its share of the vote in the 2017 General Election.

Within the Labour movement, older radical understandings of religion were kept alive in the run-up to Corbynism. Dennis Skinner, like Corbyn, was one of the few figures from the old Labour Left to survive the Blair-Brown years, as well as being a former miner with connections to the once prominent Nonconformist (in this case Methodist) traditions in the Labour movement. In his memoirs, he referred to the connections often made in the Labour movement between Methodism and Marxism and how lay Methodist preachers were a significant presence in pit communities. As Corbyn would regularly do (see Chapter 2), Skinner referred to the Parable of the Good Samaritan (Luke 10.29–37), arguing that it was not about individualist improvement ('a load of crap') but rather collective good of the sort he saw in the pit ('solidarity and struggle') and in trade unionism. This parable, Skinner claimed, was about helping 'someone in need' and was an example of 'a socialist story'. That this was a distinctly leftist reading was not simply that it was a reading in stark opposition to Thatcher's reading but because it was in opposition to vaguer liberal assumptions too. Indeed, in this context, Skinner noted that 'the Tories and Liberal Democrats are incapable of representing working people' as shown by the then ruling 'squalid ConDem coalition'. He went further still, arguing that there should be no compromise with capitalism and capitalism must be confronted. This was all part of what was needed for the 'transformation of Britain' in the interests of working people and their families, and he moved on to push for public ownership of electricity companies, rail, and the whole of the NHS.[31] New Labour, this was not. But neither was it the sort of view expected to ever again be brought to the fore of English politics.

Nevertheless, emerging among a younger generation were popular leftist sympathisers in the media such as Owen Jones, who, against Cameron's claims about British values and history, invoked a radical Christian tradition in much the way Tony Benn might have done. As well as referencing 'radical movements like the democratic Levellers and socialistic Diggers' and the Tolpuddle Martyrs, Jones highlighted the Peasants' Revolt of 1381, claiming that 'the Lollard priest John Ball publicly questioned the class system: "When Adam delved and Eve span, who was then the gentleman?"'[32] Among the non- or extra-parliamentary (and often youthful) precursors of Corbynism, Occupy was particularly important in perpetuating radical understandings of religion, Christianity and the Bible. One of the most prominent images used in Occupy London Stock Exchange was Jesus throwing out the moneychangers, such as in protesters' visual portrayals. Veteran Marxists like Terry Eagleton suggested that the protesters were effectively followers of Jesus but went further by arguing that Jesus' actions in the Temple showed that he 'was at one with a later Jewish prophet, Karl Marx, whose concept of alienation involves just such a break between the product and the producer'.[33]

A more immediate precursor to the return of the socialist under-standings of religion – and perhaps even representative of a younger generation despite his older age – was Russell Brand and his rise to prominence in English political discourse. This included a clandestine meeting with Miliband (himself gently pushing a critique of neoliberalism) during the 2015 General Election and, in light of his anger at the pointlessness of voting, also involved guest editing the *New Statesman* and famously being interviewed on the BBC's flagship current affairs programme, *Newsnight*, by its then star Jeremy Paxman. Among this stir, Brand (with his own Jesus-chic) foregrounded the idea of Jesus as the ultimate revolutionary, alongside related understandings of any number of religions. This was particularly clear in his 2014 book, *Revolution*, where Brand's use of Christianity and the Bible looked firmly in the tradition of leftist English Christianity, even if he used his own distinctive language. He prioritised the story of Jesus in the Temple, which was understood to be an attack on the influence on public life of a corrupt financial elite, and proclaimed Cameron a hypocritical 'cunt' for promoting privatising tendencies in the NHS and thus not, Brand claimed, practising the teachings of Jesus.[34] To discredit him, Brand's sustained use of Jesus, the Bible and Christianity was largely ignored, misrepresented, or occasionally dismissed as self-indulgent or distorting in the media who instead went for easier targets and anything implied to be non-English/British-sounding or too liberal Hollywood (e.g., Hare Krishna, Hinduism, Buddhism, mysticism, transcendentalism).

What is significant about the reluctance to attack (acceptable forms of) Christianity and the Bible in the media was that use of them could provide a degree of protection *if* its use were perceived to be authentic. Brand remained easy for the media to dismiss in this respect, irrespective of a consistent lack of fairness in representing his views (see Chapter 5). Corbyn, however, was not. At worst, there were plenty of jokey and ironic comments about him being comparable to that other JC. The rise of the movement was predictably attacked for many things, but it is striking that Corbyn turned to Christian rhetoric and so the summer of 2015 saw the return to front-line parliamentary discourse of openly socialist understandings of the Bible, Christianity and religion that had not been so prominent since the heyday of Tony Benn. 'Revivalist meetings' was a common description of the popular Corbyn meetings (often held in churches). His parliamentary ally and a self-identified atheist, Clive Lewis, claimed that there was a 'religious element' to Corbyn's support, presumably understood in terms of the enthusiasm for Corbyn.[35] Rhetorical combinations of socialism, nostalgia, religion, biblical allusions, William Blake and Jerusalem, a specifically English or British radical tradition, and so on, were also easy enough to find. By the time Corbyn had been elected leader of the Labour Party, his close parliamentary ally Cat Smith was openly claiming that 'Jesus was a radical socialist' and, as one of her examples, she used the image popular in Occupy: Jesus 'turning over the tables in the temple'.[36] Smith would not be the only Labour figure to think in such terms. And as party leader, Corbyn himself began referencing the Bible, Christianity and Islam immediately and in relation to overtly socialist arguments. We will return to this in the next chapter.

Religion on the Right

If Corbyn represented a post-crash revolt on the Left, there was another development happening which became (not entirely fairly) associated with the Right, and the UK Independence Party (UKIP) particularly: Brexit. Brexit, especially in relation to immigration issues, would mark another shift which would nuance how religion would become understood and constructed in English political discourse. After the Coalition gained power, UKIP began to rise significantly in the polls (even polling ahead of the Liberal Democrats), with Nigel Farage becoming an ever-more prominent figure. Farage, of course, regularly attacked the European Union (EU) but he was also regularly attacking mainstream 'careerist' politicians and a political class who were seen to have betrayed the electorate, particularly on issues of immigration. That this rhetoric was to some degree successful should not now be a surprise. While there were immediate reasons for hostility towards the political class, particularly after the 2009 parliamentary expenses scandal, this rhetoric tapped into longer-term socio-economic changes in Britain. It had some traction among older working-class voters (and, now, non-voters) in post-industrial Britain, who lived away from the cosmopolitan centres, with views clustered around Euroscepticism, immigration, national identity, changing culture, a lack of social mobility, and intense dissatisfaction with the political class. This should be set against the backdrop of the fate of industry under neoliberalism, the rise of precarious employment and low pay, and a generation not trained or raised for such changing circumstances. While UKIP were initially deemed to be a threat to the Conservatives, it is now clear why they were an especially potent threat to the seemingly more cosmopolitan Labour Party who had been losing support from their working-class base for some time as they seemed more interested in voters with middle-class pretentions who might swing an election.[37]

Brexit certainly owed something to these socio-economic changes in British society. As we will see in the next chapter, Theresa May tried to capitalise on such tendencies after the fall of Cameron, not least in her toying with nativist or ethnonationalist portrayals of certain traditions like Easter and Christmas. One version of this thinking certainly had a presence in UKIP, such as in one memorable anti-EU pamphlet by Christian Soldiers (UKIP) which was seen around the time of the EU Referendum and at UKIP conferences. Accompanied by the 'shield of faith' and the 'sword of truth', it had the revealing title, 'Bible believing Christians who support Britain's membership of the European Union (EU) are committing spiritual treason against Almighty God and His Kingdom.' The contents of the pamphlet were not what might ordinarily be expected in mainstream English political discourse, even at the Eurosceptic end of the Conservative Party. The 'malevolent' and 'ungodly' EU, it warned, wants to 'abolish our Christian Nation State' and the 'ancient Laws and Freedoms bestowed on us by God'. Perhaps aware of an especially niche audience, much space was also devoted to young people who 'have never known the wonderful freedom & joy that comes from living in a Christian nation' and were forced 'to bear the heavy EU chains forged in the fiendish fires of subversion by Quislings and Traitors'. Indeed, the EU building of Strasburg was 'deliberately designed as a replica of the ancient biblical Tower of Babel', while the woman riding the beast in Revelation 17 was deemed an important image for the Babylon-emulating EU. The pamphlet was rounded off with an anti-EU prayer for the reader's further use.

Needless to say, this type of Christianity was not the sort that was ever likely to be a vote winner or chime with the disillusioned of Brexit Britain, and nor was it ever likely to have been used by Farage. But Farage saw Christianity as integral to Britishness, though he couched his use of the language of religion in his usual idioms and did not overemphasise anything too problematic for the British press ('Whilst I would not ever present myself as being a person of deep religious conviction I absolutely believe in Christian values that have made this country great').[38] But there was a key Other in Farage's rhetoric which, while certainly present in other political traditions, was rarely foregrounded in such a contrasting manner or without a typical qualification about the benefits of Islam. On schools and the Office for Standards in Education, Children's Services and Skills (OFSTED), the 2015 UKIP Manifesto stated that 'we will continue to monitor British values, but with a view towards combatting extremism and radicalisation, rather than criticising widely-held Judeo-Christian beliefs'.[39] As the results of Chapter 3 suggest, there was the implication that 'extremism and radicalisation' involved 'Muslims', at least for those with the right ears to hear. There is further evidence to support this identification of (certain) Muslims in contrast to nativist or cultural Christianity, at least in the way an interview was reported in the *Telegraph*. Farage was quoted as calling for 'a much more muscular defence of our Judaeo-Christian heritage' which, in a now established use of such a phrase, was deemed to be about 'our identity', and that 'we're open to different cultures but we have to defend our values'. Failure to promote this message by the Archbishop of Canterbury and politicians 'is appeasement of the worst kind'.[40] By way of contrast, he was reported to have said that Muslims who speak no English or wear the veil have no place in UKIP and he was further critical of female genital mutilation. As we will also see in Chapter 3, this singling out of gender and equality issues in relation to national identity (not to mention an allusion to the war with the loaded term, 'appeasement') was a move that had much in common with new tendencies in far-right discourse, particularly groups like the English Defence League (EDL). And, as we will see in the next chapter, this playing with a nativist or ethnonationalist 'Judeo-Christian beliefs' in contrast to a problematic Islam was something which May took seriously and repeatedly.

Where we are now

By the time of the 2017 General Election, it was clear that the ideological fallout of the 2007/8 crash was unpredictable. The socio-economic changes that gave rise to UKIP and Brexit would benefit May's Conservatives as UKIP once again began to sink. But the decline of UKIP also, albeit to a lesser extent, helped Corbyn's Labour in the election. Also perceived to be influential was an emboldened younger generation who had experienced or perceived austerity in different ways. With the very mild recovery of the Liberal Democrats, the 2017 General Election marked not only a return to two-party politics but a return to distinctive ideological differences between the two main parties in English political discourse. The impact of the financial crash on understandings of religion had not always been immediate. By the time Cameron became Prime Minister in 2010, it seemed that the dominant assumptions about religion were relatively settled and, if anything, he was merely intensifying what he inherited. Religion and associated terms (e.g., Christianity, the Bible, Islam) were, for instance, ideally assumed to support the economically and socially liberal political settlement. Christianity might be English or British but, as we will see in the next chapter, its liberalism effectively represented 'all faiths and none'. If we fast forward to 2015 and the rise of Corbyn, then socialist understandings, long pushed outside parliamentary discourse, had surprisingly returned to mainstream politics. Fast forward to 2016 and the EU Referendum vote and Cameron was out, and space was now open for different nuances in the understanding of religion with, as we will also see, more nativist or ethnonationalist understandings normalised and ready to be developed by May. While there were plenty of longer-term causes, the 2007/8 financial crisis ushered in the most volatile period in contemporary English and British politics in recent decades. Many of the ideas associated with all these different movements and moments were contradictory, and voting patterns were not always reflecting the old binaries of Right and Left. Still present in this contemporary chaos were understandings of religion which remained an implicit (and occasionally explicit) authorisation for different and emerging ideological positions. The rest of this book will look further at how different understandings of religion were changing in this period of social, economic and political chaos and what understandings were vying for dominance by the time of the 2017 General Election. Next, then, we will turn to the positions of the main party leaders established by June 2017.

2

Brexit Means Christmas, Christmas Means Socialism, and a Time for 'Homosexual Sex': Shifting Notions of Religion from the Frontbenches

Introduction: the meaning of Christmas

At the end of the divisive year of Brexit, it was perhaps fitting that Nigel Farage confronted the Archbishop of Canterbury, Justin Welby, at Christmas. Farage tweeted (@nigel_farage, 25 December 2016): 'Merry Christmas. Ignore all negative messages from the Archbishop of Canterbury and have a great day!' Welby, a Remain advocate, had just preached his Christmas Day sermon at Canterbury Cathedral which talked about 2016 as a year 'awash with fear and division', alongside concerns such as the wellbeing of a family scavenging for food by lowering their child into a supermarket dustbin.[1] Christmas is a time for many things including, as Farage showed, political figures expressing certain views which contribute to shifting understandings of religion in English political discourse. Indeed, political leaders of each party typically give a Christmas message which in turn reveals how political positions are intertwined with assumed meanings of Christmas and Christianity. In this chapter, I will look at how the political Christmases of the recent present compare with the political Christmases of the not-too-distant past. Political Christmas messages are a particularly useful starting point because they give us closely comparative examples with which to analyse the changes that are taking place. This will provide a starting point for illustrating how the recent political and economic crises contributed to such shifting understandings of Christianity in particular before looking more widely (i.e., beyond Christmas) at how political leaders understand and develop such language.

In terms of English political discourse, Christmas also provided a relatively rare opportunity for politicians to talk openly about ideas associated with religion with less chance of alienating voters who might matter. We might tweak Christopher Deacy's argument that Christmas is some kind of secularised manifestation of 'religion' to argue it is a festival that, understood in a certain way, is assumed to have some kind of cultural and ideological authority tied in with notions of Englishness and Britishness.[2] And by 'culture' I am thinking more in terms of Slavoj Žižek's claim that people do not necessarily 'really believe' but some may follow rituals typically categorised as 'religious' out of respect for our community or 'culture', whether nonbelieving Jews keeping kosher rules out of respect for tradition or, indeed, annually playing along with the game of Christmas, irrespective of what we really make of the historical Santa Claus.[3] This ironic distancing allows belief without (necessarily) believing very much or for ideology to continue without claiming to be too ideologically committed. Put another way, as Žižek partly did, when we heard stories about statues or buildings being destroyed by the Taliban or ISIS for being idolatrous, the outrage was not typically because of an offence to a deity but because of an offence against a reified notion of cultural heritage. And if any monster were to desecrate Christmas, some (such as certain journalists and politicians at least) might view this as an attack on 'our culture' while not necessarily worrying whether Santa is really crying into his sherry.

We should keep such thoughts in mind throughout this chapter and thus we should not expect too much material alien to mainstream liberal discourses, material that might be found in (say) the stories presented in accounts of Jesus' birth in the Gospels of Matthew and Luke. Do not expect to be reading too much about Asaph the father of Jehoshaphat, angelic appearances, the meaning of Jeremiah's words about Ramah, the details of Mary's sexual practices and marital status, John the Baptist's drinking habits, why Elizabeth was a disgrace, leaping in the womb, Jesus' circumcision, the offering of a sacrifice of turtle doves and pigeons, and possibly not even bringing down the rich and the powerful, though Jeremy Corbyn may have had other ideas. These were not the areas of the Christian archives that needed worrying about too much in liberal parliamentary politics. Instead, expect sometimes ironic respect for an authoritative source of cultural heritage which will support a given political position, but which will not overdo anything perceived to be peculiar or alien in political discourse.

Theresa May's Christmas

In her Christmas 2016 message, Theresa May used cliches familiar to political leaders from Christmas past. There was the standard stress on the importance of volunteers and armed services while Christmas also provided an annual opportunity for the Conservatives to try and promote themselves in an area where they are typically weaker in terms of trust: public services ('those in our health and care services'). The message of the birth of Christ was as vague as ever ('forgiveness, love and hope').[4] All of this could have (and more-or-less did) come from David Cameron and would not be out of place among almost any modern prime minister or party leader because, from this perspective, Christmas has to remain sufficiently liberal, normative and agreeable. But there was something about May's Christmas that was distinctive, and which began to shift notions of the meanings of ideas we might associate with Christianity and religion. Indeed, we can turn to May's own comments about religion to see how such assumptions became marked by Brexit in particular.

On becoming Prime Minister, May almost immediately repositioned herself (or was repositioned in the media) as integral to Brexit: 'Brexit means Brexit' quickly became repeated and her rhetoric would include advocating a 'red, white and blue' Brexit. In terms of Brexit and under-standings of religion, we might recall what happened to May's words in different interviews for *Desert Island Discs* and the *Sunday Times*.[5] Here, she made seemingly innocuous comments about 'faith' (e.g., 'It is part of who I am and how I approach things') and a vague favourite of politicians: 'doing the right thing'. In the *Sunday Times* interview, before she moved on to discuss being a practising member of the Church of England and having associated values, she also mentioned getting on with the terms of Brexit. This reference to Brexit meant that a connection between God and her words could now be made by others, all the while providing May with plausible deniability in that she did not *quite* make an explicit connection in the interview, a suspected tactic used by politicians to get a potentially divisive story in the press.[6] Let us take two different per-spectives in the subsequent reporting of this story:

Theresa May says God and her faith are guiding Brexit decisions. (*Huffington Post*, 28 November 2016)

> Guide me, O thou great Theresa: Theresa May says her faith in God will guide our path out of Europe as she admits Brexit is keeping her awake. (*Sun*, 27 November 2016)

The idealised *Huffington Post* reader was not a May voter so there was no real damage likely to be done to May while the Brexit-supporting *Sun* went for a typical twist of appreciative irony in their supportive headline. But, luckily for May, the recurring theme of her as 'the vicar's daughter' worked in terms of perceived authenticity in a way that Christianity did not for Blair (much to his disappointment), partly because it did not involve too much unpalatable religion. Indeed, the repeated notion of The Vicar's Daughter conjured up the old-fashioned gendered, palatable and indeed 'English' image of doing the everyday practical work about the church (e.g., arranging flowers, administration, providing biscuits, cleaning the tea cups) while the (male) vicar might be expected to do the sermons, theology, dogma, and other oddities.[7] Compare also the following write-up from the *Financial Times* where any potentially unpalatable features of church life (e.g., details of theology) were left unmentioned and the image presented as one fit for public service:

> 'She feels that she has been called to do this. She has a very strong sense of vocation and destiny and a very clear sense of right and wrong,' says Prof Linda Woodhead, an expert on the Church of England at Lancaster University. 'Like her father, she has huge grit and determination and stamina to see through the moral vision she believes in.'
>
> That firmness of purpose has been evident in Mrs May's drive in her previous job to cut immigration and to tackle what she sees as the failings of Britain's police force. It will now be tested as her government decides how to pursue Brexit.[8]

With the *Financial Times* and the *Sun* carrying out the types of media propaganda we will discuss in Chapter 4, Brexit was tied in with perceptions of May and religion. No doubt May and her press team knew what they were doing with the repeated mention of her church upbringing, though the effect would remain the same even if the press led the way. By the time of May's 2016 Christmas message, it could hardly avoid being a Brexit message. The message itself looked to a hope for 'a bold new role for ourselves in the world and to unite our country as we move forward into the future' as 'we leave the European Union'. Interestingly, and perhaps not unexpectedly, the *Daily Express* fulfilled its duty and read this as 'a message directed to bitter Remaoners [*sic*]'.[9]

But this sort of support for a Brexit Christmas did not come out of nowhere. Like the high street, May's Brexit Christmas had already started to gather momentum in September, as the following exchange in the House of Commons shows:

> **Mr Shailesh Vara (North West Cambridgeshire) (Con):** The Prime Minister will be aware of coverage regarding a report to be published by Dame Louise Casey, the Government's integration tsar. The report will speak of British laws, culture, values and traditions, such as Christmas, being threatened by political correctness from council officials. Will the Prime Minister take this opportunity to send a loud and clear message that the best way to secure a harmonious society is not only for mainstream Britain to respect minority traditions, such as Diwali, Vaisakhi and Eid, but for council officials to appreciate that minority communities should respect the views and traditions of mainstream Britain, which means that Christmas is not 'Winterval' and that Christmas trees are not 'festive' trees?
>
> **Prime Minister, Theresa May:** I agree with my hon. Friend. I will not comment on or pre-empt the findings of Louise Casey's review, which is an important piece of work. I will simply join my hon. Friend by saying that what we want to see in our society is tolerance and understanding. We want minority communities to be able to recognise and stand up for their traditions, but we also want to be able to stand up for our traditions generally, and that includes Christmas.[10]

We know, then, that Christmas means Christmas and not Winterval. One notable aspect of this exchange was that it played into discourses about 'political correctness', ownership of language, and, of course, the alleged threats to Christmas itself. This was a favoured discourse of the Right for some time – including tabloid campaigns to save Christmas – though one which did not correspond with what actually happened behind the stories. As Oliver Burkeman has shown, these stories were consistently reported inaccurately in newspapers and there was no concerted campaign to replace Christmas with Winterval, Luminos or Winter Celebrations, and nor had there been a plot for Christmas cards to have less Christ and more Seasons Greetings.[11] Contrary to some press reports, terms like 'festive', 'season' and 'Christmas' were used interchangeably for decades and on Christmas cards for long before that. However, while there may have been no significant attack on Christmas, issues of accuracy for the ideological position associated with strands of the political Right were as relevant as the strange details of much of the Christmas story in the Gospels of Matthew and Luke have been for politicians. Such rhetoric certainly tapped into a common tradition embraced by all leading politicians – namely, that Christianity, the Bible and Christmas are a part of English or British cultural heritage – but May's spin on it was clearly one that might broadly be associated with the Conservative Right, right-wing tabloids, or, indeed, UKIP.

Here, we can contrast the ghostly presence of Christmas past. Following the lead of New Labour, David Cameron's Christmases were more typically economically and socially liberal in emphasis. Of course, there were certain general overlaps between Cameron's Christmas and May's Christmas. Cameron also included nostalgic and nationalistic elements in his Christmas messages (e.g., the importance for churches, Britain as a Christian country) and vague and agreeable explanations about the meaning of Christmas (e.g., giving, sharing, taking care of others). But there were notable differences. Cameron's 2015 Christmas message foregrounded military interventions and the situation in Syria. This was not a feature of May's main Christmas message, which might have been because of a not untypical rhetorical distancing from the foreign policy of the predecessor or hesitancy in committing to such positions since Trump was about to take over as president.

But Cameron had two further distinctive aspects either downplayed or replaced in May's Christmas message. First, Cameron's Christmas was part of his intensification of the inherited neoliberal assumptions about Christianity and the Bible that he received from Thatcher onwards. Cameron placed a strong emphasis on those providing services (e.g., volunteers, charities) perceived to be beyond those closely connected to the state which may seem innocuous enough, but he also mentioned specific instances of foodbanks and the 2014 floods for which his government received much criticism. For Cameron's Big Society logic, this outsourcing of the state should be seen as a Good Thing because canoeing priests or foodbank volunteers are exactly what we should be expecting of Christian British values. Cameron may have acknowledged homelessness, but he followed this immediately by praising those who help the vulnerable at Christmas. Put another way, as Cameron did at Easter 2014, 'Jesus invented the Big Society 2,000 years ago; I just want to see more of it.'[12] This emphasis was muted in May's Christmas. This is not to say that she was seriously challenging the neoliberal settlement, but this rather represented the political expediency of appealing to the elusive 'Brexit voter' (e.g., and put crudely, pro-NHS, pro-decent wage, priority for British vulnerable, anxieties about immigration, dislike of liberal elite politicians, etc.) which was an emphasis of May's rhetoric from the start and was also being taken up by UKIP.[13]

Second, we need to recall these comments by May: 'We want minority communities to be able to recognise and stand up for their traditions, but we also want to be able to stand up for our traditions generally, and that includes Christmas.' A year earlier, Cameron certainly made nostalgic claims about Britain being a 'Christian country' and the related values represented by Jesus' birth ('peace, mercy, goodwill and, above all, hope') but it was because of these 'important religious roots and Christian values' that 'Britain has been such a successful home to people of all faiths and none'.[14] Indeed, in 2014, Cameron made similar comments. Britain may have churches large and small up and down the country but they 'will hold open their doors and welcome people of faith and none to give thanks and celebrate together'.[15] The phrase 'all faiths and none' (or variants) was a favourite term for Cameron (used also by his Coalition partner, Nick Clegg) as his particular way of simultaneously explaining that the Bible and Christianity, and the values they, like other religions represent, were also the source of his notion of what made up (neo)liberal multicultural British or English nationhood. Furthermore, as noted in the previous chapter, for Cameron, human rights, equality, monarchy, parliamentary democracy, protest, freedom, abolition of slavery, emancipation of women, responsibility, hard work, charity, compassion, humility, self-sacrifice, love, pride in working for the common good, honouring social obligations to one another, and the first forms of welfare provision were not first from the development of the state but, tellingly, from the Bible and Christianity. And yet these values 'speak to us all – to people of every faith and none'.[16] The paternalistic rhetoric was obviously a nationalist move in its own right, even if different to May's nod in the direction of a soft ethnonationalism. In fact, we might say that Cameron's myth of British and Christian superiority was more obviously part of the pre-Trump, pre-Brexit liberal embrace of others without inclusion or at least mention of, as Žižek might put it, any problematic, illiberal Otherness typical of neoliberal multicultural discourse.[17] There is more to say on this in relation to Cameron and we will return to issues of such 'post-racial' discourse in the next chapter.

But, in a new world of Trump and (understood a certain way) Brexit, May's rhetoric, following the lead of Shailesh Vara, was blunt in its identifying the Other and its difference, seemingly left open without explicit judgement. Note in May's response the strong distinction between minorities ('their traditions') and the assumption of a normative British identity which, if not exactly 'white', then 'our traditions' (particularly Christmas) were emphatically not Diwali, Vaisakhi or Eid. The Brexit-inspired Othering of those deemed Asian minorities ought to be clear enough and it was similar to what we saw with Farage in the previous chapter, albeit with more openly positive things to say about Islam and Muslims. Perhaps this flirting with an ethnonationalist understanding of Christmas was unsurprising given her early premiership of a red, white and blue Brexit, a desire to deal with the threat of UKIP, an influential cohort of Leave MPs on the backbenches, and, most tellingly, the Conservative government floating the idea of companies identifying non-British workers.[18]

Another parliamentary exchange gained greater press coverage:

Fiona Bruce (Congleton) (Con): Comments this week by the equalities commissioners about not being worried about talking about Christmas at work were important, because many Christians are now worried, even fearful, about mentioning their faith in public. Will the Prime Minister therefore join me in welcoming the recent Lawyers' Christian Fellowship publication 'Speak Up!', which confirms that in our country the legal rights of freedom of religion and freedom of speech to speak about one's faith responsibly, respectfully and without fear are as strong today as ever?

Prime Minister, Theresa May: My hon. Friend raises an important issue which matters both to her and me. I think the phrase that was used by the Lawyers' Christian Fellowship was 'the jealously guarded principle' of that ability to speak freely, as she says, respectfully and responsibly about one's religion. I am happy to welcome the publication of this report and its findings. Of course, we are now into the season of Advent. We have a very strong tradition in this country of religious tolerance and freedom of speech, and our Christian heritage is something we can all be proud of. I am sure we would all want to ensure that people at work do feel able to speak about their faith, and also feel able to speak quite freely about Christmas.[19]

By invoking Christmas, an assumed aspect of normative culture was once again seemingly under threat. Quite who or what was threatening Christmas was left unsaid, while audiences and inherited mythmaking about 'political correctness' and national identity could fill the gaps where required. Certainly, it may be puzzling to some to think that Christmas was ever under threat. We might argue that Christmas carols, nativities, public Christmas trees, private Christmas trees, unsafely decorated houses, drunken Christmas parties, abuse of office photocopiers, Noddy Holder, Shakin' Stevens, Kim Wilde, VH1 in December, the announcement of Christmas adverts, buying presents for people you barely know or care about in fear of recriminations, secret Santa, the Queen's message, Christmas TV, complaining that Christmas starts earlier each year, social isolation, loneliness, and so on might suggest a context in which people can indeed 'feel able to speak quite freely about Christmas'. But this would be beside the point. It was again the construction of a threatened normative culture that was the message here but one which simultaneously laid claim to the values of 'religious tolerance and freedom of speech'.

This implicit myth of potential persecution and threatening Others had obvious resonance in an age of Brexit understood in terms of race and immigration. And it is once again striking that there was, in this instance, no mention of other traditions holding the same values, as was the case with May's predecessor. May's rhetoric functioned as a challenge to Cameron's 'liberal' take on Christmas, Christianity and the Bible. It was a harking back to another kind of nostalgic Conservative view associated with Thatcher and Enoch Powell where there was an even stronger ethnonationalist take on Christianity.[20] It is perhaps fitting that the ubiquitous Vicar's Daughter image represented a new spin on the gendered presentation of another prime minister with whom May was compared and who was remembered (not entirely accurately) as hero of the Brexit cause: Thatcher, the good Christian housewife and the daughter of a hardworking grocer and Methodist preacher.[21] In her 2016 Christmas message, May continued the favoured narrative of The Vicar's Daughter which was now told with a festive touch. Here, we got hints of the presentation of May as the result of a kind of idealised no-nonsense, disciplined and middle-class upbringing ('Having grown up in a vicarage, I know how demanding it can be for those who have to work over the Christmas period').

Indeed, May also gave an interview about her Christmas (which gained wider media attention) with one of the few publications that could compete with *A Christmas Carol* for seasonal nostalgia: the *Radio Times*.[22] This Christmas, transmitted through May's class habitus, was understood to be both nostalgic and British, infused with what might be assumed to involve sensible, middle-class values and manners. She had a quick drink 'with friends in our village'. Charity began at home when the churches in Maidenhead then put on 'lunch and entertainment' for older people, particularly those who might be alone. For the Christmas meal itself, she would always prefer to cook not the traditional turkey but the even more traditional goose. For TV, she preferred the Christmas staples of Doctor Who, Agatha Christie and Poirot (starring David Suchet, of course), though she would never eat in front of the television. The interview also brought up The Vicar's Daughter cliche. In this respect, the interviewer asked if 'the religious side' of Christmas was important and the answer was an unsurprising 'yes'. And 'religious' here was deemed to be 'going to midnight Mass on Christmas Eve and church on Christmas Day morning' enhanced by the recollection that as a child she 'had to wait until my father had finished his services before I could open my presents' which 'felt like a very long wait' as friends 'would be able to open their presents first thing in the morning'.

As with the *Financial Times* interview, this was part of May's post-Cameron branding as an idealised *Daily Mail* reader's unflinching, get-the-job-done prime minister where her Christian upbringing and context was assumed to be directly transferable to her politics. As Thatcher's early image was partly an attempt to distance herself from the then political establishment, one function of the mythmaking around May was to show that she was not part of the 'liberal elite' nor a 'citizen of the world', nor the stereotypical metropolitan types rejected (at the very least if certain media narratives were to be believed) in the EU Referendum. Indeed, in addition to the assumed background of this being the soul of British culture, heritage and identity, there was a Thatcherite downplaying of gender itself being significant while simultaneously constructing an idealised female figure of Middle England. So, when asked if she had any TV role models, she could reference British National Treasures (the great Diana Rigg and Joanna Lumley in *The Avengers*) but add that 'I don't think I thought about it in those terms. I have never had a female role model – I've always just got on with doing what I am doing.' From this perspective, foregrounding too much of anything that might sound like feminism could easily have been deemed a little *too* liberal elite in certain influential circles.

What emerged was Christmas as a cipher for a picture of a normative culture, politics and heritage which was deemed tolerant but represented in distinction from 'minorities' and led by a no-nonsense woman, not that gender politics should remotely matter, or so this logic went. This was clearly one prominent option among Brexit-based understandings of religion and Christianity, and one with resonance on the Right (see Chapter 3). Yet, despite May being Prime Minister, this did not mean it was the understanding of Christmas, Christianity and religion that would become overwhelmingly dominant. Indeed, by 25 December 2016 any overtly hard Brexit rhetoric was now becoming a Conservative problem. The previously safe Conservative seat of Richmond Park happened to be strongly pro-EU and saw victory for Liberal Democrats in the by-election at the beginning of December (and would only *just* return to Conservatives in the 2017 General Election). With a then seemingly revitalised Liberal Democrats with their strong Remain message and a small parliamentary majority for the Conservatives, it was perhaps little surprise that May's Christmas speech had a subtle qualification: 'with our international partners, we must work together to promote trade, [and] increase prosperity'. At the end of 2016, the rhetoric of 'the 48 per cent', incorporating liberal and/or more affluent Remain voters who did not necessarily like Labour and Corbyn (particularly for supporting the outcome of the Referendum vote), still held some political force in the press and should not be underestimated as an influence on May's assumptions about terms associated with Christmas, Christianity and religion.

By Easter 2017, the Conservatives were taking over UKIP's anti-EU rhetoric from the Right while simultaneously not wanting to isolate pro-EU (and potentially Conservative) voters entirely. In this context, it was striking that May (still stressing her credentials as The Vicar's Daughter) addressed Brexit concerns with a nod in the direction of Cameron's festive rhetoric:

> This Easter I think of those values that we share – values that I learnt in my own childhood, growing up in a vicarage. Values of compassion, community, citizenship. The sense of obligation we have to one

another. These are values we all hold in common, and values that are visibly lived out every day by Christians, as well as by people of other faiths or none.[23]

This was not quite the stark contrast of 'their traditions' and 'our traditions' mentioned by May in Parliament with reference to Christmas and at first sight this might seem to be as inclusive as Cameron's 'all faiths and none'. However, notice that it was not '*all* faiths and none' but '*other* faiths and none' which marked a clearer difference and was consistent with her earlier 'their'/'our' Christmas rhetoric. It is also worth observing the context of May's Easter because just prior to this speech May became involved in a minor controversy about whether the National Trust and Cadbury should have included 'Easter' in their logo for their jointly sponsored egg hunt, in addition to the various mentions of 'Easter' on their website. She thought it was 'absolutely ridiculous' that they did not and that Easter was a 'very important festival for the Christian faith', citing that she was both a vicar's daughter and a member of the National Trust (another potential signifier of a certain patriotic stereotype) in support.[24] This apparent War on Easter was precisely the sort of debate that we see enraging figures on the far right, keen to identify it as distinctively English/British and under threat from Muslims, lefties and even, occasionally, Jews (see Chapter 3). Nevertheless, the nod to 'people of other faiths or none' reveals some of the other ideological pulls on May. It was not likely that she would have been rhetorically divisive in an official government message for a religious festival. This would have been even more pertinent given the Westminster terror attack a month earlier when Khalid Masood murdered and injured people with a car and murdered a police officer with a knife which he claimed was a response to military intervention in 'Muslim countries'.[25]

All this belonged to what would become May's overall electoral strategy – namely, to hold together different interested parties after the Brexit vote – and one which appeared, in the short term at least, to pay dividends. According to YouGov polling published in March 2017, an overwhelming majority still would have voted in the same way. However, what was also revealed was that a significant majority of people (69 per cent to 21 per cent) thought that the government should accept that Brexit now ought to go ahead, with 49 per cent confident in May's negotiation skills (39 per cent against) and 52 per cent thinking her proposals were positive for Britain.[26] We might contrast this with only

15 per cent thinking Parliament should vote on whether to accept a deal. These tendencies appeared to be reflected in the May 2017 local elections with the Conservatives performing strongly and seemingly absorbing UKIP voters. The Richmond Park defeat now appeared to be a typical mid-term, anti-government protest vote as the slim 52–48 Referendum split was already becoming a distant memory for a good chunk of Remainers. But May's General Election rhetoric and growing coalition were also partly designed to appeal to the working-class Right, disgruntled with their economic lot under neoliberalism and who might have been attracted to UKIP or even groups further rightward. The 2017 Conservative Party Manifesto notably attacked 'untrammeled free markets', a (somewhat vague) offer of protection to 'people working in the "gig" economy' and, in language which we will see in Chapter 5 was typically assumed to be a deviation from purer 'religion', the rejection of the *cult* of selfish individualism' (my italics).[27] In other words, this apparent embrace of protectionism was a rhetorical and implicit othering of the dominant economic system that was integral to the anger partly underpinning support for UKIP by those who felt abandoned by New Labour (see Chapter 3).

On calling the snap General Election in June 2017, May was set for a landslide which would have marked a significant ideological as well as electoral victory. But statistics on attitudes are not, of course, some infallible indicator of electoral success or a necessary indication of what would be decisive for people when actually at the ballot box. Indeed, the Election itself turned out to be something of a failure for May for numerous reasons, including insufficient appeal for a younger vote with such voters having different interests while also being affected by precarious working patterns and cuts in, for instance, education. And, while his party attracted Remainers, Corbyn was also fighting with May for the UKIP vote. With what looked like the return to two-party politics, an alternative to May emerged, spearheaded by Corbyn. And with this came a cluster of alternative understandings of religion, Christianity and Islam.

Jeremy Corbyn's Christmas

Days before May had delivered her first Christmas speech, Corbyn was experiencing his second Christmas as Labour leader. A year earlier, Corbyn had already given his socialist tradition a Yuletide spin in his

2015 Christmas message published in the *Sunday Mirror*.[28] In this instance, Corbyn made a move familiar to the construction of an English or British radicalism by using the Bible to protect Marx from perceived corruptions and make him palatable to English political discourse.[29] He thus ended with both 'Jesus said: "It is more blessed to give than to receive"' and a carefully worded socialist saying with biblical precedent (Acts of the Apostles 4.32–35) which, in one form, was famously used by Marx (though here simply referred to as 'a similar maxim that inspired our party'): 'From each according to their means, to each according to their needs.' A number of traditional themes from this overtly socialist construction of Christianity were present in Corbyn's 2015 message (e.g., low pay, refugees, child poverty, firefighters, hospital workers), and his concept of 'solidarity' and 'unity' (traditional language of the Left, of course) was grounded in Christmas and the Bible and, most unusually for a modern Labour leader but once an assumption among certain Nonconformist Christians, equated with the s-word – socialism: 'the Christmas story holds up a mirror to us all. "Do unto others as you would have done to you" – that is the essence of my socialism, summed up in the word – "solidarity".'[30] Socialist understandings of the Bible might have returned to the Labour Party, but the annual snow and tinsel meant they were now officially mainstream in English political discourse.

For Christmas 2016 Corbyn delivered a video message where he focused specifically on the 'shocking rise in homelessness' and how, 'since 2010, rough sleeping has doubled and increased by 30 per cent in the last year alone'.[31] His message was notably different in emphasis from those of his predecessors (and in line with his left-wing mentor, Tony Benn) in that he emphasised specific instances of injustice and the victims of the intensification of neoliberalism, in this case an attack on the scale of homelessness in 'the sixth richest country in the world'. We might compare, or perhaps contrast, this with Ed Miliband's 2014 address. Miliband (like Clegg) placed issues of solidarity more safely into the distant past, to the First World War and the famous truce and football match. Indeed, for Miliband, this football match was sort of Christian but presented in a way that could equally have been spoken by Cameron: 'In the midst of a tragic conflict the generosity, hope and sense of human solidarity that is characteristic of the Christian faith and culture came to the fore.' What is also notable was that Miliband referenced the more politically radical tradition of the Labour Party where the Bible and Christianity were once used to justify and provide authority for the trade unions, hostility to the establishment, egalitarianism, nationalisation, collectivism, founding of the NHS and welfare state, and so on. However, the more overtly leftist version of this tradition had seemed to have lost its power since the days of Tony Benn who would mention leftist specifics in the present in his application of the Bible and radical Christianity (e.g., the then imminent Iraq War, Sharon's treatment of Palestinians, hostility against asylum-seekers, etc.).[32] Miliband rather followed this Labour tradition to oppose general things like 'suffering', 'injustice' and 'poverty' through solidarity but filtered them through the New Labour years by keeping things vague and without any specific application other than examples from a century prior:

> We need the same sense of compassion in the face of the suffering and hatred that afflicts parts of our world. I am proud that the Labour movement has such deep roots in the Christian tradition of social activism and solidarity in the United Kingdom.[33]

Certainly, there were faint echoes of an older socialist tradition but, ideologically, this was not significantly distant from Cameron's understanding of Christianity and notions of Big Society.

At this point the more overtly socialist tradition had indeed long been kept at a safe chronological and ideological distance since the 1990s when Labour began to embrace Thatcherite economics with traditional rhetoric generalised to avoid overtly left-statist policies.[34] However, as Corbyn's Christmas messages showed, the return to referencing precise – and potentially antagonistic – leftist causes of the present (particularly homelessness) as part of a radical Christian tradition were soon to be resurrected. Indeed, in sharp contrast to previous Labour leaders, Corbyn was forthright in presenting his socialism unwrapped in his Christmas message, particularly in 2015. More broadly in Corbyn's Labour, Corbyn and allies such as Cat Smith ('Jesus was a radical socialist')[35] were as explicit as any contemporary frontbench politician for decades in advocating socialist understandings of religion and Christianity. But in advocating an explicitly socialist understanding of Christianity, Corbyn, as we will see in receptions of him in the press (Chapter 5), effectively symbolised an alternative to neoliberalism eternal and the suppressed leftist Other of the then dominant political settlement. Indeed, one MP sympathetic towards Corbyn told me that Jesus in their understanding was too radical for Parliament and, rather than become an MP, Jesus would be more suited to Occupy, a view common enough during Occupy – including Occupy London Stock Exchange where Jesus throwing out financial figures from the Temple gained a degree of prominence.[36] This same Corbyn sympathiser went further still and claimed that the Bible was a 'manifesto' for turning capitalism on its head and cited Jesus' actions in the Temple as evidence.

Returning to the Christmas speeches, what was also different was that Corbyn was the only major political leader urging more state intervention in some form in an era where austerity was the dominant feature of mainstream English political discourse since the 2007/8 crash (whether Conservatives, Liberal Democrats or pre-Corbyn Labour). Where Cameron in his festive messages rhetorically stressed that foodbanks were a positive example of outsourcing the state, Corbyn pressed for greater state support (as he did in 2015): 'Labour has pledged to put an end to rough sleeping in our first term of government. We'd do that by doubling the number of homes available for people who've been sleeping on the streets. We'd also supply support for homeless charities, and the people who work and volunteer for them.' All this was grounded in the Bible and presented as being encapsulated by the Christmas story: 'They remind us of Christmas values: love for your neighbour, working together and hope, hope that things can be different.'

The reference to 'love for your neighbour' is significant because it occurs in the Parable of the Good Samaritan (Luke 10.25–37), as well as other biblical passages (Leviticus 19.18; Mark 12.28–34; Matthew 22.34–40; Galatians 5.14). When Corbyn alluded to the Bible it was almost always to the Parable of the Good Samaritan and the working out of 'love for your neighbour' through the notion of not 'walking by on the other side', typically to promote welfare or social housing. For example, Corbyn invoked the Good Samaritan in his (first) leadership victory speech in September 2015, just as he did regularly in his popular rallies (whether in the leadership election or the General Election). The context of the allusion in September 2015 was following on from his opposition to the Welfare Reform Bill which had partly propelled him to leadership of the Labour Party. He added, 'we want to live in a society where we don't pass by on the other side of those people rejected by an unfair welfare system. Instead we reach out to end the scourge of homelessness and desperation that so many people face in our society.'[37] In addition to an implicit critique of much of the Labour Party, there was an anti-Thatcherite emphasis in this allusion as it ran contrary to Thatcher's famous claim that 'no-one would remember the Good Samaritan if he'd only had good intentions; he had money as well'.[38] Corbyn's anti-Thatcherite move in relation to the Good Samaritan, poverty, and the role of welfare was one he made elsewhere.[39]

Corbyn's 2016 Christmas message was not an obviously Brexit one. 'British values' were mentioned but this sort of phrase was (and remains) extremely common in political rhetoric. Nevertheless, Brexit certainly had a haunting presence. The absence of overt Brexit themes was striking, particularly when the other party messages from 2016 addressed such topics head-on. But Corbyn had his own form of the inevitable festive family clashes and decisions about who needed most attention. The traditional Labour vote from post-industrial Midlands and northwards was, put crudely, a Leave vote while the newer metropolitan heartlands of Labour were more typically Remain. Of course, how this might transfer into elections was not going to be straightforward (and still is not). Without any benefits of hindsight, Corbyn's explicit support for the Referendum result through whipping his party into voting for the triggering of Article 50 to leave the EU was partly a tactical move designed to hold on to places like Stoke and to attract some of those who had defected to UKIP. Though often overblown (see Chapter 4), there was an anti-immigration discourse associated with the Leave vote and we have already seen that May toyed with this sort of angle.

To complicate matters further, and as his Christmas messages indicated, Corbyn was a long-time, dedicated supporter of migrant and refugee rights while having to face the easily misunderstood and controversial problem for the Left: the end of freedom of movement upon leaving the single market in relation to management of migration, wages and exploitation of labour. Was the Left to focus on a cheaper migrant workforce across the EU or unionised and higher wages for workers in the UK (including those coming to work in the UK) post-Brexit? Though the issue was not precisely the same, it might still be significant that in his 2016 message Corbyn focused on one of his other long-term interests to try and work a way through, or around, this problem: homelessness *in the UK*. In this respect, we might note how he highlighted his visit to Centrepoint, 'a charity that does vital work in London, Bradford, Sunderland, and other places, giving opportunities to homeless young people and helping them off the streets into a better life' (by contrast Liberal Democrat leader, Tim Farron, went to a refugee centre in Paris for his Christmas 2016 message). Corbyn may not have personally believed that charity began at home, but we might speculate that the location of his message may have been designed partly to appeal to, or not isolate, those who did.

In this respect, it remains important to highlight that when Corbyn invoked 'our values' or 'British values' in relation to political assumptions about Christianity and the Bible, he could be located in a tradition of invoking Christianity, the Bible, and even religion, as something distinctive to the British or English Left. To repeat, this has historically been used to present a British or English socialism uncontaminated by continental variants deemed problematic, as well as an acknowledgement of Nonconformist influence on the Labour movement (see Chapter 1). It is significant that Corbyn concluded his first speech as Labour Party leader with reference to Keir Hardie – one of the figures most obviously remembered in the British Christian Socialist tradition – and his words, 'My work has consisted of trying to stir up a divine discontent with wrong.'[40] There are other more precise explanations behind the invocation of this tradition of English or British socialism. It is notable that this tradition was employed by Corbyn just after claims that he lacked patriotism because he silently reflected on the generation of his parents rather than singing the national anthem at a Battle of Britain memorial service, because his tie was too loose, and because he had not bowed to a sufficient degree for sections of the press at the Cenotaph on Remembrance Sunday. Related to this, it is also telling that a version of the tradition associated with Tony Benn (see Chapter 1) was utilised in light of the electoral threat from UKIP. For instance, Sam Tarry, co-director of Corbyn's re-election campaign, explicitly sought to counter the threat from UKIP with reference to the 'freedoms' fought for by 'the Peasants' Revolt, the Tolpuddle Martyrs, the Chartists, and the suffragettes and others' as part of the 'radical tradition' to emphasise 'an English Labour Party' with a 'socialist vision' which is a 'patriotic one, because nothing is more patriotic than building a society for the many; not the few'.[41]

In terms of a homegrown English or British radicalism in the tradition of Christianity and radical biblical interpreters, this was something Corbyn likely inherited directly from Tony Benn. Benn had developed an ongoing interest in the English Civil War and understanding the Levellers as radical democratic interpreters of the Bible as he began to shift firmly to the Left in the early 1970s.[42] Corbyn, who was personally and ideologically close to Benn, described the leftist gatherings at Benn's house in his early career as his 'university education', and where, according to John McDonnell, they 'would discuss everything under the sun'.[43] Given that Benn had also been publishing on such radical traditions around this time, it is highly likely that here we have probably the most significant influence on Corbyn in this respect. Just months before becoming Labour leader, Corbyn himself gave a speech on the Leveller John Lilburne with a strong Bennite bent. What is particularly significant is that Corbyn's speech was designed to provide an alternative British or English history to Michael Gove's proposals for a history prioritising certain kinds of British values of leaders, battles, and national 'superiority' (Corbyn's term), which for Gove included an understanding of the King James Bible as a core part of British heritage and democracy, with the sting of any politically dangerous or unpalatable texts, history or weirdness removed.[44]

Instead, Corbyn proposed that the English Civil War should be centrepiece of education because it overthrew 'the undemocratic divine rights of kings' and 'asserted the power of elected Parliament over the monarch and the barons'. Corbyn foregrounded the importance of the Quakers who were 'extremely dangerous to the established church and the power that went with the established church'. However, this was not restricted to a liberal democratic argument or a critique of church hierarchy. For Corbyn, Lilburne and the Levellers were ahead of their time in the promotion of religious freedom, democracy, and 'the general ideas of socialists as a whole'. They belonged, he argued, to a radical democratic tradition that cannot be removed from a challenge to the 'whole class structure of society'. He related this to the corruption of democracy by money, privilege, place and patronage, as well as the failure of national democracies to hold to account 'global corporations and global finance'. He finished his talk with a quotation from the Levellers' Manifesto, 'An Agreement of the Free People of England', with obvious biblical allusions:

> We doe not impower them to impresse or constraint any person to serve in war by Sea or Land every mans Concience being to be satisfied in the justness of that cause wherein he hazards his own life, or may destroy an others ... Thus, as becometh a free People, thankfull unto God for this blessed opportunity, and desirous to make use thereof to his glory, in taking of every yoak, and removing every burthen, in delivering the captive, and setting the oppressed free; we have in all the particular Heads forementioned, done as we would be

done unto, and as we trust in God will abolish all occasion of offence and discord, and produce the lasting Peace and Prosperity of this Common wealth.[45]

This, Corbyn suggested, should be taught in schools as a celebration of what has been achieved and what can be done; this should be presented as British or English 'history from below' to challenge Gove's take on national history. That radical English or British traditions with an emphasis on egalitarianism rather than ethnicity were part of the ideological background to Corbyn's politics ought to be clear enough. However, when Corbyn became leader, extended discourses on the Levellers were not likely to form a readily known set of cultural references. Instead, and in line with a more simplistic presentation of his message, Corbyn turned to the most popular and pithy biblical allusion from the Good Samaritan and used the vehicle of Christmas to promote a more radical socialism.

Alongside the popular presentation of Corbyn as jam-maker and allotment-keeper (a domesticated and recognisable English type as much as The Vicar's Daughter), this British or English radical tradition provided Corbyn with a degree of protection (albeit limited) from the ongoing media attacks (see Chapter 5). But not even Christmas could provide Corbyn with full protection if he was going to be understood as partaking in Yuletide misery worthy of Scrooge himself. Indeed, it was worse still as he was even portrayed as *betraying* Christmas, or at least evoking the sort of Nonconformist English Christianity of cursed memory: Puritanism. Despite being published after Corbyn's Christmas message in the *Sunday Mirror* (19 December 2015), an article from the *Telegraph* (23 December 2015) reported that Corbyn would not give a Christmas message on Christmas Eve and had been 'accused' of cancelling Christmas.[46] This seemingly impossible future feat was, presumably, prevented by the little Christmas miracle of an MP willing to do the accusing and, presumably, saving our future Christmases. While the article eventually went on to print denials of Corbyn being anti-Christmas, it is worth quoting the main part of the article:

Jeremy Corbyn has been accused of 'cancelling Christmas' by refusing to issue a Christmas message.

The Labour leader has decided to break with recent tradition and not issue a message tomorrow on Christmas Eve.

Instead he will make his thoughts known ahead of New Year's Day.

Mr Corbyn's predecessor Ed Miliband issued messages to the nation on Christmas Eve both in 2014 and 2013.

Mr Corbyn's decision to not to [sic] send a Christmas message to Britain's Christians is in stark contrast to when he sent a message to British Muslims to mark the Muslim festival of Eid in September and a Tweet to mark the Hindi festival of Diwali last month.

David Cameron, the Prime Minister, is expected to follow tradition and issue a Christmas message tomorrow.

Andrew Bridgen, a Conservative MP, said: 'This is the new politics – Corbyn cancels Christmas.'

'It is just a hint of what the British people would have to look forward to under a Corbyn-led Government.'

Instead of discussing the contents of Corbyn's Christmas message, it was instead stressed that Corbyn was anti-Christmas and he was presented as the kind of 'politically correct' person who would say 'Happy Holidays' or the like, pander to Muslims and immigrants, and, paradoxically perhaps, do something only Oliver Cromwell would dare do. But, with the hindsight of May's Christmas a year later, we can see how Corbyn and Corbyn's Christmas effectively symbolised the kinds of things from which we need protecting, at least according to certain sections of the press.

The actual contents of Corbyn's Christmas message certainly functioned in an antithetical way when contrasted with the hostility to refugees in some discourses on the Right. Perhaps the most notorious recent example was the infamous *Daily Mail* cartoon (17 November 2015) published after terrorist attacks in Paris which were claimed by ISIS. The perpetrators were later revealed to include French and Belgian nationals of Moroccan and Algerian descent, some with Syrian connections.[47] Nevertheless, the cartoon caricatured refugees by representing The Muslim through silhouetted figures of weaponised Mujahideen fighters in Afghanistan, women in the hijab, presumably the occasional innocent refugee, and rats (which, as was pointed out, were strikingly reminiscent of antisemitic cartoons from Nazi Germany), all crossing the open (EU) border.[48] Against the backdrop of these kinds of ideas, Corbyn's invocation in his 2015 Christmas message of the popular Left/liberal reading of the Nativity as a story of refugees only heightened the problem of this retelling for his opponents: 'Christmas is also a time for reflection, and it is worth considering the poignancy of the Nativity story. It is about offering shelter to a family in need and to those who find themselves – refugees fleeing evil.'[49] From the logic of some sections of the Right in dealing with Corbyn, it was difficult to criticise The Jam-Maker and Allotment-Keeper for positively using something with the cultural value of Christianity and Christmas, and certainly when it was a popularly received understanding of the Bible. To get around this problem in the competition for ownership of Christmas, the *Telegraph* article had to avoid criticising the popular retelling of the Nativity story by acting as if it were never retold by Corbyn at all, while manufacturing an anti-Christmas controversy in its place.

Excursus: the Good Samaritan in Syria

To get a more rounded picture of Corbyn's assumptions about religion, we also need to look more broadly at the question of foreign policy, Islam and the Labour Party, though as we will see this also relates to Corbyn's understanding of Christmas. Here, the Good Samaritan in a different guise was present elsewhere in Corbyn's Labour, but this time fully militarised. In his speech (2 December 2015) supporting the bombing of Syria, Hilary Benn, probably the most high-profile Labour front-bencher hostile to Corbyn's agenda (and son of Corbyn's mentor, Tony), justified intervention with reference to the very same parable and the very same words and sentiment within the parable, while coming to the exact opposite position on military intervention to that of Corbyn. And note that the addition 'of the road' made this allusion to Luke 10.31–32 more explicit than other uses we have seen (and perhaps more so among those with memories of the hymn 'Cross Over the Road' from school assemblies):

As a party we have always been defined by our internationalism. We believe we have a responsibility one to another. We never have, and we never should, *walk by on the other side of the road.* And we are here faced by fascists ... They hold our values in contempt. They hold our belief in tolerance and decency in contempt. They hold our democracy ... in contempt ... Socialists and Trade Unionists and others joined the International Brigades in the 1930s to fight against Franco. It's why this entire House stood up against Hitler and Mussolini ... we must now confront this evil.[50]

If nothing else, this example shows how exegesis can be driven by a given political ideology while the biblical text can simultaneously provide the authority. But the authority of Hilary Benn's position, and the assumption of Corbyn as counter to the political mainstream, was further enhanced by the rounds of applause and positive media spin Benn's speech was given (and played in full on BBC Radio 4, on 3 December 2015).[51] The construction of ISIS/Daesh was also part of this implicit dialogue about understandings of religion. ISIS were constructed not only as 'fascists' but as being 'evil'. Unsurprisingly, ISIS-as-evil was common enough and found in some other relevant contexts. It was a similar construction to that of Cameron who, as we will see further in the next chapter, saw ISIS/Daesh as a monstrous perversion of a purer liberal democratic Islam. But also like Hilary Benn, Cameron alluded to the parable of the Good Samaritan in justifying military intervention against ISIS when he claimed that '*we cannot just walk on by* if we are to keep this country safe ... we have to confront this menace ... we will do so in a calm, deliberate way but with an iron determination' (my italics).[52]

This liberal-interventionist Good Samaritan had the further function of providing the authority for establishing who had the legitimate monopoly on violence which explains why, in the Syria debate of December 2015, Cameron was keen to drop terms like 'Islamic State' by claiming the organisation was neither Islamic nor a state.[53] As with his assumptions about 'true religion' or 'real religion', only 'true states' could legitimately use violence. This also meant that the opposition was categorised in fantastical terms (e.g., 'they are monsters ... the embodiment of evil') and that such opposition could not be categorised as True Muslims (who ought to be good liberal democratic citizens). Cameron's presentation of evil obviously had a sympathetic audience. But simplifying the situation by blaming 'evil' and a 'warped version of Islam', and denying that the invasion of Iraq and its aftermath was the 'source' or 'root cause' for the rise of ISIS, also masked the complex histories and geopolitics involved in the emergence of ISIS and localised terror attacks in Britain, France and Belgium (see Chapter 3).[54] And so, in Cameron's last Christmas message (2015) just after the Syria vote, he talked only of the most immediate causes of refugees in Syria (ISIS/Daesh and the new enemy, Assad) and the problems faced by Christians 'from Africa to Asia' worshipping despite fear of persecution, in order to justify the claims that the armed forces are 'in the skies of Iraq and Syria, targeting the terrorists that threaten those countries and our security at home' and 'on the ground, helping to bring stability to countries from Afghanistan to South Sudan'.[55]

Hilary Benn's use of the Good Samaritan and his understanding of 'evil' were rhetorically and ideologically similar to Cameron's. The difference was that Benn, like Blair before him (and recall that Benn supported the Iraq War), used the language of the Labour tradition and its internationalist history to make what is effectively the same interventionist point. ISIS were now deemed fascist, the types of people socialists, trade unionists and, ultimately, the Labour Party would have fought. It is striking that Benn grounded this intervention (like plenty of interventionist politicians before him) in the emotive story of British resistance to Hitler and in the great socialist story of the Spanish Civil War. This is not, of course, to deny fascist tendencies in strands of such thought but an emphasis on fascism alone does not explain those complex histories feeding into groups like al Qaeda and ISIS. The myth-buster might also be tempted to point out that the British state was not so forthright in confronting fascism in the Spanish Civil War and, as we will see in Chapter 6, one group fighting ISIS in Syria and claiming the heritage of the International Brigades – the Bob Crow Brigade – were not happy with Hilary Benn. But, again, historical realities are beside the point because comparing ISIS with Franco and Hitler and the British state with the aims of the International Brigades was part of an attempt to convince the Labour Party of the need for ongoing military intervention. This was Labour mythmaking and part of a stable, non-complex historical lineage, much the same way as Blair invoked the 'apocalyptic' tradition used in the development of the welfare state and NHS to justify intervention in Afghanistan.

Corbyn's understanding of ISIS and how to deal with them was first tested as leader in the 2015 debate over military intervention in Syria and in the Christmas messages shortly after. By way of contrast to Cameron's militaristic Christmas message, Corbyn, as we saw, placed the stress on the Nativity being about offering shelter to 'refugees fleeing evil' and with a possible reference to alternative ways of dealing with fascism in the claim that globally there were 'more refugees today fleeing horror than at any time since the Second World War'.[56] Elsewhere, Corbyn was more explicit as he too played the same game of understanding ISIS as a 'perversion of Islam', as he did in his first major interview as leader on BBC1's *Andrew Marr Show* (27 September 2015) and in his speech following Shami Chakrabarti's report into antisemitism and racism in the Labour Party where he distinguished between 'our Muslim friends' and 'various self-styled Islamic states or organisations'.[57] But this idea of a distortion of a truer form of Islam allowed Corbyn to continue the anti-war stance of much of the Labour Left and to come to the exact opposite conclusion to that of Hilary Benn and Cameron and other users of this kind of binary (e.g., Thatcher, Blair, Boris Johnson), that is, to justify *non*-military intervention in the Middle East and North Africa.

In Corbyn's logic, ISIS being a deviation from a purer Islam meant that negotiations would be impossible and so, Corbyn argued on the *Andrew Marr Show*, the alternative way to deal with them involved stopping funding, arms and oil revenues. This was a logic that gave Corbyn some protection from, and indeed temporarily reversed, the allegation of 'terrorist sympathiser' after the terror attacks in Manchester and London in the run-up to the 2017 General Election as he unusually pushed foreign policy to the fore as one explanatory factor behind terror. This turned out to be either a popular explanation or not unpopular enough to be a vote loser (or a bit of both). Indeed, given Corbyn's politics and views on foreign policy he was one of the few politicians who could push this line with some perceived authenticity. Further, a message from anti-fascist, anti-ISIS volunteers associated with the Bob Crow Brigade was sent from Syria unequivocally backing Corbyn (SMASH ISIS, VOTE CORBYN), supporting his idea of stopping funding at the source.[58] On the Red London Facebook page, one proxy for the Bob Crow Brigade, the message from northern Syria (8 June 2017) developed Corbyn's logic about a perversion of Islam even further by attacking Western support (including that of May) for 'Salafi Jihadism' and stating that such a label was more appropriate than 'extreme' Muslims because those causing terror were a 'tiny, tiny group from Saudi Arabia'. By contrast, Corbyn was the only leader prepared to criticise the 'right people'.

The Corbynite logic partly helps explain the mistake Owen Smith made in trying to court the Left in his leadership challenge to Corbyn. While Corbyn claimed that ISIS could never be involved in peace talks, Smith made the following claim (17 August 2016) which would prove damaging for his admittedly already damaged campaign (and which would lead to a firm condemnation from the Bob Crow Brigade – see Chapter 6):

My view is that ultimately, all solutions to these international crises do come about through dialogue, so eventually if we are to try to solve this all of the actors do need to be involved. But at the moment Isil are clearly not interested in negotiating. At some point for us to resolve this, we will need to get people round the table.[59]

As it became clearer when Smith tried to clarify his position and in the ensuing controversies, the notion of talking with ISIS in this discourse had perhaps been confused with the logic behind talking with the different groups in the Irish peace process or Corbyn's much-publicised engagements with Hamas and Hezbollah, as well as overestimating leftist sympathies with certain strands of Islam. But if this were the case then it ignored the perception that even if the Irish Republican Army (IRA) or Hamas were deemed problematic, they remained connected with specific causes that had some sympathetic resonance on the Left (and among some further right), for example, Irish and Palestinian struggles, even if such groups were perceived in mainstream political discourse to be going about things the wrong way. ISIS, in this kind of discourse, were understood as being too far removed from Muslim, Iraqi or Syrian struggles and more interested in a purer fascism or death-cultism.

As with the debate over bombing Syria and the role of the Good Samaritan, competing understandings of ISIS and Islam were (whether participants knew it or not) intertwined with what people thought about Corbyn and were part of the battle for the soul of the Labour Party and English or British socialism. After the 2017 General Election with a gain in seats and a hung Parliament, Corbyn was, for the first time as leader, welcomed by the Parliamentary Labour Party, or at least to a greater degree than before. With this, Corbynite, anti-austerity, anti-war, inclusive, and socialist assumptions about religion, Christianity and the Bible (minus, of course, notions of Jesus the King, ruler of an eternal kingdom, and receiver of expensive gifts of frankincense, gold and myrrh from those presumably of no small means) were stronger than they had been for decades and were now standing nose-to-nose with May's more ethnocentric assumptions as they competed for dominance in post-2008 English political discourse. But this also meant that the Remain vote had not been picked up by the Liberal Democrats in any significant way and that accompanying understandings of religion were muted in dominant discourses. Even so, there was one dimension of dominant understandings of religion, Christianity and the Bible that still cut across political divides and, as Tim Farron would find out, it was one that was not going away: social liberalism.

Tim Farron's Christmas

As his 2016 Christmas address showed, Farron was, for a post-Thatcher politician, unusually forthright in his Christian beliefs, though as leader he did not ultimately stray too far from general liberal assumptions about Christianity and the Bible. As he claimed, 'But do you know what? As a Christian, I think Christmas is about God who gave himself up for us and came to earth in order to do that, who urges us to follow him and to believe that we should do to others what we have done to ourselves.'[60] There are good reasons why Farron wanted to keep certain controls on where he would open his Bible: he had to deal with questions about whether he thought homosexuality – or, more precisely, 'homosexual sex' (to use the favoured term) – was a sin. It is possible that he did think it a sin during his time as leader, but this was not the sort of thing a political leader of a party could readily admit (UKIP aside, perhaps). Farron therefore made the classic liberal distinction (noted favourably by some activists and cross-party MPs I interviewed) between his personal (Christian) morality and his public political liberalism which tolerates other groups and individuals, irrespective of whether they are personally agreeable. This, for Farron, was crucial to him being both a Christian and a L/liberal. In addition to claiming that we are all sinners, to get around the problem of potential media condemnation, as seen in the particularly difficult *Channel 4 News* interview on this topic shortly after becoming leader, Farron's approach was typical enough in political discourse and a move made by both Blair and Obama (as well as Russell Brand): he stressed a more 'liberal' part of the Bible over an 'illiberal' part. When confronted by the interviewer with the decidedly illiberal Leviticus 18.22 ('You shall not lie with a male as one lies with a female; it is an abomination'), Farron's solution was to point to Jesus instead and to favour a biblical passage more amenable to contemporary liberalism, Matthew 7.3: 'You don't pick out the speck of sawdust in your brother's eye when there is a plank in your own' (Farron's paraphrase).[61] The problem for Farron was that, unlike Blair, Obama or Brand, no one really believed he was personally accepting of homosexual sex as un-sinful.

Still, one Liberal Democrat activist I spoke to after the interview said that there was much support within the party membership for Farron and, by making the familiar move to a more palatable aspect of the Bible, that Farron was instead deemed to be particularly strong on issues of social justice. Nevertheless, the presence of liberal constraints on Farron's public presentation of Christianity was effectively confirmed by politicians I interviewed, and notably ones from different perspectives. One MP from a different party told me that Farron handled the situation well while another wished Farron could be more explicit in his views but claimed that the problems of keeping his party onside and 'secularism' (presumably understood as pro-homosexual sex and 'religion' understood as anti-homosexual sex) made it difficult for him. By way of contrast, a senior politician (also from a different party) and former frontbencher thought that Farron should simply oppose homophobia and support homosexual sex or else he must be deemed an irrelevance to political debate. There was likely an allusion to this sort of thinking when it was reported from the 2015 Labour Party conference that Angela Eagle criticised Tim Farron for being 'an evangelical Christian who believes in the literal truth of the bible' at a time of 'a huge revival of fundamentalist religious belief' but he 'just doesn't want to talk about it a lot because he knows how much it will embarrass his own party'.[62] We might note here that terms like 'literal', 'fundamentalist' and 'evangelical' function (as they often do in political discourse) as markers of a distortion from a correct, liberal understanding of a 'purer' religion. In each of these diverse cases, there was the assumption that being open in opposition to homosexual sex was not an option for a leader of one of the main parties. Despite such pressures, Farron's dealing with this issue early in his leadership by effectively refusing to comment on the problematic biblical verses seemed to have worked for him initially in that the issue did not haunt the party too loudly until the 2017 General Election. Here, the pressure on Farron to come clean about his compatibility with a more acceptable liberalism presumably weighed heavy as he first said that being in a gay relationship was not a sin and later (facing up to the theological technicality directly) that homosexual *sex* was not a sin, as the pressure of the election mounted, not that he necessarily believed what he said.[63]

Given the anxieties about potentially illiberal views relating to religion, it is notable in this respect that Farron gave a self-deprecating reference to the use of the Nativity in his 2016 address ('I could try and crowbar in a kind of Nativity message') which functioned as an attempt to make his religiosity sufficiently normalised for mainstream liberal discourses. But it was nevertheless striking when he would push details of his Christianity in his understanding of Christmas. The main stress was a clear anti-Brexit theme for which there was also potential for political capital (for the Liberal Democrats, at least) in light of popular assumptions about the 48 per cent who voted Remain: pro-immigration. Whereas Corbyn was in a homeless shelter in the UK, Farron was, tellingly, in Paris at a holding centre for refugees, particularly *children*, many of whom wanted to come to the UK, a striking move after the recent images of children in Aleppo. Indeed, Britain ('a place of peace and of security and tranquility') was emotionally contrasted with the countries of the refugees ('appalling circumstances, from war, from oppression, and torture'), with another emphasis on age ('They've seen some terrible, terrible things, these young people'). The rhetorical function of this, particularly the emotional pleas about youth, is clear enough and we might contextualise this by recalling the harrowing picture of the three-year-old Aylan Kurdi washed-up dead on a Turkish beach.

Despite the self-deprecation, Farron was immediately clear about grounding the authority of a message of support for refugees in the Bible by endorsing the obviousness of a popular liberal reading of the Gospel texts and Nativity story (which, ironically enough, echoed arguments used in Parliament in support of same-sex marriage): 'Yes, Mary, Joseph and Jesus became refugees. Yes, they were living under the oppression of a wicked regime.' But it was at this point that Farron stressed his Christian credentials and then added further biblical justification: 'God [via Jesus] … urges us to follow him and to believe that we should do to others what we have done to ourselves'. The application of this, of course, was to reverse the situation and imagine if the UK was 'a war-torn and terrible place to live' and 'we' had to make decisions about 'our children'. To justify this, Farron, like all politicians, made sure that his understanding of the Bible, Christianity and God were 'consistent with our heritage'. And if there were any doubt that this was part of a competing ideological battle for the soul of Britain in light of the divisive Referendum vote, then note Farron's plea and implicit defence against the Right's monopoly on nationalism: 'And I guess I'm somebody who is not at all squeamish about my patriotism and very proud to be British.'[64] This was effectively staking claim to be the Christmas for the 48 per cent, a plea for the intensification of the liberalism that influenced Cameron in face of the challenge represented by May's more nativist Christmas. And this is highlighted further when we compare the previous two Christmases.

Though it lacked the stamp of Brexit, Farron's Christmas 2015 likewise discussed the plight of refugees and the idea of the Nativity story being about refugees. There may even have been a hint of moving beyond the Coalition years with Farron's Christmas message playing to his base. Shortly before Farron's 2015 address, I spoke to some younger Liberal Democrat activists on issues of faith and with hindsight it is now clear how well Farron's message on refugees would have resonated. The language of 'social justice' was typical and, as one activist put it to me, the reasons why Christianity was most important to the party were because of the sort of social justice represented by groups like Christian Aid and Tearfund. Yet at this point, Farron's speech was notably more general, as were his vague calls to end homelessness (contrast Corbyn's more precise proposals). Indeed, his 2015 address contained the usual political generalities about hope, football, TV, charitable help, family, and so on.[65]

In some ways, his logic in 2015 was close to Cameron's soft paternalist Christmas in that Christmas did not represent blunt religious difference. Farron even included a Cameronism: 'people of all faiths and none ... no matter what our faith, or values or beliefs are, my hope this Christmas is that we are all inspired ...'. Similarly, we might also go back a year before to Nick Clegg's Christmas which was vaguer still but with a form of liberal multiculturalism we saw with Cameron.[66] Clegg gave his address from a primary school in London which was reminiscent of a textbook primary school Religious Studies/Education class on the sorts of things religions do (e.g., 'festivals'), albeit minus much content (and presumably school children were then one of the few student groups not expected to be critical of him in public after reneging on his pledge to abolish tuition fees). He explained that at the 'heart of this festival is the birth of Jesus Christ' and that it is 'a time of joy and celebration for Christians around the world', and yet, as ever, this 'festival' was about 'uniting people of all faiths and none'. Indeed, the liberal multicultural point was symbolised in the video by the prominent positioning of a girl with both a head covering and Santa hat while Clegg and the children all made mince pies against a backdrop of Christmas decorations. In case we did not pick up on that message, Clegg hammered the point home in his claim that 'the core values this story represents – love, charity, hope – are universal'. Against this backdrop from a time of pre-Brexit innocence, Farron's 2016 stark Christmas message about actual refugees and Britishness represented a shift in L/liberal understandings of Christianity.

But there was no significant Remain boost and sympathies towards migrants went sufficiently in the direction of Corbyn to contribute to the capping of Liberal Democrat gains in the 2017 General Election. Farron remained an issue for the national press and political discourse for his (Christian) views on homoerotic sex which in turn revealed a dominant ideological trend still at play in English political discourse for all politicians. Brian Paddick quit as shadow home secretary 'over concerns about the leader's views on various issues that were highlighted during GE17', and was soon to be followed by Farron himself.[67] Farron's explanation was striking. He talked about being 'torn between living as a faithful Christian and serving as a political leader' and that a 'better, wiser person' perhaps could have dealt with this tension better, remaining 'faithful to Christ while leading a political party in the current environment'. Nevertheless, he concluded, that to be a leader of 'a progressive liberal party in 2017' and 'a committed Christian' who wanted 'to hold faithful to the Bible's teaching' was 'impossible'.[68] It is notable that Farron published similar sentiments on the right-leaning *Spectator* blog, one of the venues where such (apparent) views would get a more sympathetic hearing in mainstream English political discourse.[69] Following increasing public acceptance of homosexuality, the example of Farron shows how deeply embedded the Blairite qualification to the understanding of religion and the Bible had become in English political discourse, not least after same-sex marriage became legal and was defended in Parliament with reference to Jesus (see Chapter 1). While in June 2017 Corbyn and May represented two different understandings, this form of liberalism should be seen as a third dominant understanding that has only strengthened its position since 2008. It is no surprise that the Liberal Democrats chose a replacement like Vince Cable who, in an interview on *Good Morning Britain*, identified as a Protestant and immediately replied that homosexuality was not a sin.[70]

Oddities after the Election

And yet there would be a mild twist to this story after the Election. Jacob Rees-Mogg – the anachronistically aristocratic social media star, Conservative MP, Catholic and Brexiteer – had been a promoter of religion in politics in a way which, in one sense, was at odds with the mainstream of political debate over the past decade. In an interview on *Good Morning Britain* (6 September 2017), Rees-Mogg was challenged on his Catholic beliefs, same-sex marriage and abortion, in much the same way as Farron was. Indeed, Rees-Mogg defended himself in a similar way on same-sex marriage. Referring to a different New Testament passage from that of Farron but imbued with the same logic, he turned to the story of the 'woman taken in adultery' (John 7.53 to 8.11), and the example of

Christ who said, 'he who is without sin cast the first stone' (Rees-Mogg's paraphrase). In other words, as an individual Catholic, he saw the 'teaching of the Catholic church', particularly 'in matters of faith and morals', as 'authoritative' but simultaneously claimed that he should not be judging those who live different lives. Moreover, as same-sex marriage was the law of the land such rights were protected irrespective of his personal views. Rees-Mogg was blunter than Farron in admitting his views and it is striking how Rees-Mogg pushed their shared logic to criticise the Liberal Democrats for not tolerating a 'Christian as their leader' while the Conservatives would do so (with notable assumptions about what 'Christian' must entail).[71]

Whether Rees-Mogg's bluntness could ever work on the front-benches where Farron's obfuscation failed depends on a variety of factors, including whether enough potential Conservative voters would not find his social and religious 'conservatism' sufficiently off-putting. We should probably also factor in a key dimension of Rees-Mogg's persona that could assist his constructions of his Christianity: his use of irony, as well as the ironic reception of Rees-Mogg. Despite his own worries about the future of politicians who openly identify as Christian, he is reported to have said:

> I think it's highly unlikely that God is particularly interested in the minutiae of party politics but if he were, everyone knows that God is a Somerset Conservative … Joseph of Arimathia [*sic*] is well known to have brought Christ to visit Glastonbury when Christ was a schoolboy – that would indicate a Somerset connection and all sensible people in Somerset are Conservatives so we get him as a Somerset Tory.[72]

Whether the relative popularity of Rees-Mogg could amount to anything is, for now, in the realm of counterfactual history. However, his views on homosexuality were not personally costly as of 2017, partly because of his ironic, posh persona. Such irony (coupled with the increasing power of social media) maintained his ideas while simultaneously deflecting any problematic oddities or controversies in the construction of religion in much the same way as Boris Johnson has functioned throughout his career. What Rees-Mogg represented was the potential for Conserva-tive reconfiguring 'tolerance' to include the coexistence of 'illiberal' and 'liberal' notions.

Nevertheless, Conservatives close to Cameron and his liberal rhetoric were not without their ongoing influence on such matters. The Conservative recovery in Scotland led by Ruth Davidson pointed to a powerful countervailing tendency. Shortly after the result of the 2017 General Election, she pointedly tweeted, 'As a Protestant Unionist about to marry an Irish Catholic, here's the Amnesty Pride lecture I gave in Belfast ...' (@RuthDavidsonMSP, 9 June 2017). Here, Davidson reflected wider concerns among liberal Conservatives (north and south of the border) about working closely with the Democratic Unionist Party (DUP) after the result of the hung Parliament. The issue was emphatically about the problematic 'religiousness' of the DUP because here was a party from Northern Ireland with some MPs and activists open about their socially conservative Protestantism. This was not the sort of thing found in mainstream English political discourse and Northern Ireland was typically categorised as a quite different context.

In terms of English political discourse, particularly in the liberal press, there was, as we might expect, a tendency to see the DUP on religion as potentially excessive for our times. Zoe Williams remarked that 'someone read their manifesto and said it was basically the Bible with fortnightly bin collection'.[73] On the issues of gender and sexuality, the *Mirror* went with the front-page headline of 'Coalition of crackpots', referring to 'the fundamentalist DUP' and contrasting them with liberal, pro-LGBT rights Conservatives.[74] Williams' article was likewise about homophobia and, given what we have seen, it should not be a surprise that this was a flashpoint. Other precise areas of excess that caused concern for sections of the press involved attitudes among DUP members on evolution and creationism. Lucy Pasha-Robinson discussed a DUP assembly member attending an event presenting 'the biblical case for the sound teaching of children' that offered 'helpful practical advice on how to counter evolutionary teaching'.[75] Other reports focused on DUP connections with the Caleb Foundation, a creationist lobby group. Chris York, for instance, reported that members and activists believe that the Earth 'is less than 10,000 years old despite the fact that it is most certainly not' and that thus they 'subscribe to the literal interpretation of the Book of Genesis, that the planet was created by God in six days'.[76] As should be familiar, the idea of following a 'literal interpretation' is the kind of qualification used to denote a deviant position problematic for, or alien to, the present liberal assumptions of English political discourse when cast in terms of religion, and York was not the only example of this emphasis.[77]

That this sort of understanding was deemed as unsuitable for English political discourse can be seen in terms of constructing it as *foreign*, particularly *American*, casting the DUP as representing the rednecks of the British Isles. This was perhaps no surprise given the recurring issues of evolution, abortion and creationism. Michael Hugh Walker not only referred to the foreign country of the past when he called the DUP 'our favourite intrepid adventures from the year 1644' but also referred to them as the 'Bible Belt bad boys of Ulster'.[78] Like other areas of the press, *The Economist* provided an explanation about who the DUP were. While it was keen to note the balance between 'pious voters' and 'secular ones', it still referred to this as 'a mixture of old-time religion and secular nativism'. Indeed, *The Economist* referred to the argument that the DUP were 'a "theocon" grouping whose ideas are unusual in today's western Europe' who would be 'much more familiar' to 'an American, especially from the deep South' and whose 'version of climate-change scepticism ... echoes voices on America's religious right'.[79] We might push this analogy a little further. As it happens, the vagueness of (pre-Trump) liberal democratic uses of religion and the Bible among American presidents of recent decades (e.g., Clinton, Bush, Obama) had much in common with mainstream English political discourse. But where they differed sharply was the electoral divisiveness of issues like abortion, evolution and creationism which did not have traction in English political discourse. Quite whether any of the fears about DUP religious excess will come to prominence in English political discourse or will be managed out of public sight is for future historians. As of 2017, foregrounding issues such as evolution or abortion were likely to be as popular as fox hunting but the potential for the DUP (or a similar tendency) to bring about shifts in understanding religion and related terms (whether in support, opposition or puzzlement) ought to be clear.

Concluding remarks

In her 2014 Christmas address, the then Green Party leader Natalie Bennett mentioned 'millions grappling with debt', job uncertainty, zero-hours contracts, 'savage and random benefit sanctions', and job losses in the public sector after 'the essential services in which they worked were cut', and those suffering in Syria, Iraq and Libya.[80] In one sense, this language had been a staple of the Left in English political discourse but it was virtually absent among the main parties in Parliament, including pre-Corbyn Labour, and certainly so in the pre-Corbyn Christmas addresses. On the pre-May Right, UKIP were promoting a kind of ethnonationalist Christmas and Christianity in distinction from the practices of other 'minority' (and notably 'Asian') groups. Again, this had been a staple of the Right in English political discourse but absent from Cameron's paternalistic multiculturalism. But all this was before the emergence of Corbyn and Brexit, both of which represented a crisis in the social and economic liberalism that became dominant in mainstream parliamentary discourse over the past 40 years and marked the Christmas messages prior to 2015/16. Corbyn's Labour – and to a lesser extent the Liberal Democrats under Farron – were now addressing topics more typically associated with the Labour backbenches or the Green Party (e.g., low pay, how to tackle homelessness, the War on Terror and socialism), while May's Conservatives were now (successfully) competing with UKIP for who got primary ownership of a certain kind of Britishness and Englishness. Further encroaching on UKIP territory, the Conservatives also emphasised economic protectionism by constructing socio-economic individualism in terms of deviancy from an assumed purer 'religion' through the language of 'cult'. In contrast to Corbyn's attempt to appeal to the Leave towns of the North and Midlands, and May's attempt to appeal to Brexit Britain, Farron used Christmas as an anti-Brexit, pro-immigration vehicle to appeal to the seemingly dwindling pro-EU 48 per cent whereas his predecessor tried to out-Cameron in presenting a vague liberal multicultural Christmas. But as Farron found out, it was instead the strength of the socially liberal qualification to understandings of religion developed under Blair, particularly issues relating to homosexuality and sex, that his time as leader has revealed most.

3

Muslims, the 'Perversion of Islam', and Christian England on the (Far) Right

Introduction: the changing far right

By the time of the 2017 General Election, then, the competing constructions of terms relating to religion were in flux. The next two chapters
will look at some (and only some) aspects of the story behind where
we got to by mid-2017, beginning with the developments on the Right
and how far-right ideas about ethnonationalism, Christianity, Islam and
Muslims were, or became, ideas close to the mainstream and embraced
– with qualification – by the Conservatives after the divisive EU Referendum in 2016. What we will ultimately see in this chapter are the ways
in which certain discourses about the 'perversion of Islam', so common
among leading politicians, had some connections with ideas associated
with the contemporary far right, despite both sides typically distancing themselves from one another. Implicit throughout both far-right
and more centrist versions were newer ways of racialising minorities,
in this case in terms closely related to religion, and more specifically
'Islam' and 'Muslims', as well as how this obfuscated issues about class
and foreign policy.

   This apparent focus on categories relating to religion (rather than
race) already suggests that the most prominent ideas associated with the
common notion of 'far right' changed over the past century, at least in
the choice of who was deemed worthy of discrimination. As the leader
of the British Union of Fascists (as well as spending time as Labour and
Conservative MP) Oswald Mosley was the most prominent figure in
setting the far-right agenda when fascism was on the ascendency in the
1930s. His followers gained the support of Viscount Rothermere and
the *Daily Mail* in the infamous headline, 'Hurrah for the Blackshirts!',
as well as rumoured support from within the Royal Family. While the
far right was consistently on the fringes of mainstream English political
discourse, the example of Mosley and the Blackshirts shows it could be

connected with tendencies and interests in mainstream and elite politics, as its future would continue to show. While antisemitism was a recurring feature, post-war far-right discourse tended to focus on immigration from the Caribbean and Asia and found its most prominent voice in the then Conservative MP, Enoch Powell. Powell would become something of an iconic figure on the far right which emerged again as a coherent group throughout the 1970s in the National Front (NF). The NF were likewise hostile towards immigration from the Caribbean and Asia, but antisemitism and neo-Nazism were also notable tendencies, including in the thinking of its leader, John Tyndall. The NF had an intimidating street presence but were also at one point the fourth biggest party in the UK before Thatcher's 1979 General Election victory appropriated, and marked the end of, their prominence. Thatcher, for instance, was hardly unknowing in her claim in 1978 that people 'are really rather afraid that this country might be rather swamped by people with a different culture'.[1] In the 1980s and 1990s, the far right still had a public presence but more typically through clashes on the streets with anti-fascist groups. The next major group to emerge to prominence in English political discourse was the British National Party (BNP) who from the end of the 1990s until 2014 would be led by Nick Griffin, with potential credibility coming through being a graduate from Downing College, University of Cambridge. After some success in local council and European parliament elections in 2008–09, the 2010 General Election marked the end of the BNP as a relatively significant political force.

The far right in English political discourse has historically been focused on classifying and othering groups in terms of biological, racial and ethnic difference. However, changes in emphases (though not unprecedented) marked the post-2008 era and a rhetorical shift towards assumptions about religion in the far right's choice of public enemy: Muslims and Islam. This should perhaps be no surprise given the developing Orientalist interest in Islam and Muslims in British, American and European political discourse since the 1970s and intensified after the fall of the Soviet Union and then 9/11 and the War on Terror, all picking up on colonial and postcolonial legacies.[2] The one far-right group who epitomised this shift were the English Defence League (EDL). With a working-class base, overlaps with football violence and 'casual' culture, and some connections with the BNP, the EDL effectively formed in Luton in 2009 under the leadership of Tommy Robinson (the pseudonym of Stephen Yaxley-Lennon) with a focus on protesting against Islam as an ideology and viewing Britain and England as Christian, tolerant, and having a cultural heritage incompatible with Islam. The opposition to 'Islam' per se (rather than 'radical Islam', 'perversion of Islam', etc.) was common in EDL literature, epitomised by the 'What Is Islam?' page on their website. The EDL officially distanced themselves from what they (and others in public discourse) deemed 'racism' and, in certain quarters, even took a pro-Israel turn, seemingly in sharp contrast to the antisemitic past of the far right. They claimed to be hostile to an ideology rather than a race and to welcome people from any ethnic background, including the promotion of their Jewish and Sikh divisions. In contrast to the historic far right, they also officially embraced social liberalism (e.g., equality of gender and sexuality) and had subgroups such as the LGBT division and the female EDL Angels (who were the focus of a BBC documentary in 2014). Since the departure of Tommy Robinson in 2013, the EDL began to decline, at least in terms of numbers at demonstrations, but they maintained a strong web presence used for organisation, group discussion, publicity, developing opinions, and so on, which has provided one of the most significant platforms for anti-Muslim and anti-Islamic ideas to be disseminated in the UK.[3]

By 2017 the far right was again fragmentary, but the anti-Islam, anti-Muslim, anti-immigration emphasis remained strong in such contexts and beyond. In more mainstream politics, such ideas were taken up by UKIP which had minor electoral successes and one major political success in Brexit. In the Referendum campaigning of 2016, the violent impact of such discourses became apparent to a wide audience when the Labour MP Jo Cox was murdered on 16 June 2016, by the far-right sympathiser Thomas Mair who was heard shouting the words 'Britain first', which happened to be the name of another far-right group with a strong online presence. A year later (19 June 2017), Darren Osborne drove a van into a group of people near the Finsbury Park mosque and witnesses heard him shout, 'I want to kill Muslims'. Such acts did not come out of nowhere. While complicity was typically denied, groups with a prominent online presence, such as Britain First and the EDL, and related social media discussions (e.g., on Twitter), further showed how anti-Islamic, anti-Muslim, anti-immigration, anti-EU ideas, and occasional pro-Christian nationalist ideas, were regularly reinforced. In this chapter, I want to look at such groups and related social media activity to get behind the official 'post-racial' statements and see what kinds of ideas were deemed acceptable. In particular, I will look at how these groups and their participants constructed and contextualised terms such as 'Islam' and 'Muslim', including in relation to Christianity and nationalism. As ever, this will not involve making judgements on what 'true' Islam is or is not but rather it will involve looking at how such language was being used to promote ideological positions and maintain, develop and challenge social formations. I will then move on to the ways in which these constructions of 'Islam' and 'Muslims' (among others) functioned in more mainstream political discourse, with particular attention given to the national media. I will discuss how all this relates to the 'perversion of Islam' trope dominant in mainstream parliamentary politics and the ideological function of why people like to hate groups like the EDL. Throughout, I will look at how these emphases relate to racialising discourses so readily denounced by groups like the EDL.

Muslims, Islam and the online far right

From January 2016 to March 2017, I looked at four like-minded and public far-right groups of this newer variety on Facebook with a combined total of over 1,700,000 followers (no doubt with some manufacturing of the numbers), and Twitter activity sympathetic to such groups, their ideas and their representation of, for instance, 'Islam', 'Muslim', 'Christianity' and 'Christian'. In presenting the views of commenters, I will keep everything anonymous and I will not quote directly or summarise specific comments (other than those of anonymous administrators and memes) in order to not contribute to notoriety and to maintain such anonymity, despite such material all being publicly available. Instead, I will summarise repetitive and dominant views, many of which were repeated with daily regularity, very rarely challenged and seemingly with minimal trolling. Where necessary I will also state where a view is uncommon or rarely repeated. My aim is not typically to establish percentages or statistics for how common the theme of Islam or the like was (though, to be clear, hostility to Islam and Muslims was, unsurprisingly, a daily or even hourly feature) but rather to gain some insight into the ways in which such issues were presented and understood before moving to wider trends in English political discourse. Nor should this be seen as *necessarily* representing views typical of (say) an EDL or Britain First member or sympathiser and, although there were consistent overlaps on the issue of Muslims and Islam (and much else) between the groups I looked at, we do not have such access to their personal views and certain online views may have involved behaviour not performed in other social contexts. What I would stress instead is that this was a look at the ways in which certain online performers worked with such constructions and how they related to wider discourses. It should also be added, and in line with the emphasis in this book, that while claims to Britishness were certainly made, the focus in the material I analysed was much more typically centred on England, or a Britain with England at its centre.

What was overwhelmingly clear was that the dominant position on Muslims and Islam was not that ISIS, 'jihadism', 'Islamism', or terror were constructed as a perversion of purer Islam (as virtually all mainstream politicians and the occasional far-right leader will emphasise), but that such violence and illiberalism was integral to Islam with the popular notions of 'Islam is a religion of peace' and 'moderate Muslims' regularly mocked. While geographical differences among Muslims could be acknowledged, they were more likely to reveal a deeper, ahistorical truth about Islam. So, whatever disliked practices (say) Afghan Muslims might perform, they were indicative of what was being reported about Muslims in another country. When the Qur'an was mentioned, it was not likely to be spared as it was regularly seen as the source of the problem and occasionally deemed an 'instruction manual' for terrorism, following a common online cliche. One repeated online view was that ISIS or their sympathisers were snakes in the grass – with the grass being Islam or Muslims generally. Muslims and Islam *as a whole* could then be regularly referred to in the historically familiar language of racial demonisation relating to, for example, vermin, female (and occasionally male) genitalia, filth, excrement, animals, insects, non-humanity, sexual deviancy, murder, mass threats and evilness. All this appeared to be fairly typical of similar online activity.[4]

Plenty of specific examples of supposed evidence of larger Muslim wrongdoing could be found. A common view (with clear echoes of older racialised language) was that ungrateful Muslims take advantage of welfare, housing and benefits, including the promotion of stories about Muslim men practising polygamy and producing countless children for financial gain which they would not be able to do in 'their countries'. Practices deemed to be especially 'Muslim' (and therefore unBritish/ unEnglish) were the wearing of the burqa and niqab, the observance of Ramadan, avoidance of pork, and following sharia law. Sharia was not only regularly deemed to be counter to British or English law (occasionally classified in terms of the Magna Carta) but as taking over the country and due to be dominant within one or two generations, if it had not done so already. This was, of course, assumed to be symptomatic of Islam more generally which was 'taking over', had sexually assaulted the country and was threatening 'our way of life' in an unprecedented manner, with Easter, Christmas, Parliament and the Queen potential casualties. If the whole country had not already turned Islamic, then certain places apparently had, notably Tower Hamlets, London more generally, Birmingham and parts of Yorkshire, with Muslim mayors popping up everywhere due to Muslims block voting and the majority of the population being inert, or so the narrative went.

This distinction between British/English and Muslim/Islam could be seen in relation to television, particularly the BBC. This included suggestions that Muslims should not be represented because 'we' were British and 'they' were not and were unlikely to assimilate with this mythic notion of Britain. Similarly, the administrators of the groups regularly and publicly provided a series of related links and memes for viewers to read. Festive days provided ethnic identity markers and there were suggestions that if St George's Day were to be a Bank Holiday then Muslims should not celebrate it. In memes about how full Britain supposedly was, immigration (represented by Muslims) was typically contrasted with what was perceived to be British. This could include London-centric images (e.g., Big Ben), the Union Flag, the armed forces and food. Food was a regular point of ethnic, cultural, religious, and national self-identification, and identification of the Muslim Other. Criticisms of halal food were extremely common. Halal was variously thought to be taking over cafes, restaurants and supermarkets, as well as regularly presented as cruel to animals. Avoidance of pork was the most referenced specific example of food deemed especially Islamic or Muslim, including the idea that a pig was one of the few non-Muslims who had ever found something positive in Islam. There were, as expected, plenty of related derogatory claims about bestiality. But what of its opposite, that is, English and British food? A bacon sandwich, often accompanied by a cup of tea, was probably the most commonly assumed national food promoted by the group administrators with obvious anti-Muslim, anti-Islamic implications. Other things were obviously nostalgic, such as a Sunday roast dinner, fish and chips, and shepherd's pie. On certain repeated memes, including one calling for 23 June (i.e., the date of the Referendum vote) to be made British Independence Day, other foodstuffs found included a cup of tea, jam tarts, beer, and a fried breakfast of the sort that might induce a Great British Heart Attack.

With such intense stereotyping and with a group so relentlessly dehumanised (and, notably, feminised), verbal images of grotesque violence towards Muslims was grimly unsurprising. This was partly because the dominant view – and indeed the whole point of such groups – involved Islam and Muslims being deemed incompatible with what was understood to be Englishness, Britishness, or even European or Western civilisation. And if the problems were thought to be so drastic then so were the proposed solutions, from stopping benefits and housing through banning the burqa to burning down sharia courts. Other suggestions included simulated or actual violence against Muslims. Similar hopes were expressed for Muslims (or the interchangeable 'migrants') to die, be disinfected, or be sent to internment camps. Unsurprisingly, this could be cast in militarised language of a country under attack and an enemy against which 'we' need to fight, a rhetorical move found in related online activity.[5] It was constantly remarked that Muslims, or at least Muslims who find British or English culture, history, laws and traditions offensive, should be deported or 'go back' in order to stop the erosion of 'our' culture or halt the 'flooding' of the country or continent. Precisely where such people ought to go were countries, continents or geographical areas typically assumed to be majority Muslim (e.g., Turkey, Afghanistan, Pakistan, Saudi Arabia, Africa, Middle East) where they can, so the argument frequently went, attack each other or let Muslims sort themselves out, and with the bricking up of the Channel Tunnel one possible solution to the perceived problem according to one popular meme. Voting to leave the EU was also integral to rectifying the perceived problem because the EU was typically seen as betraying British or European values through its alleged erosion of cultural identities, national sovereignty, and openness to mass migration. Predictably, this was largely discussed in terms of the threat of Islam, Muslim immigration and 'terror', with some occasional but regular claims that the EU would soon be Islamic. This sort of anti-EU feeling was ubiquitous, and thousands of comments were overwhelmingly in favour of leaving the EU.

The idea that this new far right was about attacking ideology or religion rather than race occurred regularly in posts, comments and tweets, even to the point where it was claimed that it was *Islam* that was really racist, even the most racist ideology in human history. But rarely was this embrace of anti-racist rhetoric straightforward in that familiar racial issues would not be far away. One popular online meme, for instance, provided a kind of idealised colour-coded chart of skin and hair colour for different European nations contrasted with what these nations had become 'after multiculturalism' (i.e., non-white), while others complained that Britain or England had become a society where races had mixed too much. While not a common target in the way Islam and Muslims were, antisemitic slurs and stereotypes familiar on the far right and now updated recurred in comments sections, such as Jewish people as a force driving liberalism, Jewish people running the EU and targeting the UK with immigrants, and Jewish people attacking Easter and Christmas. Even on ostensibly pro-Israel discussions, comments could be found about Israelis or Jews wanting to undermine the West through allowing Muslim infiltration. Although only an occasional target, particularly in comparison to Islam and Muslims, the familiar racist labels could be found with reference to skin colour. When Black Lives Matter had come to the fore, it was disparaged in some public social media activity, with comments that what it was really about was black criminality and anti-white racism. The label 'racist', as well as 'antisemitic', could be reversed and turned on other groups, ideologies or imaginary movements known for, or associated with, anti-racism (e.g., the Left, multiculturalism, socialism, 'cultural Marxism') while simul- taneously claiming, for instance, that Apartheid was a positive thing for black South Africans or that black culture has contributed little to human civilisation. What we clearly see here was an appropriation of progressive language while simultaneously making the same sorts of racialised points of the traditional far right that previously did not nec- essarily require the veneer of liberalism.

This sort of racialised rhetoric was not as central as it was once on the far right, at least in the groups I studied. But when such comments emerged they were defended as being 'honest' or 'fact', rather than racist, or otherwise were just ignored. Slurs were, as might be expected, more commonly aimed at Muslims and Islam and, despite official rhetoric and anger at allegations of racism, were likewise racialised. For a start, the nativism of 'our race' (presumably assumed to be white and normative) could be constructed in opposition to 'Muslims' who were, so certain arguments went, racist towards whites and that it was now acceptable to be prejudiced against whites. Similarly, terms such as 'indigenous population' were used to describe those deemed to be true British/

English and not Muslim. One popular meme claimed, with a Union Flag-covered face, that however British 'you' think you are, 'I' am more British because of 'my' soul, being and spirit made up from the British Isles. Another repeated meme asked, 'what happened?', and was accompanied by a picture of London in 1950 (featuring white people) and a picture of London in 2016 (featuring deliberately non-white Muslims). 'Arab' and the old racist label 'Paki' could be used interchangeably with 'Muslim' (hardly untypical among EDL supporters, as other empirical examples show[6]), and there were even simultaneous and common claims that none of the labels used were racist and that it was impossible to be racist towards Islam or an ideology. But, if it is not already clear, such unchallenged comments probably highlight what was present throughout such obsessions with Islam and Muslims, namely, that they were not easy to disentangle from the inherited racialised rhetoric. It is often remarked that the far right once donned suits to give themselves credibility as the new slicker leaders masked some of the old racial politics and violence. The same might be said, at least in the instance of my sample, of donning the rhetoric of 'ideology' and 'religion' to perpetuate inherited racial ideas and an assumption of normative whiteness deemed under threat.

Unsurprisingly, then, a related opposition was Muslim versus Christian, or variants such as Islam versus Christianity, the Qur'an versus the Bible, or Muhammad versus Jesus. Other than isolated commenters claiming to be church-going Christians or promoting salvation through Christ alone, the overwhelmingly dominant sentiment was more about Christianity as a marker of white nativism and not Islam. England, Britain and Europe could be deemed 'Christian' and emphatically not Muslim while in response to debates happening in France, there was acceptance that France was not Muslim but (Judeo-)Christian *and white*. There were debates on Islam apparently being represented more on the BBC which was thought problematic because as the BBC was British, religious programming should be of a Christian nature, or at least not Islamic. Similar sentiments could be found in related discussions (e.g., representations of the cross in public, Easter and Christmas). Militaristic and muscular Christian imagery was embraced particularly in popular memes, such as Crusaders (with the obvious anti-Islamic connotations), a quotation from St Augustine about truth defending itself like a lion and accompanied by a picture of a lion (with connotations of a certain kind of Englishness), and Jesus – Our Commanding Officer introduced on a picture of a soldier in chainmail, carrying a broadsword, and with a red cross on his tunic as he kneeled before Jesus. Indeed, the use of the cross (likewise with connotations of a certain kind of Englishness) is found among various online groups, including in 'official' presentations, logos and crests of the EDL and Britain First.

There was a regular sentiment of identifying with a (Judeo-)Christian culture with the additional suggestion that Christianity was still something people typically practised in a benign manner. So, for instance, the Bible could be deemed to promote a Christian culture of restraint and humility in the practice of faith (e.g., praying quietly and in private) in contrast to ostentatious Muslims who upset the private-public distinction. The Qur'an could be deemed as something especially volatile and commanding Muslims to kill unbelievers in the present, whereas the Bible (especially Jesus and the New Testament) was more typically presented as nonviolent, even if plenty of commenters did not identify as Christians in the sense that they would claim to follow the Bible or go to church. When persecution was mentioned, it was Christians who were most persecuted around the world (usually by Muslims) and the group with whom British or English people should identify. On the rare occasion when the claim was made (typically by an outsider) that violence was associated with Christianity, this would be ignored, met with indifference (were not all religions terrible?) or, as with a discussion of the claim that Anders Behring Breivik was a Christian, met with flat denial or a counterclaim that such people are not truly Christian and so violence cannot be seen as integral to Christianity, an explanation not deemed transferable to Islam and Muslims.

It is also worth noting that discussions of Christianity would more typically come up when the posts were overtly about religion or Christianity being under threat. Otherwise, mention would be made in the occasional comment rather than sustained debate. Moreover, there were a minority of commenters who hated all religion and when the issue of homosexuality or violence and religion was discussed, commenters could be found referencing the 'Old Testament' or 'the Bible' (specific books, chapters and verses were not cited in homosexuality debates as far as I could see, though a vague reference to stoning to death as a punishment or Adam and Eve might). Unlike most debates, there was no obvious pattern to how the discussion would progress once the 'Old Testament' (their term) was mentioned. Some would argue that the 'Old Testament' condemned homosexuality and condoned violence but, unlike the Qur'an, the New Testament and/or Jesus overrode such illiberalism.

Some would be glad that homosexuality was thought to be banned in Christian scriptures and even conceded this as a point of similarity with Islam. Some would simply dismiss the Bible in its entirety. What, of course, united all this was that homosexuality was indeed an issue of some significance for contemporary liberal discourse about religion, a point we saw in the previous chapter.

As with race, the appropriation of liberal rhetoric in areas of gender and sexuality could be found, as could simultaneous disdain by some commenters. Islam and Muslims were regularly denounced for being misogynistic, and discussion points were raised about homophobia and the murder of people for their sexuality. Muslim men were consistently presented as rapists and unable to control their sexual urges, including the occasional explicit contrast with British or English men who were deemed more restrained. Muslim men in certain countries (e.g., Afghanistan) were used as an illustration about the supposed essence of Islam, with Muslims more generally used to represent Islamic views on sexuality, particularly claims about paedophilia (often concerning boys), a regular derogatory allegation levelled at Muhammad. While criticisms of homophobia could be found and puzzlement could be expressed as to why liberal LGBT+ people apparently want Muslims here despite what Muslims were thought to think, overtly homophobic sentiments were also found among the respondents, a tendency hardly uncommon among contemporary European far-right groups drawing on conservative traditions.[7] Responses to a story about one Arab-majority country banning media representations of homosexual or homoerotic content were mixed but drew a surprising amount of support.

While homophobia could be shared openly, overt misogyny was less likely to be. Clearly, the perception of hating women per se was unacceptable, while hating homosexuality was tolerated far more. However, misogyny was regularly implicit. There were instances of Islam and Muslims, as well as their alleged socialist sympathisers, being denounced for being 'sexist' and yet when the topic of domestic abuse was raised, it was regularly about women being violent against men and men being falsely accused of sexual assault. This is not to undermine the seriousness of such issues, but given how problematic reporting sexual assault is for women in the UK and how entrenched domestic abuse against women is, the emphasis in this discourse on male recipients and *only* (as far as I could see) on Muslim perpetrators against women was notable. Such violence against women was tied in with discourses about the veil, burqa or niqab, so integral to the polemics of contemporary far-right groups (and beyond). In the thousands of comments I analysed on whether 'the face veil' and burqa for women should be banned, the overwhelming answer was 'yes', and not only because 'the face veil' was understood to have been forced upon women by men (typically on pain of death). Discussions of women claiming to be covered in order to avoid male arousal would regularly be accompanied by denunciations and mocking of the women on the grounds of their looks. Regular commenters wanted veils banned because male terrorists might be hiding underneath, a notably gendered assumption about violence and religion to which we will return in Chapter 6.

Muslim men could be feminised or de-masculinised, in addition to being constructed as being sexually predatory upon women. A repeated slur was the drag combination of Muslim men being bearded and dress-wearers. With feminisation or de-masculinisation being a common slur, presumably tied up with heterosexist and heteronormative assumptions, it is no surprise that such ideas could be turned on English or British people who were not behaving as they should towards Muslims and Islam. For accommodating Muslims without resistance, the British or English could be accused of turning into 'pussies'. David Cameron could regularly be denounced in emasculating terms ('not having the balls' was a particularly common phrase) for not standing up to immigration or Muslim practices. Conversely, female politicians in France and the UK who did criticise immigration, Islam and Muslims could be seen as playing a more masculine role than Cameron (in particular). Thatcher – who had a polarising reception in such social media outlets – was deemed to have had more than enough masculinity to stand up to Muslims, Merkel and the EU, and might have prevented Muslim immigration (if she were still living). This was even a point accepted by some of those hostile to Thatcher.

The masculinisation of Thatcher was, of course, nothing new and, in these contexts at least, worked with the assumption that a 'strong' leader – even a military leader – was necessary to deal with what was obviously perceived to be a colossal problem. Easily the most revered strong leader was Churchill, a staple in far-right (and mainstream) nationalist nostalgia in recent decades, and this is no surprise given the regular evocation of the central myth in English political discourse – the Second World War – though here the emphasis was more on beating 'the Germans' (rather than fascists) and on a nativist, nostalgic and idealised view of a white, uncomplicated, Muslim-free nation. Other figures deemed worthy leaders were Putin, Trump, Henry VIII, Lech Walesa, Farage, and even Mussolini, most of whom were presented as being openly hostile to Islam and Muslims in a way a mainstream politician in English political discourse usually was not. But another staple in far-right (though less so in mainstream) nationalist nostalgia was almost as popular as Churchill: Enoch Powell. Powell is an important example because he too was deemed to suffer by being labelled 'racist' even though he was allegedly right all along about immigration. The reference point was, of course, Powell's 1968 'Rivers of Blood' speech, despite Powell making claims and retelling stories (which are not foregrounded in the social media outlets I looked at) about a 'Negro' and how 'the black man will have the whip hand over the white man' in 20 years.[8] This too is an important reception of Powell to bear in mind given that contemporary far-right discourses claim to be hostile to 'religion' and 'ideology' rather than 'race', and is a reminder that the connections with the more overtly racialised rhetoric of the past are not easily disentangled. In this respect, it is telling that there were even occasional claims that Hitler was indeed evil but was not actually a figure of the Right. Instead, he could be classified as of the Left, a move notably designed to allow credibility while simulta-neously criticising migration, Muslims and Black Lives Matter.

Theresa May was not deemed a worthy leader, almost always because she was perceived to be too tolerant of Islam, as was Corbyn, though he was lampooned for a variety of reasons (e.g., mad, soft, naive, stupid, unpatriotic).[9] But one figure in particular was the recipient of scorn and distrust: the Mayor of London, Sadiq Khan, who was presented as a kind of Salafist sleeper agent who had cunningly worked his way to the heights of power. Khan was regularly presented as a terrorist sympathiser or even terrorist mastermind, an insult to (sometimes Christian) Britain, and symptomatic of a Labour Party now deemed to be Muslim, and who was even more suspect for not leading a purge of Muslim terrorists from London and may already have been leading a jihad on London. Khan's words, even after terror attacks, were scrutinised and deemed to be deceptive in that he was not *really* sorry people had been killed. After suggestions that he was secretly happy when Muslims kill British or English people, there were calls for him to resign and hopes expressed that he would have been shot instead. All this may come as a surprise to those more familiar with Khan as a liberal politician on the soft Left of Labour who voted in favour of same-sex marriage. But that he identified as a Muslim shows how problematic any evidence that a Muslim might not be a terrorist was in such social media outlets, hence Khan *must* be hiding his sinister ambitions. Again, this sinister hiddenness was an updating of old slurs, particularly antisemitic and anti-Arab ones (e.g., the 'hidden Jew', sly fighters), which persisted among right-wing groups throughout the twentieth century before their more liberal rebranding.

Islam, Muslims, Englishness and Britishness

Constructing Christianity in relation to English or British identities has, of course, both recent and long-term histories. With reference to the British Social Attitudes data from 2008, Ingrid Storm has shown that just over 23 per cent made a connection between 'British' and 'Christian', particularly as a kind of ethnic marker ('it is important to be Christian to be truly British'), despite declining identification with Christianity and low levels of church attendance in the UK. Indeed, such connections seem less likely among regular churchgoers and, Storm further argued, those who were not regular churchgoers were more likely to view immigration as a threat to national identity.[10] There is also, of course, a long, Orientalist tradition of constructing English, British or Western culture (and thus in-group and self-identity) as tolerant and enlightened and Muslim culture as intolerant and despotic.[11] Similarly, the construction of religion (or related categories) on the non-Muslim side of the opposition in online discussion was part of a long established genealogy. In the far-right discussions I examined, it was notable that although there were occasional quotations from the Bible, as well as occasional outright rejection of religion, the source of authority when understood in terms associated with religion were typically the more general 'the Bible', 'the New Testament', 'Jesus', 'Christianity', and so on, which were probably more culturally amenable to their accompanying construction of English or British heritage and Western civilisation. The contrast between these general terms, on the one hand, and Islam, Muhammad or the Qur'an, on the other, stretch back centuries in the history of Christian-Muslim relations. More specific notions of the Bible, New Testament, Jesus, or Christianity as compatible with, even the source of, democracy in contrast to illiberal, tyrannical, despotic Islam, the Qur'an, or Muhammad, have developed since the seventeenth century and the emergence of English and British parliamentary democracy (as well as through national interests in the Middle East), as Yvonne Sherwood has shown.[12] This has also been a feature of European far-right thinking, notably in the manifesto of Breivik. Perhaps the most infamous visual example of this in contemporary far-right groups in the UK was the Britain First, cross-carrying 'Christian Patrols' among Muslim communities in East London in the aftermath of the Charlie Hebdo murders in January 2015.[13]

To further understand the levels of hostility towards Islam and Muslims, we can also turn to the kinds of issues that were integral to UKIP and the far right in recent English politics. BNP association with neo-Nazism and antisemitism, and their explicit emphasis on ethnonationalism and racial identity, may indeed have put them at odds with UKIP who, in official pronouncements at least, were not likely to be so blunt and are (thus) more likely to find electoral success than a group too closely associated with the (foreign) Nazis in popular imaginations. But between the EDL and UKIP there was more official ideological overlap on the issues of immigration and official renouncing of racial identity, as well as an emphasis on Islam and integration and making occasional connections with Christianity and Britishness/Englishness (see Chapter 2). As we saw, Farage was one of the figures deemed to be the kind of strong leader required for some commenters in the far-right groups. As a movement, the EDL were in decline but, along with UKIP, they reflected significant long-term changes in concerns among the English electorate in relation to attitudes towards immigration. As Robert Ford and Matthew Goodwin have argued, the UKIP 'revolt on the right' owed much to support from older, less educated voters from blue-collar backgrounds lacking the relevant employment training and opportunities for the changes taking place in post-industrial Britain, and with some of the blame for their predicament aimed at immigration levels and the complicity of the political elite. This, Ford and Goodwin added, was also intertwined with a broader view gathering momentum for decades: an anti-establishment hostility towards a political class who had not been thought to address concerns, had come from more privileged backgrounds, held more socially liberal views, and were more likely to target middle-class swing voters. Based on the Continuous Monitoring Study, Ford and Goodwin also showed how, between 2004 and 2013, 30 per cent of voters were both Eurosceptic and opposed to immigration, 30 per cent were Eurosceptic and politically dissatisfied, while 20 per cent shared all three attitudes.[14] While not necessarily prioritising the EU, it became a symbol for such discontentment as was revealed in the result of the EU Referendum in 2016.

In this context, Muslims and Islam were readily available reference points for discussion of immigration and partly because recent discourses about immigration have involved the Middle East and Syria in particular. This was broadly complemented in the levels of distrust or hostility towards Islam consistently found in various polls. Paul Baker, Costas Gabrielatos and Tony McEnery, for instance, pointed to the British Social Attitudes survey from 2003, showing 62 per cent of people believed that Muslims have greater loyalty to Muslims abroad than to non-Muslims in the UK, and the Exploring Islam Foundation which found that 43 per cent (sample: 2,152) did not believe that Muslims had a positive impact on British society, half linked Islam with terrorism, and 13 per cent linked Islam with peace.[15] To this we might add that, in interviews from 22–24 April 2016 (sample: 2,012), ComRes found that 46 per cent disagreed with the claim that 'Islam promotes peace' (32 per cent agreed), 56 per cent disagreed with the claim that 'Islam is compatible with British values' (28 per cent agreed), 33 per cent agreed with the claim that 'Islam promotes violence' (51 per cent disagreed), 28 per cent agreed with the claim that 'Islam is a violent religion' (57 per cent disagreed), and 43 per cent agreed with the claim that 'Islam is a negative force in the UK' (40 per cent disagreed). One notable feature of the ComRes poll seemed to tally with the results noted above concerning an older demographic attracted to ideas associated with UKIP and a driving factor in the Brexit vote, in that the 18–24 age group was consistently more likely to have positive (or less negative) attitudes towards Islam, such as 42 per cent agreeing that 'Islam promotes peace' (compare 25 per cent for the 45–54 age group), 41 per cent agreeing with 'Islam is compatible with British values' (compare 27 per cent for 45–54), 18 per cent agreeing with 'Islam promotes acts of violence in the UK' (other age groups: 32–39 per cent), and 31 per cent agreeing with 'Islam is a negative force in the UK (rising from 37 per cent to 49 per cent from ages 25 to over 65s), though 25 per cent agreed with 'Islam is a violent religion', only slightly below the average.[16] In this respect, it is perhaps worth noting that the sample I analysed was overwhelmingly over 35, at least as far as it was possible to tell through social media profiles. As we will see below, and as we have touched upon already, there is some indication that such interconnected attitudes towards Muslims, Islam and immigration had some support among some sections of disaffected working classes.

Such attitudes went much further. Given that part of the role of the national media is to make a profit and to provide a platform for influencing political discourse, it should not be a surprise that the national media was part of these debates with such a market available (and one which is found among middle classes too, of course). Indeed, it is widely remarked that media assumptions (particularly on the Right) about Muslims and immigration helped mould the assumptions among far-right groups. The normalisation of such assumptions in what might be deemed more mainstream culture is also shown through further empirical study. Analysing 200,037 articles between 1998 and 2009, Baker, Gabrielatos and McEnery looked at the representations of Islam and Muslims in the traditional national press (*Sun, Star, Express, Daily Mail, Guardian, Telegraph, Mirror, Independent, People*).[17] While there were predictable spikes in such representation after 9/11 and 7/7, this period marked a gradual increase in interest. To give some indication of frequency, they noted that between 2000 and 2009, the word 'Muslim' (and plural) occurred 121,125 times (approximately 33 times a day on average), with about half of the articles referring to conflict.

It was how Islam and Muslim were understood that is pertinent. The representations were frequently negative particularly among right-leaning newspapers, with regular examples of the 'us' and 'them' binary working, presumably, with the assumptions that the ideal reader was not Muslim, and that Muslims were perhaps not really British. Muslims were regularly generalised as 'the Muslim community' who were easily offended and received preferential treatment. Muslims were similarly generalised as belonging to 'the Muslim world' in contrast to 'the West'. Various uses of 'Islam' were modified with language such as 'militant', 'fanatic' and 'extremist', with seemingly less negative terms like 'devout' denoting deviancy or hypocrisy. One of the more startling findings was that when using 'Islam' and related words (e.g., 'Islamic', 'Islamist') as a means for detecting the relevant articles for their analysis, they found that 'terrorism' and related words (e.g., 'terror', 'terrorist') were more frequent. The language of 'moderate' in relation to Muslim and Islam was less common (and even this term implies a non-moderate Islam/Muslim), occurring one in every 237 cases and for every case of 'moderate' in relation to Muslim/Islam there would be 21 mentions of 'extremism'. Among the more liberal press (*Guardian, Independent*), there were more attempts at nuance. But one example is particularly relevant, namely, the *Guardian* keyword: 'Islamist' (occurring 2,388 times). 'Islamist' was used to denote a particularly strict form of Islamic rule, and one which had some parallels with the notion of what an idealised liberal democratic Islam should be according to mainstream English political discourse. We will return to this sort of use below.

That there was overlap between national media outlets and far-right social media activity discussed above ought to be clear enough. Indeed, linking online newspaper articles was the favoured type of post which, typically, involved a link with a brief editorial comment, if any at all. The most commonly cited media outlet for posts was the UKIP-supporting *Express* (which Baker, Gabrielatos and McEnery found to be most likely to discuss immigration and the imposition of sharia law), though *Breitbart* and the *Daily Mail* were popular too. The reason for the choice of news outlets should be obvious enough (i.e., they were all likely to push negative stories about Islam, the EU, immigration, etc.), but they also revealed some of the complexities involved in reading practices. For instance, a news story (or a seemingly innocuous question such as whether praying in certain places should be allowed) might ostensibly have described some issue that was perceived to involve a Muslim person or a perceived problem with Islam, even if no such mention of 'Muslim', 'Islam' or the like was made. This sort of dog-whistling could be seen in a widely circulated story in the *Express* about companies changing the phrase 'Easter eggs' to 'chocolate eggs', much to the reported fury of Conservative MP Bob Blackman, among others. According to the *Express*, who were perhaps a little too enthusiastic with their interpretation of the statistics, the 'overwhelming majority of Britons are angry' about this alleged development after a YouGov survey of 2,050 people found that a mere 11 per cent agreed with the removal of the phrase.[18]

The demographic breakdown of the 11 per cent was not specified in the *Express* piece (other than people who might represent 'political correctness gone mad') but when the link was provided without commentary, the participants filled in the gaps, largely with 'Muslims' and related ideas (e.g., sharia, Muslim and/or Middle Eastern cultural takeover), and various provocative responses to them, though also with the occasional reference to political correctness and profiteering companies, at least in the hundreds of comments that I read. The problem was deemed so acute that there were hopes that this would bring an end to Cameron's government. The ideas discussed should be familiar in light of what I have summarised about far-right social media. A flipside to all this was that Britain or England was, ideally at least, Christian. Jesus, Christianity and a Christian 'heritage' or 'culture' were presented regularly as the opposite of Islam and political correctness (at least in 20 per cent of the comments I viewed but which could of course have changed had people been asked directly), typically as something belonging to 'us' and with people identifying as, for instance, Christians, not especially pious Christians, atheists, or nothing overt. Out of curiosity, I counted a sample of those who proclaimed a hatred for 'all religion', including several wanting all religions banned, and they totalled about 12 per cent, just 1 per cent more than those who were happy with the removal of 'Easter' from the marketing of Easter eggs. Although we should of course restrain ourselves from reading too much into this, perhaps it might indicate that filling in the *Express'* gaps with Muslims and Islam tells us more about the gap-fillers than the realities of the 11 percenters, some of whom might have been represented among the ranks of far-right sympathisers. But this mattered little when developing a new mythology of difference.

Gender and Islam

As the presentation of Islam and Muslims in relation to terror, extremism, militancy (etc.) was normalised in terms of deviancy from liberal democratic assumptions, so too were assumptions about Islam, Muslims and gender. However, the mythmaking once again broke down in the insider debates among far-right groups. As we saw, misogynistic comments, concerns for things such as domestic violence against men, and even support for homophobic attitudes ordinarily perceived to be 'Muslim', were found. In this sense, we should probably be thinking about the pull from reactions against shifting notions of gender relations over generations, as well as the more overtly misogynistic tendencies that can be found on the harder far right. But there were not sustained discourses more typical among certain European far-right groups where feminism and homosexuality were seen to be a threat to the nation.[19] In addition to the appropriation of liberal discourses among far-right leaders, we should factor in the role of women in far-right groups. While some women would likewise make misogynistic comments, and support typical views of gender and Islam, sustained Breivik-style anti-feminism or discussion of 'men's rights' may well have been restrained due to the mix of genders among participants and the prominent organisational roles of figures like Jayda Fransen (who was acting leader of Britain First) and women in the EDL, including the EDL Angels. Andrea Dauber, who has uncovered some of the participation of women in far-right groups, has pointed out that for UKIP, the BNP and the EDL, between 28 per cent and 36 per cent of their supporters were women.[20]

There were certainly women present in online activity. Taking a small sample of 200 from those groups I analysed, there were 30 per cent presented as female commenters and 70 per cent male, though in their study of the EDL Facebook group participants in 2011, Jamie Bartlett and Mark Littler found that 81 per cent were male and 19 per cent were female.[21] Whatever measurement we take, clearly far-right online activity was still a predominantly male domain which partly accounts for its masculinised rhetoric but it was nevertheless possible that the minority female presence had some restraining influence on the violent rhetoric towards women, and particularly so given that the perception of Muslim misogyny was a regular topic. However, gendered and sexualised threats to boundaries were still present among those I analysed in the claims about a failure to live up to such notions of masculinity when required. This led to claims that 'we' have lost our masculinity (e.g., become 'pussies') in failing to defend the nation against hordes of queer Muslim perverts, sexists, rapists, paedophiles and sex pests, a view which overlapped with other European far-right tendencies.[22] Strong Great Men (or Great Masculinised Figures) were, therefore, required to defend the borders. Put differently, this also perpetuated stereotypes of gender and sexuality in its own distinctive way.

The seemingly contradictory tendencies of benign Christianity and/or the nation, and the militarisation of the nation, Christianity, or Jesus, probably also owed something to the treatments of gender and sexuality in the far-right material I viewed. In this sense, we can understand how the militaristic and masculinised (e.g., truth as a lion, the crusader as a male soldier, the fetish for strong, masculine leaders) could coexist with assumptions of innocence: purity of intentions (connected as they were with notions of truth, honour, Christianity) about protecting 'our' values of tolerance and promised physical acts against the threatening, intolerant Other were deemed necessary self-defence. We might compare how such attitudes played out in individual instances which revealed the 'harder', violent notions of masculinity coming to the fore on certain street protests, and certainly among the EDL according to popular imaginations at least. In their case study of three young male EDL supporters from working-class backgrounds in their wider social contexts (e.g., pubs, snooker halls, workplaces, homes), James Treadwell and Jon Garland looked at the structural and psychological factors at play in the ways in which they constructed masculinity and male-on-male ('lads' versus 'lads') violence. These involved perceptions of marginalisation, failure and disadvantage which were connected by the individuals with their own acts of violence directed at Asians/Muslims. Among the structural issues were models of contemporary masculinity and violence which involved control, authority, individualism and aggression. In this instance (as with other EDL members), it was closely linked with football hooliganism, although in such cases it also involved a mimicking and reworking of wider social concepts of masculinity and dominant media narratives about Muslims and immigration of the sort we saw in online groups and stirred up by the EDL in contexts of poverty. Personalised issues included self-perceptions of heroism and pride at attacking the male Muslim and the perceptions of Islamification. However, this process was cyclical in that it simultaneously reinforced social exclusion and marginalisation and contributed to the negative stereotyping of white working-class men as violent racists, even if they were not entirely atypical in their attitudes either.[23] While the specific contexts of online discussion, reading newspaper headlines, snooker halls, and EDL rallies were not the same, they provided mutually reinforcing discourses and the common argument about connections between rhetorical violence and physical violence is not without merit in this instance.

The veneer of equality and respectability was crucial to outward-facing groups like the EDL or Britain First and this would provide some evidence that their surprising interest in women's rights functioned to invent a mythology of England, Britain or the West as a site of an acceptable form of gender equality (e.g., women must be unveiled) while simultaneously categorising Muslims accordingly. This interest in gender and sexuality in relation to the state and Muslims was clearly part of wider debates in contemporary political discourse. Baker, Gabrielatos and McEnery's study of the representation of Islam and Muslims in the national press also found a disproportionate emphasis on Muslim women rather than Muslim men and unsurprisingly the emphasis lay on the appropriateness of being veiled, with more right-leaning newspapers likely to condemn the clothing with reference to issues of oppression, community relations and extremism.[24] The perceived Christian or British/English culture that was deemed kind to women and tolerant of homosexuality while being militarily hostile to hypocritical, oppressive or sexually deviant Muslims can unsurprisingly be viewed as part of a wider Orientalist, racialised and imperialist discourse that gathered momentum during the War on Terror.[25] What Alana Lentin and Gavan Titley claimed of the construction of a certain post-9/11 New Labour discourse would apply to such EDL or Britain First mythmaking, namely, that 'locating anti-feminist practices and homophobia as resistant characteristics of racialized groups' has 'become central to unfolding and prolonging the Muslim problem over time, while locating a liberal progressive telos in the articulation of integrationist nationalisms'.[26]

Christianity and (the perversion of) Islam in liberal parliamentary discourse

As this would suggest, the common claim that the far right is a more extreme version of nationalist tendencies in mainstream political discourse and among the wider public is a claim with some validity. Yet despite the levels of relative popularity of negative discourses about Islam and Muslims, it remains that the opposition of Christianity/England/Britain versus Islam would be much more difficult for mainstream politicians to the left of UKIP to maintain, not least because a significant number of Muslims are voters and subjects. When Pegida activist Anne Marie Waters – who openly claimed that Islam is 'evil' and that 'Islamic culture does not fit with ours' – was nominated to be UKIP's parliamentary candidate (and later ran for leader), it provoked outrage and, given UKIP's election campaign and rhetoric in 2017, this may have been deliberately provocative.[27] The notion that the Bible and Christianity represented democratic values, English nationalism and heritage may have ran deep in mainstream English political discourse but the Islamic Other was nuanced in a noticeably different way to Waters and those we saw on the far right and in the right-wing media.[28] Instead, what was deemed to be 'true' Islam and the 'true' reading of the Qur'an belonged to the same liberal democratic tradition as the more trusted Christianity and the Bible while acts of violence or illiberalism associated with Islam became a 'distorted' or 'false' version of Islam.

Even Theresa May, who, as we have seen, toyed with the notion of Christian symbols and nativism, was always unlikely to present Islam per se as a problem. In her speech to Parliament after the Westminster attacks in March 2017, she spoke about 'Islamist ideology' and 'Islamist terrorism'. Furthermore, the notions of a 'perversion' of a purer faith and un-Islamic and un-religious acts came out in questioning from the Conservative MP Michael Tomlinson:

> **Michael Tomlinson:** It is reported that what happened yesterday was an act of Islamic terror. Does the Prime Minister agree that what happened was not Islamic, just as the murder of Airey Neave was not Christian, and that both were perversions of religion?
>
> **The Prime Minister:** I absolutely agree. It is wrong to describe what happened as Islamic terrorism; it is Islamist terrorism – a perversion of a great faith.[29]

This notion that Islam has been perverted is one we have seen before, and it is one which political leaders stressed in the light of terror attacks. As Tommy Robinson was blaming Islam for the murder of Lee Rigby in Woolwich (May 2013), the then Mayor of London, Boris Johnson, claimed (contrary to the murderers) that 'it is completely wrong to blame this killing on the religion of Islam' and the cause was 'wholly and exclusively in the deluded mindset of the people who did it'.[30] David Cameron categorised the murder as 'a betrayal of Islam … There is nothing in Islam that justifies this truly dreadful act.'[31] Elsewhere, Cameron categorised ISIS/Daesh and its adherents similarly as 'not Muslims' but rather 'monsters', a 'fanatical organisation', a 'warped ideology', 'warped interpretation of theology and scripture', 'extremists who want to abuse Islam' and who provide a 'perverted, illiberal and hostile interpretation of this great religion' which is 'a religion of peace'.[32] After the bombings in London on 7 July 2005, Tony Blair, who welcomed a supporting statement from the Muslim Council of Great Britain, likewise talked about how the attacks were done in 'the name of Islam' but (and with a striking May-like use of 'we') that 'the vast and overwhelming majority of Muslims, here and abroad, are decent and law-abiding people who abhor this act of terrorism every bit as much as we do'.[33] In a speech shortly after, where he elaborated further, he re-emphasised that 'all civilised people, Muslim or other, feel revulsion' at such acts which represent 'a strain within the world-wide religion of Islam, as far removed from its essential decency and truth as Protestant gunmen who kill Catholics or vice versa, are from Christianity'.[34] Indeed, it was Blair, probably more than any other mainstream political leader, who normalised the language of a 'perverted and false view of Islam', particularly in relation to foreign policy.[35] Clearly, then, this notion of a 'perversion of Islam' or a 'false Islam' has become standard rhetoric after attacks or acts of violence. As one former government advisor told me, it is unlikely that a politician actually has any serious in-depth knowledge of the history of Islam but distancing the majority of Muslims and Islam from terror and violence is a necessary function in the immediate aftermath of an attack in trying to establish calm against, in, and support from Muslim communities.

There was another feature of this move to stress terror as a 'perversion of Islam' which involved the legitimation of the state monopoly on violence. One of the curious features of the material I looked at among far-right groups was that there was both a tendency to see Christianity and the Bible/New Testament/Jesus as representing peace and to use Christianity and Jesus in militaristic terms. Although there was no attempt to reconcile these potentially contradictory notions in the material I saw, it was suggested that there may be an underlying logic in the dominant idea that the country and English identity needed physical self-defence, hence the language of being 'under siege' and so on. This was part of a broader cultural logic shared with mainstream political discourse which isolated the perceived perversion of Islam as the threatening Other requiring self-defence through attack. For Cameron in his justification for bombing ISIS/Daesh, 'we' were certainly prepared to use violence in a 'calm, deliberate way but with an iron determination'. Yet equally this had to be because of provocation and because he also claimed that 'minorities, including Christians' were especially persecuted, and 'today ... our religion is now the most persecuted religion around the world'.[36] But the myth of innocence went further still in staking a claim to being peaceful, with none other than the Prince of Peace invoked to justify the violence necessary to keep Britain safe:

> Right now, our brave armed forces are doing their duty, around the world: in the skies of Iraq and Syria, targeting the terrorists that threaten those countries and our security at home; on the seas of the Mediterranean, saving those who attempt the perilous crossing to Europe; and on the ground, helping to bring stability to countries from Afghanistan to South Sudan. It is because they face danger that we have peace. And that is what we mark today as we celebrate the birth of God's only son, Jesus Christ – the Prince of Peace.[37]

As we saw in Chapter 2, to support militarism further in the Middle East and North Africa through this tension of peace/self-defence, Cameron, followed by Hilary Benn in his advocacy of bombing Syria in December 2015, alluded to a biblical character who helped the recipient of violence: the Good Samaritan. The parable in Luke 10.25–37 was implicitly read by Cameron and Benn in terms of the Good Samaritan as a potentially violent figure, prepared to seek out the violent robbers and beat them to death. Here Cameron and Benn were effectively making a pitch for British and Western states having the legitimate monopoly on violence against an Other which, in its opposition to the British state and competing claim to violence, could not be deemed truly Muslim or truly Islam, both of which must be assumed to be compatible with liberal democracies in their essential forms.

In mainstream parliamentary discourse, then, the construction of the perversion or distortion of Islam, or a false version of Islam, took the place of Islam, essentialised as the violent, illiberal Other, and contrasted with a benign Christianity. In this sort of reading (which was dominant in the main parliamentary parties) Islam and religion properly understood was, like Christianity, to be seen as part of British or English liberalism. Cameron, following Blair, supported those he claimed were challenging 'warped' versions of Islam and promoting Islam as liberal, tolerant, inclusive, and compatible with democracy, freedom and equality. Indeed, such values represented the idealised British state and subject for Cameron and it was only once the notion of 'religious brotherhood' was separated from them that Islam and religion effectively became 'warped'.[38] Of course, this understanding of Islam and the state was not just for non-Muslim politicians and it was a (neo)liberal democratic and nationalist game that those who identify as Muslim could also play in the public arena, just like those other interest groups who might identify as Christian, Jewish, Sikh, religious, atheist, secularist, spiritual, satanic, pagan, and so on. So, for instance, in a debate with Jack Straw on BBC Radio 4's *Today* programme (21 April 2014), Talha Ahmad of the Muslim Council of Britain accepted the notion that there was a distinction to be drawn between devout Muslims and a miniscule extremist minority who proselytise exclusively, label nonbelievers as 'infidel', and deny women equal rights, and that 'decent' Muslims would all agree. Furthermore, Ahmad argued that the pursuit of faith involves respecting everyone's space and that Muslims are 'obedient', in this case to the rule of the liberal nation state.

Why we all love to hate the EDL and other myths of innocence

In 'Why we all love to hate Haider', Slavoj Žižek recognised that one ideological function of the popularist Right can be to supply the 'negative common denominator of the entire established political spectrum' and 'furnish the proof of the benevolence of the official system'. One function of a controversial figure like Jörg Haider was partly to legitimise the international liberal consensus while strangling any radical alternative, particularly anti-capitalist movements and class struggles, which become de-legitimised through association with similar concerns among the 'populist' Right.[39] Of course, we could say similar things about the notion of 'radical' Islam. In contemporary political discourse, the language of extremist or radical Islam effectively supresses and discredits the history of a 'radicalism' in politically leftist Islamic traditions, and potentially leftist challenges to established political discourse more generally.[40] But in terms of the English and British far right, we might recall the presence of Nick Griffin on BBC's *Question Time* in September 2009, a figure who united the established political spectrum in opposition. Rather than see Griffin's platform to debate with mainstream politicians and commentators as a bizarre aberration or an extreme example of free speech, it might be more helpful to view this as a perhaps necessary showcasing of liberal benevolence as the recession and cuts were beginning to hit. Griffin was predictably wild and would go on to discredit himself with ease in his discussion of a moderate Ku Klux Klan (KKK) member, his discomfort with homoerotic kissing, and desire for correct British lineages belonging to the islands since the Ice Age, no less. Also on the panel, however, was Jack Straw who was a regular defender of Britain's involvement in Afghanistan and Iraq, the Foreign Secretary when the Foreign Office were discrediting the British Ambassador in Tashkent for criticising the human rights' record of Uzbekistan (a then British ally), critical of Muslim women with their faces covered when speaking to him, an enthusiastic member of the New Labour establishment happy to employ anti-immigration rhetoric, and a representative of the ruling Labour Party who were embracing austerity. Nevertheless, in this context the feral Griffin meant Straw's views were within the bounds of the political consensus, with Straw functioning as a voice of moderation, reason and decency as he condemned the far right to generous applause.

In the case of the EDL, condemnation among politicians and journalists was easy to find. So, for instance:

> I have described some parts of our society as sick, and there is none sicker than the EDL. (David Cameron)
>
> [Tony Blair] totally disagrees with what they have said. (Tony Blair Institute)
>
> We should all be aware of the damage that the EDL's divisive message can do to communities. (Theresa May)
>
> The English Defence League is not welcome in Birmingham. They will never be welcome in Birmingham. (Party leaders on Birmingham City Council)

And, though not quite as hostile, at the far right of the media consensus, opinion writer Richard Littlejohn settled for describing the EDL as 'a pretty unsavoury outfit', even if the EDL got more of a sympathetic hearing on the right wing of the national media than the BNP ever would.[41] This is emphatically not to say that such comments were incorrect in and of themselves but they can still be viewed in terms of their ideological function or, put another way, what they were likely to omit in the condemnation. By focusing on or implying issues relating to racial and racist issues, and registering their disgust at such racism, the established political system could sidestep possible complicity in the creation of such discontent – after all, who outside the far right is likely to oppose anti-racism?

However, what studies of the EDL (e.g., ethnographic, investigative journalism, statistical) show is another aspect of the story not typically highlighted in mainstream political discourse involving consistent reference to social and economic dislocation, poverty, unemployment, precarious employment, low pay, community neglect, hatred of politicians, perceptions of being betrayed by the Labour Party of their parents, and so on, all set against a backdrop of a loss of a once comparably stable employment in industry. Indeed, we might follow Winlow, Hall and Treadwell in noting how the EDL were in some ways a product of liberal complicity with the neoliberal settlement and accompanying (largely exclusionary, and now entrenched) class interests and representation in politics, popular culture, education, universities (etc.).[42] To admit this too much would be tantamount to admitting that the political consensus failed the working class. Nevertheless, politicians tried to court such a vote (we might recall Gordon Brown's 'British jobs for British workers') and such an attempt was represented in the 2017 Conservative Manifesto with its striking criticisms of 'untrammeled free markets', an offer of protection for those working in the 'gig' economy, and the rejection of the 'cult of selfish individualism', combined with May's toying with ethnonationalist language, all of which should be collectively seen as part of a seemingly growing Brexit consensus in the run-up to the General Election and an attempt to attract the concerns of the working-class Right who might otherwise have turned to UKIP (Chapter 2). All the while, of course, they were simultaneously not wanting to be associated with the far right which could be done by criticising the relatively uninfluential EDL and maintaining the convenient language of a 'perversion' of Islam.

Despite the consistent hostility towards racism and groups deemed racist in connection with attitudes towards Islam and despite the consistent construction of anything illiberal being a deviation from 'true Islam', the pervasive myth of innocence in mainstream political discourse served another function. In addition to pushing economic issues to one side, such discourses also allowed the perpetuation of what we might otherwise call racialised policies while simultaneously claiming the opposite. Here, we might point to the work of David Theo Goldberg on race and racialising discourses in the age of neoliberalism and how anti-racist rhetoric in political institutions and intellectualised concepts still perpetuate unconscious and implicit racialising distinctions, despite good intentions.[43] In the aftermath of the Woolwich murder, Tony Blair and Boris Johnson presented the image of a diseased or poisoned Muslim or Islamic body which posed a societal threat. Blair referred to the 'problem within Islam' alternatively as a 'strain within Islam' that 'is not compatible with pluralistic, liberal, open-minded societies' while Boris Johnson, using similar reasoning, referred to 'the virus of "Islamism"' and the 'virus of extremism' among 'a minority of Muslims', and how we should 'try to help immunise the vast, innocent and law-abiding majority of the Muslim population'.[44] For all the positive rhetoric they employed about Islam and Muslims, was it really so far removed from the far-right comments we saw earlier about extremist snakes in the Islamic grass? Moreover, the emphasis on certain perpetrators of violence or those matching definitions of 'terrorism' (and not some other group that might fit the definition, whether domestic abusers or nation states) as *especially* problematic meant that a particular group got such intense political and media attention which in itself perpetuated difference and distinction.[45] To this it might be added that the 'perversion of Islam' and 'true Islam' tropes were a part of such distinctions, essentialist identities, boundary- and difference-making in relation to the construction of the state, Europe, the West, and so on that was typical of the construction of more familiar racialised distinctions – after all, *we* know what *they* are supposed to look like, what clothes *they* are supposed to wear, which group *they* belong to, and even what skin colours *they* are supposed to have.[46]

A subtle, dog-whistle approach to marking out communities without explicitly racialising them is rarely difficult to find in the rhetoric of leading politicians, irrespective of the rhetoric of inclusiveness we saw in, for instance, Cameron's construction of Christmas (Chapter 2). For all his strong rhetoric about a 'perversion of Islam', Cameron still targeted Muslim groups and communities for tolerating, or lacking resilience to, extremism and for embracing cultural segregation.[47] In March 2005, the New Labour Minister Hazel Blears talked about 'dealing with the terrorist threat' which at present 'is most likely to come from those people associated with an extreme form of Islam, or falsely hiding behind Islam' but this 'inevitably means that some of our counter-terrorist powers will be disproportionately experienced by people in the Muslim community'.[48] After stepping down from parliamentary politics, Tony Blair argued that extremism in Islam ran deeper in Muslim communities than is conventionally admitted. Blair used the phrase a 'problem within Islam' and even had Tommy Robinson suggesting that they both shared similar views (which Blair denied). Blair's wording even provoked a rebuke from the Conservative MP Gavin Barwell who, to add to the potential blurriness of the categories 'Islam' and 'distortion of Islam', claimed Blair's wording was problematic even though he agreed with what he said.[49]

In this respect, one of the striking features about Arun Kundnani's book, *The Muslims Are Coming!*, is that it effectively focuses on the use of language relating to the 'distortion of Islam' trope, particularly in the analysis of terms such as 'extremism' and 'radicalism'. For Kundnani, societies like the UK view Muslims in such a way and developed detailed theories to explain the processes of young Muslims becoming terrorists, with the assumption that the cause of terrorism is such 'Islamism'. The ideological battles over the War on Terror were firmly placed onto a group assumed to be racially and culturally distinct and with the default assumption that the term 'terrorist' is to be especially associated with the political violence of *Muslims*. What this meant was that *Muslims* and the alleged behavioural signs of a particular (*Muslim*) 'ideology' became the especial recipients of state surveillance, including participation of universities, prisons and online communities in the process of surveillance. The most extensive example of this was the Preventing Violent Extremism programme (or Prevent, as it is popularly known), a programme designed to stop the growth and execution of terrorism and inaugurated under Tony Blair's government in 2006, though it built on earlier counterterrorist initiatives. Prevent was to promote 'British values' such as tolerance and democracy and provide resources for Muslim communities and online groups, as well as countering 'extremist' propaganda in Pakistan and the Middle East. Whatever the motivations of the individuals involved in developing Prevent, Muslims were, as Kundnani stressed, the group singled out ('an ideological battlefield whose human terrain was Muslim citizens'), an effective subcategorisation of Muslims into 'extremist' and 'moderate', a pitting of 'Muslim against non-Muslim in competition for local favors from the state', and targeting an ideology defined by Hazel Blears in 2009 as involving a 'twisted reading of Islam' again as the ultimate cause of terrorism. As if to confirm the kinds of analysis undertaken in this book, there were even awards given to promote correct (or 'moderate') readings of Islamic tradition and of the Qur'an.[50]

The state's myth of innocence and monopolisation of tolerant patriotism invoked by the rhetoric of a 'perversion of Islam' also involved distancing mainstream political discourse from potential complicity with the results of British foreign policy (indeed, opposition to the War on Terror has been deemed a potential indicator of terrorist sympathies according to Prevent). To problematise this it is worth noting some (and only some) of the numerous long-, medium- and short-term explanations which might help us understand the rise of ISIS, al Qaeda, and their claimants in Europe, other than resorting to the basic explanations of a metaphysical 'evil', 'perversion', or 'Islam'. To generalise such scholarship perhaps too much, attacks from Boston through Nice and Paris to London and Manchester, as well as Europeans going to fight for ISIS in the Middle East, might involve localised and psychological explanatory issues such as criminal backgrounds, dysfunctional families, discourses of masculinity, youth cultures, internet networks and conversions, boredom, racialised categorisation of generations of immigrant communities as outsiders, shifting generational attitudes towards social liberalism, romance of fighting abroad, intersection with certain Salafist ideas, identification with oppression of Muslims internationally, returning fighters permitted by the British state to fight alongside ISIS or al Qaeda against 'rogue states' in Libya and Syria, and so on. In terms of the Middle East and North Africa, we might note equally complex histories of the emergence of ISIS and al Qaeda which have been discussed in scholarship, including (among others) the decline of secular nationalism in the Middle East and North Africa, the combination of a rise of slums with sharp population growth, the role of oil in economic growth and crashes, ideological influences from Left to Right in colonial and postcolonial universities in North Africa (e.g., vanguardism, anti-imperialism, terror, internationalism, popular justice), and issues relating to Saudi Arabia including the availability of Wahhabism as an ideological option.[51] But some of the issues could be (and have been) linked even more directly to Anglo-American foreign policy, such as Western support for dictatorial states, Western support for the Mujahideen (and thus the Taliban and al Qaeda) against the Soviet Union, British support for 'rebels' in Libya or Syria (and thus potential ISIS sympathisers), American bases in Saudi Arabia, sanctions on Iraq in the 1990s, the ongoing treatment of Palestinians, drone attacks, the post-bombing chaos in Libya, and, again, the invasion of Iraq and a defeated Baathist military which were most immediately connected with the emergence of ISIS.

There is, obviously, much more to be said about violence associated with groups like ISIS or killers in Britain and France but what this brief sketch shows is just how complex causal explanations might be and, of course, that Western states may not be as innocent or simplistic as the official rhetoric would suggest in loading near-sole blame on a sullied Islam. Despite all this, through invoking the notion of a 'warped' version of Islam, Cameron denied that the invasion of Iraq and its aftermath were a 'source' or 'root cause' for the rise of ISIS.[52] In response to the Woolwich murders, and despite claims of the murderers, Boris Johnson similarly argued that it was 'equally wrong to link this murder to the actions of British foreign policy'.[53] Tony Blair, who has continually had to deny connections between foreign policy, not least for potential legal ramifications, likewise suggested after the London bombings of 2005 that there was a need to blame 'this ideology and the violence that is inherent in it' because it 'did not start a few years ago in response to a particular policy', again despite the complex social and geopolitical histories and despite the explicit motives given by the bombers which mentioned Chechnya, sanctions on Iraq, the Iraq War, Afghanistan, Palestine, and Bush and Blair, as well as the standard references to Islam.[54]

We can go further still. By looking at how the different myths of innocence perpetuated by, on the one hand, Cameron and mainstream party-political figures and, on the other, far-right sympathisers such as those I looked at, we see that their respective constructions of Islam as responsible for any violence or illiberalism lack any significant historical contextualisation.[55] It was an ahistorical myth which constructed a kind of Christian and/or national innocence and, despite the qualifications, assumed a construct of Islam which is tainted in some way. This can be highlighted by a parlour game of reading 'our' recent political history in a similar way. Tony Blair used the example of Catholics and Protestants during the Troubles as a seemingly acceptable example of distortion of religion; but what if we replaced these sorts of arguments with Blair himself? Blair was clear in claiming religious motivations and the authority of the Bible, as were George Bush, David Cameron and Barack Obama. All these were invoked in decisions where, to a greater or lesser degree, countless people died, including in situations where white phosphorus was used. Now try and imagine the media and Parliament discussing, in a sustained way, notions of 'Christian violence', or even a 'distortion' of 'true Christianity', and then trying to factor this in as a part of a 'measurement' for understanding how violent a religion currently is or is not. Or, to push this further still, what about Buddhism and popular assumptions about nonviolence at its essence? Steve Jobs, a hero of corporate liberalism, identified as a Buddhist and yet Apple has been noted for its use of materials from sweatshops which were accused of contributing to workers' suicides.[56] Given the lauding of Jobs' charisma and influence at Apple, should we make a connection between his corporate Buddhism and his acceptance of Apple's use of sweatshops? Does this mean that there has been a dangerous streak of 'religious extremism' running through Apple? Or are suicides not the right kind of violence and not to be classified as 'terror' or 'extreme'? Can someone who holds liberal democratic values not count as tolerant of religious extremism? Could we go one step further and ask 'the British community', 'the American community', 'the Western community', 'the Christian community', or 'the Muslim community' to stand up to the known practices of Apple instead of tacitly supporting them by buying more iPhones? This is not, of course, to say who or what should or should not be blamed but it is to suggest that liberal-capitalism-as-benign implicitly belongs to this myth of innocence too.

Conclusion

What we have seen is that with politically acceptable uses of 'religion' as an analytical category it was 'Islam' (or 'Islamism', 'perversion of Islam', etc.) that was most likely to be the one which could be used as an explanatory force and certainly more so than the seemingly innocent 'Christianity' (or 'Buddhism', or indeed 'capitalism'). This was something shared across the spectrum, from the far right to mainstream politics, and measured in relation to its compatibility (or not) with given perceptions of English or British nationalism, even if there were obviously differences in nuance. A part of these myths of innocence was to deflect and avoid complicity of the nation state while covering over the complexities of the situation that gave rise to contexts whereby such actions can occur. Assessing the parliamentary political impact of the relative popularity of such distrusting views relating to 'Islam' is not straightforward. The EDL may have fragmented and been vilified in mainstream politics but its views were not only disseminated on social media, but were replicated in the right-wing national media (or vice versa). UKIP struggled to make an impact in electoral terms yet equally it saw its greatest political success in Brexit, which cannot be removed from such ideas, even if they were also overblown by certain Remainers. Indeed, since Brexit, it was May's Conservatives who took over the views from the Right on Englishness, Britishness, nationalism, and so on (as we saw in May's handling of Christmas). Yet May also modified liberal views by incorporating the notion of a 'perversion of Islam' inherited from Cameron and much of mainstream party-political discourse. Effectively, the gaze remained on Muslims and Islam even while acting otherwise and thereby providing liberal credibility as all the while some of the far-right interests in relation to Islam had become normalised.

We should not underestimate the significance of ideology in this respect. The uses of 'Islam' and a 'perversion of Islam' both played a role in justifying treatment of Muslims domestically and internationally, whether state approved (e.g., surveillance, profiling, bombing in North Africa and the Middle East) or street violence. The flipside of this – that is, claiming state, Christian and nationalist monopoly on tolerance, democracy, rights, and so on – likewise fed into this narrative. The disclaimers by groups like the EDL or by politicians that this focus was not racist but a hostility to ideas is only relevant in the sense that it was a mystification tactic. Put differently, such disclaimers allowed groups like the EDL and politicians to target specific communities who were assumed to look, act, dress, behave (etc.) in certain ways without the stigma of how this sort of social categorisation might otherwise have been labelled: racist. Class and material contexts of violence were also part of the function of 'Islam' in political discourse, albeit in different ways. Politicising Islamic aberrations purely in terms of overenthusiastic religious extremism blocked out or discredited leftist constructions of Islam and, most pertinently, the material contexts of violence. Moreover, stigmatising the concerns of groups like the EDL in mainstream liberal political discourse also meant avoidance of complicity in creating the social, economic and political contexts that gave rise to such working-class movements like the EDL with a hatred for parliamentary politics. But this also gave rise to the popular cliche, 'the white working class' as responding to socio-economic change with racism, Islamophobia, or anti-immigration rhetoric which came to the surface in the EU Referendum. In the next chapter, we will see that this is hardly the whole story, at least in certain working-class constructions of religion, Christianity, Islam and Muslims in relation to issues of immigration, nationalism and Brexit.

4
Brexit Barrow: Religion in Real Time During a Summer of Political Chaos

Introduction

It was 2016 Brexit that really brought issues of class, ethnicity, race, immigration, and even religion to the fore of elite English political discourse of the media and political classes. These issues were presented in different, often contradictory ways. Was not a vote for Leave a cipher for (often older) white working-class racism and hostility to immigration and connected with the hostility towards Islam, Muslims and 'Asians' that we saw in the previous chapter? Did uneducated white working classes not know what was good for the country economically? Were the (presumably assumed white) working class of the North, Midlands and Wales (not to mention fellow deviants in the South) not appreciative of the vibrant liberalism of the metropolitan centres? As we have seen, it is not as if these views were entirely absent from certain working-class interests. But statistics and journalistic opinion are inevitably incomplete and, besides, because a certain percentage prioritised immigration or dislike of Islam or Muslims it also follows that a certain percentage did not. Moreover, comfortable, metropolitan middle-class elites (liberal or otherwise) were likewise susceptible to racial tropes and an obsession with Islam and Muslims, as the previous chapters have already indicated. To illuminate some of the interactions with the various political positions we have seen in the previous chapters, it is worth analysing what some of those puzzled-over people outside London think. To do this, I chose one particular northern town as a test case which, for full disclosure, is one in which I grew up and live and which did not seem to me to fit the various media and political stereotypes.[1]

Like much of northern England, Barrow-in-Furness voted to Leave the EU. 'The North' (as well as 'the Midlands') was long treated as something distinctly different from the centre of political, economic and cultural power in London and the South East. Politicians and media figures may have come 'from the North' or work 'in the North' or talk to people 'about the North', but in such cases 'the North' was constructed in relation to, or in distinction from, the centre of power. A common refrain from Remain Labour politicians and their supporters in the aftermath of the Referendum was the need to convince people in the 'traditional heartlands' of the North and the Midlands, as if these feral and formerly loyal voters just needed to be properly managed and directed to vote the right way. Indeed, it was not dissimilar assumptions that led to intrepid journalists visiting places like Burnley or, closer to the General Election, reporters in Hartlepool being described as 'embedded' as they were sent out to discover why these strange folk behaved and voted the way they did.[2] Nevertheless, plenty of journalists and politicians from all parties recognised in the lead-up to Brexit that there was a significant disconnect between the centres of political, economic and cultural power, and whatever was thought to be going on in working-class parts of the UK north of the Watford Gap.

While presenting certain Barrovian voices from around the time of the 2016 EU Referendum, I will obviously continue to focus on constructions of religion in post-2008 political discourses. In this instance I will look at how Brexit might have begun to shape the ways in which people think about such things. The aftermath of the Referendum result was an opportunity to compare the views of mainstream politicians with an unusually engaged voting public in one such 'northern town'. Not only had a large percentage of northern voters contributed to the seemingly surprise result to leave the EU, but the following days and weeks saw the Prime Minister resign, the fall of leading political personalities, an ongoing civil war in the Labour Party, and a new prime minister. However, this was not just some irrelevant political theatre for Barrovians, because with the advent of the new Prime Minister came the renewal of Trident, the submarines which had been and now would be built in Barrow. All this provided a potentially important opportunity to interview Barrovians in a context of heightened political engagement and to see how political sentiments might relate to perceptions of religion.

My goals in this respect are twofold: to analyse such data to see what kinds of perceptions about religion might exist in Barrow and compare them with some of the dominant assumptions about religion we have seen in political discourses so far. The sample size included 30 face-to-face, semi-structured interviews and broader discussions carried out mostly in June and July 2016 in houses, backyards, gardens, pubs, workplaces, streets and online messaging, with some repeated questions asked in each one. In addition, in the same period, I examined and analysed hundreds of Facebook comments, discussions and updates from Barrovian circles. As with the previous chapter, the material cited here has all been anonymised. Opinions taken from Facebook discussions and updates, while virtually all in the public domain, have additionally been paraphrased or quantified. The gender split in participants was about 50:50 between those who identified as male or female (no other gendered identities were given) and the age range was about 18–80 with few patterns emerging in terms of gender or age. The sample was random at least in the sense that I did not target people who did or did not openly identify as 'religious' and instead I wanted to see what sort of discourses about religion, Islam, Christianity, the Bible, and so on would emerge. All participants had some connection with what might be deemed working-class life and/ or the local shipyard, a near inevitability in a place like Barrow. Occupations (or not) past and present included, for instance, nurse, painter and decorator, domestic gas and heating engineer, offshore engineer, plumber, charity worker, retired, unable to work, youth worker, taxi driver, cleaner, receptionist, IT technician, pastry seller, merchandiser, and numerous former and present shipyard employees (e.g., electrician, driller, fitter and turner, typist, secretary, chemist, quality control engineer).

The questions asked of all interviewees were centred on how people might understand religion and English identity, with a particular emphasis on Christianity and the Bible, not least to see if connections with Islam might be made otherwise unprovoked. The questions allowed a degree of freedom to air opinions on the Referendum result, how people voted, why they voted (or not), what they made of what happened in the aftermath of the Referendum, and what their view of 'Englishness' (often merged with 'Britishness') might be. Ideas about nationalism are of analytical significance because, as we have seen, they turned up consistently in mainstream political discourse about religion, Islam, Christianity and the Bible. With these factors in mind, I looked for assumptions about what interviewees and Facebook commenters thought such terms might mean and, in the case of the interviewees, what they thought about David Cameron's claim on the eve of the 400th anniversary of the King James Bible in 2011 that Britain is a Christian country, a claim he would make elsewhere. Cameron's speech (cited below) brought together all his key assumptions about Christianity and the Bible as sources for British values. I will look at all these interconnected issues in turn before providing some analysis of Barrovian assumptions associated with religion and how they map on to broader understandings of religion in England.

A brief recent history of Barrow-in-Furness

First, some history is needed of the town one *Telegraph* journalist wrote was 'tucked away in a forgotten peninsula of Northern England'.[3] Admittedly, plenty of people who live in the region did not typically forget its location, but I appreciate that some readers may share the implied *Telegraph* readers' forgetfulness.

Barrow is an industrial port town in the North West of England, once in the county of Lancashire (with which some still identify) until the boundary changes in 1974 when it became part of Cumbria. It was the sort of town that became part of one narrative about Brexit: the working-class northern towns voted to leave the EU for various reasons, usually coalescing around immigration, disconnection from political and economic power, and employment issues. Indeed, the voting patterns were, like other northern towns, much higher than the 52–48 national split. Barrow was 60.6 per cent (21,867 votes) in favour of Leave and 39.4 per cent in favour of Remain (14,207 votes), with a turnout of 67.8 per cent, a slightly higher turnout than the 2015 General Election for the Barrow and Furness constituency.[4] Like much of the narrative about 'northern towns' in relation to the Referendum, the story of Barrow can be cast as one of industrial decline which gathered momentum under the neoliberal revolution. It is a town built on the iron and steel industry and immigration from, among other places, Ireland, Scotland, Manchester and Liverpool, and effectively grew from the mid-nineteenth century onward into a town with a population of just under 70,000, though the population was in decline at the time of the Referendum.[5] It would be shipbuilding that dominated the town throughout the twentieth century and into the twenty-first century, including the politically controversial Trident nuclear submarines. Until the past few years, it had a crane-dominated skyline along with Devonshire Dock Hall (DDH) where the submarines were housed and largely built amidst an array of grey, brown and dirty beige. The DDH was opened by Thatcher in 1986 and nearby but long-gone graffiti revealed its once popular nickname (with a nod to Bob Dylan): 'Maggie's Farm'.

But the locally famous yellow crane that dominated the skyline was dismantled in 2010 while the numbers employed by the shipyard had long fallen. In the 1980s the shipyard employed around 14–15,000 but in the 1990s, after the end of the Cold War, the numbers employed dropped sharply to the current figure which was closer to the 5,000 mark by 2016.[6] While Barrow may have maintained some of its manufacturing industry (albeit reduced) compared with much of post-industrial Britain, it is worth noting comparative employment and benefit rates to give a general idea about issues facing Barrovians, such as Incapacity Benefits Claimants being higher than the national and regional levels.[7]

In addition to shipbuilding, Barrow had its occasional moments of cultural prominence and they were typically part of the various assumptions about it being isolated, miserable, poor or, more romantically, working class. Indeed, in 2008 Barrow made the national press for being named The Most Working Class Place in the UK based on the number of chip shops, workingmen's clubs and bookmakers.[8] Other cultural moments include its fame for being at the end of the longest cul-de-sac in Britain, endless drug-related stories, having its bus depot featured in a *Chewits* advert, the home of the alleged Lady in the Lake murderer who also happened to be a local schoolteacher, a Legionnaires' disease outbreak in 2002, and the recipient of the undercover philanthropic Channel 4 programme, *Secret Millionaire*, which was controversial in its negative presentation of Barrow as all grinding poverty and dog turds.[9] To add to the legend, Barrow again made national news as the 'least happy' place in the UK, according to a Personal Wellbeing survey carried out by the Office for National Statistics on behalf of David Cameron. Rather than dismiss the absurdity of such 'measuring', a cover version of Pharrell's 'Happy' was made by Barrovians to show how happy (some) people (apparently) were.[10]

Of course, counternarratives could be offered but, for now, we are dealing with a narrative of decline, one which was taken up in the mainstream media and one which not all Barrovians would dispute. It is clear enough that it was yet another town which had been at the mercy of neoliberal economics which were continued in the New Labour era and which helps explain why towns like Barrow voted how they did: at least partly in protest against a political and economic elite in the South East. The voting intentions of Barrovians and those much publicised 'working-class' areas of Barrow would certainly be familiar to viewers of Sheena Moore's documentary, *Why We Voted Leave: Voices from Northern*

England, as well as readers of John Harris' regular *Guardian* series, 'Anywhere but Westminster', and Mike Carter's Orwell-esque Brexit report of his journey from Liverpool to London full of urban decay, St George flags, anti-immigration rhetoric, pound shops, boarded-up pubs, bookmakers, and Leave posters.[11] Although there are some prosperous areas, Barrow too has its pound shops, boarded-up pubs, plenty of bookmakers, and, of course, zero-hours contracts. Barrow even had certain streets knocked down in 2010 (despite some opposition from residents) for 'redevelopment' and as of 2017 there were still no replacement houses. Walking close by through the Risedale area of Barrow a few days before the vote, there too were a number of sizeable 'Leave' posters and signs and no 'Remain' ones that I could see. Unsurprisingly, then, the post-industrial town cliches could indeed be found in Barrow.

But, like any town, Barrow also had its own peculiarities. While some might want to foreground Furness Abbey (see below) as part of their understanding of Barrow, for now I want to play the game presented in standard media narratives but instead to show that Barrow (and, no doubt, equally anywhere else) did not quite fit what they may have thought about 'the North'. For a start, the idea of mass immigration in relation to (what was categorised as) 'White British' did not apply to Barrow in the same way as it did other Brexit towns, with 'White British' percentages remaining in the high 90s in the 2001 and 2011 Censuses.[12] While Barrovians may or may not have had strong views on national immigration, and while there was some immigration from outside the UK, it can hardly be said to have been a major feature of contemporary Barrovian demographics.

On the one hand, Barrow fitted the idea of what is usually labelled a traditional 'Labour town' where there appeared to have been an increasing disjunction between its established working-class vote and the main party, though it should be noted that this constituency now contained rural areas and the nearby market town of Ulverston. We might consider what Paul Mason reported in 2015 just prior to the General Election which chimes with the sentiments I heard:

> Labour has not [captured the zeitgeist of their heartlands well]. Having spent last week sitting in the clubs and workplaces of Blackpool, Preston and Barrow-in-Furness, I can see the situation is clearly [*sic*]: that even where they'll vote solidly for Labour, they'll do so without enthusiasm. Offered the chance to watch Paxman v

Miliband, the members of one Barrow working men's club switched to the rugby league.[13]

On the other hand, it was what remained of a manufacturing industry that made Barrow different from plenty of stories about 'northern towns' where industry had all but disappeared and this came through in voting patterns. The Conservatives were the second main party (not that everyone would admit to voting for them) and had some electoral success because of Trident. The Conservatives held Barrow in the 1980s but lost in 1992 when it was clear that the infamous promises of a 'job for life' were looking increasingly inaccurate in light of redundancies. Since then it was Labour (represented by John Woodcock), but their majority shrank to only 795 votes after the 2015 General Election and then to 209 votes after the 2017 General Election (though up by 5.1 per cent after the collapse of the UKIP vote). As was standard with the 'northern town' narrative in 2016, UKIP's vote had risen (by 9.8 per cent) but in the Barrow and Furness constituency they were placed third (behind Labour and Conservative) by some margin with 11.7 per cent of the vote share (compared with 42.3 per cent Labour and 40.5 per cent Conservative) before their collapse in 2017.[14] Even by the standard framing of the issues, then, Barrow already had its own significant differences and similarities which must be kept in mind throughout.

Christian Barrow?

How might assumptions about religion factor into this? Fairly recently, I had a conversation with someone from the local clergy who told me that Christianity in Barrow had visibly declined over the years. If by this he meant church buildings and attendance, then it was easy to find churches which would come to have different functions (e.g., dojo, nightclub, derelict, auction hall) or which were demolished, while the diocesan church attendance continued to decline in line with national trends.[15] This reflected my own perceptions of religion growing up in Barrow, namely, a place where there was general public indifference towards anything deemed 'religious' and where questions about belief in God, the Bible or church attendance were (or so I thought) potentially embarrassing. When I left the shipyard in 1993 to do 'A' Levels in Sixteenth-Century History, English Literature and Religious Studies, I may have been doing subjects which I thought were anti-shipyard, but it was for good reason that I either mumbled over, or neglected to mention, 'Religious Studies'.

However, it is possible that there was something that the decline of churches and my own experience perhaps missed: self-identification. In the 2011 Census, 70.7 per cent identified as Christian, which was higher than both the regional and national percentages, though notably down from 81 per cent in the 2001 Census.[16] Also worth noting is that 22.1 per cent identified as having 'No Religion', whereas other religious self-identifications (Buddhist, Hindu, Jewish, Muslim, Sikh and 'Other') did not rise above 0.2 per cent.[17] But, as is often pointed out, such statistics are hardly without their difficulties, and nor were the ways in which the questions were asked. This was one reason I did not want to seek out participants who identified as Christian or non-Christian and so to maintain the complexity and blurriness of self-identifications that were present, and analyse different discursive uses of 'religion', 'the Bible' and 'Christianity'.

Recent works by, for instance, Ingrid Storm and Stephen Bullivant, have used alternatives to Census data, turning instead to the British Social Attitudes (BSA) data.[18] This is important to note because the question significantly shifted to 'Do you regard yourself as belonging to any particular religion?' from the Census question of 'What is your religion?' This data showed a steady growth in those claiming to have 'No Religion' since such identification was recorded in 1983 to the point of outnumbering self-identification as Christian in 2009. According to this line of questioning, in England and Wales 48.5 per cent (44.2 per cent for the North West) identified as 'No Religion' (BSA 2012–14) while in 2015 the British average was 48.6 per cent (with the North West higher at 52 per cent; BSA 2015).[19] In terms of changing self-identification, this was contrasted with 71.4 per cent claiming to have been brought up Christian and 19 per cent claiming to be brought up with 'No Religion'. The decline of those identifying as 'Anglican' was the sharpest, from 34 per cent in 1983 to 19 per cent in 2014, while 'No Religion' rose from 39.1 per cent to 47.9 per cent. Bullivant had a particular interest in Catholicism and, for us, the most notable statistic is that at 15.3 per cent the North West had the highest regional percentage of people identifying as 'Catholic'.[20]

A number of relevant points emerge from this. First, the higher levels of identification with 'No Religion' are particularly notable and may suggest that the blunter Census question of 'What is your religion?'

could result in a de facto identification with (for instance) 'Christian', including a sense of ethnonational identity clustered around issues of (say) community and birth, irrespective of levels of personal attendance or interest.[21] Second, there was a sharp decline in people identifying as Christian, and an especially sharp decline in those identifying as Anglican, corresponding with a rise in those identifying as 'No Religion'. Third, the North West showed a comparative strength of Catholic identification. Despite the difficulties gaining precise data, we might reasonably speculate that this has relevance for understanding Barrow – a town with a notable Catholic heritage not only in churches but also in schools (e.g., St Bernard's Catholic High School, Holy Family Catholic Primary School), sport (e.g., Barrow Celtic Football Club) and social clubs (e.g., Knights of St Columba, St Patrick's Club). Whether popularly identified as such is not possible to answer on the basis of available data, and drinking establishments such as the Knights of St Columba provided popular late-night entertainment for, as Cameron might have put it, all faiths and none.

Indeed, the relatively small sample of Barrovian views on religion (where they even exist) may partly confirm the significance of the decision of those who use the British Social Attitudes data and the suspicions of my younger self, though we should always understand such data in terms of shifting identities and subjectivities according to context and questions asked.[22] It was clear that there was very little interest in issues of Christianity, the Bible, or religion, or at least very little interest in mentioning anything publicly. There was only occasional self-identification as 'Church of England' but no one claimed to attend church regularly (though some might have without mentioning it). Almost everyone I asked about Cameron's views on the Bible and Christianity as a source for Britishness and political ideologies (see below) responded with bafflement and some thought I was making it up. Given Storm's research on a significant minority (c. 23 per cent) understanding Christianity in an ethnonationalist sense (see Chapter 3), we might speculate that this lack of interest was perhaps partly because of a lack of immigration and ethnic diversity in Barrow. More often than not in my interactions, the discussions of the Bible, Christianity and religion were by far the briefest (in sharp contrast to views on Brexit) and in some cases people provided more detail about their age, place of birth and occupation.

With the (crucial) exception of Facebook posts on 'Muslims', and the occasional updates on guardian angels, ghosts, or heaven, it is difficult to convey just how little issues that might otherwise be perceived to relate to religion and Christianity emerged. I saw hundreds of Barrovian Facebook posts and it would not be difficult to collect themes, patterns, and popular interests including drinking, hangovers, work, animal welfare, football, rugby league, submarines, personal weight gain/loss, local history, inspirational quotes, the state of the EU, mental health, dogs, cats (less so it seemed to me), plenty of near-naked women, some near-naked men, hen nights, stag dos, nightclubs, television comedy, motorbikes, armed forces, condemning paedophiles, criticising anonymous friends and colleagues, strong political opinions, bad jokes, fishing, weddings (with the occasional background church), music, DJs, local news, conspiracy theories, holiday snaps, immigration, refugees, family pictures, or dramatic coastal photographs on the statistically unlikely sunny days. The only reactions to my own Facebook interests in the critical study of religion were more baffled responses or questions about whether I am a Christian. During this period (and well beyond), I had countless discussions with Barrovians about work, earning money for working long hours (deemed a good thing), drinking, Brexit, where to go for a walk, holidays, the weather, or undeservedly smug people being put in their place. The closest religion got to the conversation was when I admitted what I do for a living and, even then, the response was almost always bewilderment at my job and a few questions of clarification which rarely got answered satisfactorily.

Such public presentations of Christianity, the Bible and religion may well have obscured assumptions about Christianity, the Bible and religion being appropriately present in certain designated contexts (christenings, weddings and funerals). Nevertheless, and whatever we might make of the controversial secularisation theses, this all seems symptomatic of sociological and historical shifts in affiliation in the UK since the 1960s where church attendance and affiliation, as well as the political and cultural authority of the established churches, declined sharply. While this led to a national growth in those not identifying with a particular 'religion' (at least in the traditional sense) this should not be wholly identified with atheism or agnosticism (though such beliefs formed a significant part) because a range of views that might be classified as, for instance, 'spiritual', 'religious', 'spiritual but not religious', or 'supernatural', as well as varying degrees of 'believing in God' (including those who pray) also remained present among those identifying with 'No Religion'.[23] Quite how we label such a phenomenon or phenomena is much debated but need not concern us here. For now, we can say that among the Barrovian sample there was minimal engagement with ideas of traditional religious identifications and, though it was rarely hostile to concepts relating to the Bible, Christianity and religion, there were notable similarities to and differences from such understandings in mainstream political and media discourses on such topics. But before we look at the nuances among this set of Barrovians, we first need to understand these sorts of responses in the current context of Brexit. It is essential to look at the Barrovians' views on Brexit itself because the overwhelming anti-authority or anti-politician attitude that emerged will further explain the attitudes towards the Bible, Christianity, religion and, in a different way, Islam, even where attitudes were of indifference.

Brexit Barrow

A range of reasons for voting Remain or Leave (or not at all) were given. Almost all the Leave voters (irrespective of age and gender) thought Leave was simply the only choice and strange that anyone would think otherwise. The diverse reasoning on both sides would be familiar to anyone who followed the story on various media, such as those relating to workers' rights, immigration, national decision making, national autonomy, the 'Norway option', financial and cultural links with Europe, safety, fear of the consequences of leaving, anti-racism, pensions, the EU itself, financing other countries, big business, the EU treatment of Greece, and even to annoy work colleagues. But, from the people interviewed and from the numerous Facebook discussions, irrespective of political affiliation and for or against Brexit, and as was becoming increasingly clear in studies of other parts of the country, there was a near-universal disdain for mainstream politicians who were repeatedly seen as effectively the same ('bunch of bastards from Oxford and Cambridge versus another spate of bastards from Oxford and Cambridge', 'they've never really given a shit about people like us', 'they claim expenses, and that's it', 'I don't trust any of them', 'they'll fix the result', 'absolutely fed up with politicians from all sides and not listening'), as well as regularly accompanying disdain for almost anyone associated with the ruling class (EU, banks, bankers, Bank of England), media ('I don't believe much of what I read', 'don't trust [them] ... at all', 'don't give a shit about us and we all know that politicians are texting them'), and even farmers who were seen as unfairly benefitting from subsidies ('brand spanking new 4x4s'). Remain voters regularly claimed that politicians had 'no plan' for the post-Brexit situation and claims of incompetence and deceit were common. As one voter, who said she was a reluctant Remainer, claimed, 'What can I say? Same old bloody lies from both sides.' There were some answers revealing general suspicions and a contrarian attitude towards authority and their perceived threats. One Leave voter claimed that the reason Leave won was because 'the government wanted to vote in' and, she added, 'Cameron wanted to vote in, so I voted out'. Another Leave voter was contemptuous towards what he saw as 'scaremongering' (a repeated complaint among those who voted Leave), adding, 'And if somebody tells me to do something or else, I'll probably do the opposite.' But it was also clear that this theme was not necessarily anti-authority per se but more that the wrong people had long been in control. As another Leave voter claimed, his vote was nothing to do with any of the 'out leaders' but that Britain could be 'made great again' with new leaders 'and not nest featherers'.

Individual politicians were regularly singled out on all sides, especially Cameron. As far as I could see, Cameron was not once praised and was repeatedly criticised (e.g., 'massive bellend', 'smug bastard', 'cockiness', 'dodgy Dave', 'liar', 'weak', 'that [Bullingdon Club] thing, it doesn't go down well here', 'he wanted us to remain for his retirement pot', 'as much to blame as anyone for jumping ship [resigning]'), whether for his decision to resign or perceived hypocrisy, or, as we will later see, the alleged and much publicised porcine penetration during his university leisure time. One Remainer with a husband from an EU country (both of whom were from a different north-western town noted for greater ethnic tensions) worryingly recalled that when 'Cameron [said] EU nationals are ok … I just thought "oh shit"', then added that 'I have hated him more and more since this has happened. I can't believe he did this.' Nicola Sturgeon and Scottish MPs came in for occasional harsh criticism (e.g., 'that bloody Scottish gnasher') with claims that they were intent on stitching up England. Though never mentioned explicitly, it should also be recalled that scrapping Trident was central for the Scottish National Party (SNP) and the possibility of a Labour-SNP coalition was played up by the local Conservatives in the 2015 General Election. Whenever Tony Blair and Iraq were mentioned (the long-awaited Chilcot Report into the Iraq War was released on 6 July 2016), it was always strongly negative (including one hiss) and he was regularly blamed for turning Labour into something they ought not to be, a familiar view we saw emerging in working-class contexts in the previous chapter. The UKIP leader Nigel Farage was one reason some reluctant Remain voters voted the way they did, particularly his infamous anti-immigration adverts ('it makes you a bit wary to say the least … Mind you he's buggered off now at least'). Others singled out include Boris Johnson ('idiot'), Michael Gove ('that chinless bloody wonder'), Gordon Brown ('idiot', 'useless'), Neil Kinnock ('bloody windbag'), and so on. One middle-aged male Leave voter epitomised the disdain for politicians no matter what ('they're all full of shit. All of them in it for their own profit'), particularly in the claim that 'it was a bastard thing what happened to Boris by Gove. Bastard. But, still, I'm glad he did!' However, it is telling that, despite identifying as a 'traditional Labour voter' even if politicians should never be trusted, there were some positive words for Theresa May, a point to which we will return.

Strong criticisms of the local MP, John Woodcock, were also repeated ('dumped on us because it was a safe Labour seat', 'he never listens'). One late-teen Leave voter hoping to work in the shipyard said that he did not even believe that Woodcock supported Trident (despite Woodcock's most prominent view being pro-Trident). But available criticisms were mostly in relation to Woodcock's opposition to Jeremy Corbyn (e.g., 'no principles and has been stabbing Corbyn in the back since day one', 'absolute disgrace … He is arrogant and pig-headed to think that he can just waltz in and let his mates take over', 'at least [Corbyn is] trying to make this country a better place'). As this suggests, there were politicians singled out for praise. But their singling out was clearly a variant on the anti-authority, anti-politician, anti-media, anti-elite theme. Moreover, Corbyn was almost the only politician who was regularly praised prior to the confirmation of May as Prime Minister. The occasional exceptions included a hope for someone other than Corbyn to become leader of the Labour Party and there was even one (and only one) who praised Johnson and Gove. Farage gained some praise from those (unsurprisingly) with UKIP sympathies, including hope that he would play a role in Brexit negotiations, that he might topple the Conservatives and Labour, and that his provocative anti-EU performance in the European Parliament shortly after the Referendum result was a good thing.

Though not without his own fair share of criticisms ('those around him are dangerous. Gangsters. Thugs', 'I don't like him', 'he'll destroy this town'), it was Corbyn who was by far the most common politician singled out ('seems to have retained some dignity and balls', 'he's quietly spoken but to me he comes across as being sincere', 'acted admirably', 'decent bloke').[24] But again this was clearly part of the dominant anti-authority theme and contrasted with Conservatives, the then Parliamentary Labour Party, the rest of the Labour Party since Blair ('those, you know, Blairites ... Those lot are just in it for power'), and Blair himself ('whatever your politics, you know what he stands for. Unlike Blair'). Even one UKIP supporter who had previously mocked Corbyn's appearance and disagreed with much of what Corbyn had said, was impressed with Corbyn being prepared to stand up against the establishment on Iraq, Blair and the Chilcot Report. It was not always clear the extent of the support for Corbyn, but it was clear that he was deemed to be someone targeted by the political establishment and media ('made a scapegoat for [the] mess', 'it is like bullying', 'the media [treatment] ... disgusts me', 'they are trying to get Corbyn'). One Remain voter in her late sixties stressed that it was the press who 'pick out the worst bits ... hone in on something, hammer it until people believe it. Like they did with the old donkey jacket [Michael Foot].'

On Facebook, there were various posts in support of Corbyn with virtually no support posted for the then leadership alternatives to Corbyn (Angela Eagle and Owen Smith). This, of course, may have been because of my limited access to different Facebook networks but none of the interviewees or discussants showed any support for the then present alternatives to Corbyn. This does not mean that there was not private support for such people, of course, but if there was it was not the sort of thing people felt like mentioning in the networks I saw. There is also a little more data with which to work on this issue. On 28 June 2016, Woodcock uploaded a video to his constituency Facebook page explaining his opposition to Corbyn. By my count (on 5 July 2016), there were about 91 different individual commenters, most of whom appeared to be from Barrow and surrounding areas (and thus Woodcock's constituents), and with more male than female commenters (approx. 60–40 split). Some comments were not entirely clear, but most were and the overwhelming sentiment (from about 68 of the individual commenters) was support for Corbyn and/or hostility to Woodcock or his wing of the Labour Party whereas about 18 (including Woodcock himself) appeared to agree with Woodcock's message, even if not necessarily supportive of Woodcock. The issues used against Woodcock, or in support of Corbyn, were familiar ones, such as claims that Corbyn was honest and had integrity, that Corbyn supported the working class or 'the people', that he won the vote for leadership of the Labour Party, that he was electable, that the media were unfairly against him, that he was wrongly blamed for the Referendum result, that 'Blairites' or 'career politicians' were selfishly causing problems or were refusing to listen to their membership, that those opposed to Corbyn were too scared to field a candidate, and that the Iraq War and the (then) imminent Chilcot Report ware the real reasons for the criticisms.[25]

Still, the pro-Corbyn and anti-Woodcock rhetoric needs qualification. It is difficult to know how much to read into the anti-Woodcock polemic (other than as representative of the anti-politician sentiments running throughout) because it was tied in with support for Corbyn. Woodcock was one of the most prominent anti-Corbyn Labour MPs and his name in such contexts would have inevitably attracted attention both inside and outside Barrow and Furness. Conversely, one interviewee casually mentioned to me as I was leaving that Woodcock 'seemed ok'. Certainly, Corbyn was the only figure who had any significant degree of support among the interviewees, discussants, and on Facebook (prior to the announcement of a new prime minister) but this did not necessarily mean that this was then translating into widespread support in Barrow and Furness, the North West, England, or the UK. There were certainly people who identified with Corbyn's politics. From what came across among the interviewees, some admired him because of his 'underdog' status and because he was not perceived to be a part of a despised 'political elite' or the assumptions about the standard Labour politician.

But plenty of people simply did not mention Corbyn and we do not know their views. For all we know, others who had a positive view may simply have admired him but that did not necessarily mean that they were going to vote for him, while those who might have been favourably disposed towards him or held an indifferent view may have made up their minds closer to the time of the 2017 General Election. There may well be comparisons here with the popular reception of Corbyn's mentor, Tony Benn: admired for his authenticity even in disagreement. But we should also not forget that these interviews took place as the rebellion against Corbyn had just begun, which may have had an impact both positively and negatively. Moreover, as we will see, Trident was precisely the sort of issue that prevented some of his admirers accepting Labour with him as leader and, prior to Corbyn, a similar view was pushed hard in Barrow (with some success) by the Conservatives in the 2015 General Election. If more questions in the interviews had been geared towards Corbyn then maybe something clearer would have emerged. Yet it remains striking that, prior to the confirmation of a new prime minister, he was almost the only political figure who was regularly thought of positively, other than some not insignificant pro-Farage exceptions. He was the exception that proved the rule of the sample that politicians really were not trusted or liked. And, as we will see, he did not lose Barrow for Labour in the General Election as was expected and he may even have saved it through mobilising potentially sympathetic voters and by attracting some UKIP voters. We should not forget that, dominant though it still is, the shipyard was not as dominant as it once was.

However, the interviews and social media activity were also before May was confirmed as Conservative Leader (11 July 2016) and officially appointed as Prime Minister (13 July 2016). This brought certain issues to the fore which may well have been mentioned had the other interviews been carried out at this time. The last batch of interviews happened after this and after the parliamentary debate on the renewal of Trident (18 July 2016). Positive, nostalgic and romantic sentiments regarding Trident and the need for someone to launch nuclear missiles from submarines to kill fellow human beings as the ultimate deterrent were not unusual in Barrow, irrespective of gender self-identification or age. Indeed, plenty of positive sentiments and 'likes' could be found across personal and group Facebook pages of Barrovians when the vote went through for the renewal of Trident. On the popular Facebook group, 'Barrow-in-Furness in Old Photos' (with nearly 20,000 members in the summer of 2016), a picture of an older Trident submarine in the shipyard was posted shortly after the announcement of Trident renewal to 379 'likes' (or equivalent), much local pride in the comments, and only one dissenting voice. Tellingly, when Woodcock posted about Trident on Facebook the response was typically more positive than usual.[26]

It should be no surprise that such events would have had an impact on how interviewees would likewise respond and shift their emphases. With the appointment of a female prime minister, the otherwise rare (among interviewees) gendered assumptions started to become evident. Indeed, one middle-aged Leave voter was happy with May and her views on Trident, though he was also keen to make it known, accompanied by a cupped hand gesture at chest level, that he was hoping that she was the glamour model, Teresa May, who had a prominent role in the controversial video for the equally controversial Prodigy song (apparently 'about' heroin), 'Smack My Bitch Up' (1997), before being confused on Twitter with the incoming Prime Minister.[27] Another retired Leave voter thought that May needed a makeover, hairdresser and fashion advisor but she also thought May was performing well as a politician and, in sentiments rarely heard in Barrow, that 'she's Maggie with knobs on!'. But what was also striking was how self-identified Labour supporters (though not necessarily voters) warmed to her ('one of the better ones. Not a Tory really') and especially her views on Trident. One Leave voter could not vote for Labour because of Corbyn's views on Trident but she 'quite liked' May because of 'vot[ing] Trident in' and 'what she said when she'd press the nuclear button if need be'. Another perhaps highlighted what could be a potential problem for Labour in Barrow. He said that he would now vote Conservative because of Trident. He 'liked what she [May] said', that she was 'prepared to kill 100,000 innocent people – yes. You've got to be, haven't you?' He added that perhaps Corbyn would be the only reason he would vote for Labour because he admired him as a person ('I like him. I like the way he comes across. I like the way he speaks') but 'I don't agree with his views.' However, 'apart from Corbyn, I don't like Labour anymore,' he was quick to point out, because 'they aren't Labour anymore. They are just Conservatives but without the backbone.' This was not the first time such disparaging views about Labour as 'mild Tories' (as another put it) would come up.

Englishness: from 'snobby and backhanded' to the Muslim Other

Disdain for politicians and 'elites' is probably one of the few generalisations worth making from this particular study, not least because it helps us understand the logic of the answers on various issues, notably for my purposes religion, Christianity and the Bible which, through the Cameron quotation, included notions of 'Englishness' or 'Britishness'. Before we turn to how Cameron's claim about Britain as a Christian country was received, it is worth looking at some of the general attitudes towards 'Englishness' (which regularly drifted into 'Britishness') that were widely discussed with interviewees. Certainly, there were diverse views about Englishness and Britishness. One (and only one) interviewee referred to the geography of Northern Ireland, Scotland, Wales and England. A Leave voter identified as British but primarily as English, though with little elaboration. A common ironic response was to refer to England as poor at sport or being perennially disappointed by it, especially football. One Remain voter admitted it was 'pretty hard' to define Englishness, 'unless you want that shit you seen in the media, tin hats, St George's cross, rubbish at football'. Less jokey were a number of militaristic presentations of Britishness on Facebook, even in contrasting overpaid English footballers negatively with armed forces. Ironic connections were also made with food (cups of tea, fish and chips) and accents. There was no far-right sentimentality about supposed English food.

Such offhand sentiments were common enough and most claimed to not really know what 'Englishness' might mean.[28] But once again anti-authority ideas dominated understandings of 'Englishness' and 'Britishness', or even, as we saw, 'anti-Scottish' in terms of governance. However, the dimension of class was more explicit still, and usually in a negative sense. By this I mean it was thought that Englishness was typically associated with perceptions (often by 'outsiders') of middle- or upper-class behaviour and values, or southern behaviour and values (perhaps not easily distinguished from perceptions of middle and upper classes). The Royal Family also came up (with only occasional mild positivity) as did some of the most overtly antagonistic class-based views such as 'the posh English accent or whatever' ('that's not me. Can't stand it all'), 'bowler hats and suited and booted in London', 'speaking posh' which 'might have happened in an Agatha Christie book' but 'it's a load of crap', 'snobby and backhanded', and 'the Tory-like, toffee-nosed china tea cup drinker' who has an agenda which appears to be 'the separation of classes' and the maintenance of rules 'for personal gain'. Such antagonistic constructions were sometimes in distinction to what might be deemed to be more reasonable forms of 'Englishness' or 'Britishness' involving issues of tolerance, decency, common sense, resilience and fairness (e.g., 'community spirit, unflappability, a dislike of unfairness', 'this country takes it on the chin and gets on with it', 'free thinking ... not racist ... not bigoted ... listen to everyone's view').

As might have been expected in a post-Referendum context, immigration and national difference came up regularly in relation to 'Englishness', though was not quite the dominant theme in the way class was in the interviews and discussions.[29] A Leave voter in his forties suggested that 'political correctness has silenced people who won't say what their heart tells them in case they are branded racist or bigoted in some way for caring about their people and culture'. The Leave leaders were not the reason he voted but rather knew 'in my bones that England would never be free tied to the yoke of the continentals'. Even when class distinction was not explicitly invoked (as it was in most cases), related distinctions could still be made and tied in with issues of immigration.

In the case of one UKIP sympathiser in his seventies, a distinction was made between 'the British public' and 'any other country' (where 'there would have been riots, huge protests') and a few minor exceptions 'in London'. He further argued that 'the British people have had enough of politicians', but presented a further element to his understanding of national identity because 'immigration is a prime example' of why people are disillusioned. 'Whole communities have been changed', he added, but this should not be confused with racism because 'British people are quite tolerant but then get to a stage where it's too much.'

While issues relating to immigration and nationalism were common, there was a kind of photo negative equivalent of this argument, notably (but not exclusively) among Remain voters. One Remain voter, who said she would have voted Leave but thought there were too many racist attitudes among its adherents, added, 'Whether you like the fella or not, Sadiq Khan is British, and it annoys me when people says he's not', though in line with the general disdain for politicians immediately added, 'I don't like him.' Another voter who said that he was also swayed to vote Remain because of the issue of racism referred to allegations of post-Referendum racism as 'an absolute fucking disgrace' and gave the example of 'them fuckers like in Manchester on the tram or train abusing some guy' and 'the posters about get rid of the Polish vermin'. He laughed and suggested that it has 'given rise to the proper Nazis in this country' and the Referendum has brought what was 'under the surface' to 'the forefront'. Away from Remain voters, similar sentiments could also be found. One Leave voter repeatedly emphasised her respect and support for immigrants and love of Europe and that her decision was about national sovereignty and hostility towards the EU. One Leave voter who moved to Barrow from Glasgow some years ago gave different kinds of 'Englishness' where class snobbery was sharply presented (and disliked), as was 'the racist homophobic Britain First lovers with their muddled patriotism, bulldog tatts, and footy tops'. The version he endorsed was that which he sees in his social group and people he meets in Barrow and other industrial towns and cities, namely, a 'hard-working, hard-playing, welcoming, community-minded people proud to be English' but ashamed of those who behave like snobs or promote racism.

But the angriest response came from the Remain voter with an EU spouse with first-hand experiences of another town more known for ethnic tensions. She argued that 'We're just really weird … We dig our heels', people who argue about 'the metric system. Awkward. It's down to our past, the Empire. We shit on the world. We're arrogant. Ignorant. Even using "Great Britain" but people use it for how "great" we are … embarrassing'. In opposition to this construction of a kind of right-wing Britishness, the interviewee nonetheless remained 'really proud of our musical culture' but was upset that the present climate showed that being 'quite open minded' and 'tolerant' is 'declining', before concluding that now 'I really struggle with being a patriot.' She cited (with reference to personal experience) a 'backlash on attacks on EU nationals and anyone who's not white. It's no coincidence. I know it was already there, but it's got much worse since 24th June.'

For what it is worth for such a small sample size, only Leave voters mentioned Islam and Muslims in relation to issues of Englishness, immigration, or the question of Britain being a Christian country. This crossed all voting age groups, though those who expressed such views appeared to be largely (but not exclusively) male, which has some parallels with the gendered representation we saw in the previous chapter. One online discussion, with some far-right involvement, claimed that 'Muslim immigrants' were 'raping' Europe (whether this was metaphorical or not was not made clear) and the familiar claim that it would be wrong to call critics of Islam 'racist' because Islam cannot be classified as a 'race'. Another Leave voter implied that flag burning by 'Muslim extremists' should result in deportation. There was also a story (to be found also among far-right groups) about a pregnant woman in another town arrested for carrying the Union Jack because it was 'offensive' (to Muslims). Another Leave voter talked about the importance for him of the Union Jack and not a 'Muslim flag' flying in this country, regularly mocked 'Muslim terrorists', and allowed the idea of forgiveness of terrorists but only once they had been sent to God first (i.e., killed by the armed forces). Such discussions on Facebook were typically found alongside militaristic imagery and memes, and angry comments that Facebook was allegedly (indeed paradoxically) banning such memes. But not all sentiments critical of Islam and Muslims were militaristic. One exception from a Leave voter with UKIP sympathies was that he did not think that Cameron's view of the Bible and Christianity as the foundation of tolerant values 'applies to all religions in equal proportions' and that while 'the majority of Muslims are probably alright', it is the press who 'hide the baddies'. There was a claim that we should tolerate religious beliefs but that tolerance cuts both ways and that any mosque ought to be placed near pubs, gay bars and pork butchers. Another person even warned me that within 20 years Barrow would be covered with mosques, a telling fear for a town that currently appears to have no mosques and 172 people (0.2 per cent) identifying as Muslim which, according to the Census statistics, means a decrease in Muslim population by ten between 2001 and 2011.[30]

Storm's claim on the likelihood of those intertwining Christian and national identities into a kind of ethnic marker *and* with the associated construction of an immigrant Other has some relevance here. However, the kinds of cultural fears about Muslims had representation in Barrow where there were no prominent or sustained tensions on the streets. No doubt this was due in no small part to relentless representations of Muslims and Islam in the press, online, and even among politicians. We might further speculate that they typically perceived excessive 'religious-ness' of this Other (e.g., in presentations of fanaticism, martyrdom, halal, hijab, intolerance, mosque building) that made it such a ghostly threat and yet another authority to be rejected. But, equally, this too functioned as a convenient myth of innocence. This discourse thrived more easily among contemporary liberal discourses because its classificatory and dis-criminatory justifications were grounded in the rhetoric of (in)tolerance of ideas and culture rather than the now more socially taboo intoler-ance of race. In this respect, it is striking that these people were also sceptical about the level of post-Referendum racial violence. Yet as we have seen, the distinction between 'Islam/Muslim/religion' and 'race' was often different in practice and discourses represented by this minority of Barrovians belonged to obfuscating complicity with racialising Muslims. However, it is also telling that some of the overtly anti-racist responses to far-right rhetoric among interviewees also did not distin-guish between the rhetoric of 'anti-Islam/Muslim' and 'anti-racial'. For these interviewees (echoed by some on Facebook) there was otherwise no mention of Islam and such far-right thinking, and individuals who thought about Muslims and Islam in negative language were just simply deemed racist. Given the reported post-Referendum attacks, which would fit traditional understandings of racial violence, we might wonder if such Barrovian dismissal of the distinction between 'anti-Muslim' and 'anti-racial' might be on to something.

A Christian country?

There was minimal support for the idea of Britain as a Christian country (which, as we saw in the previous chapter, had some resonance nationally), perhaps because of no such prominent tensions on the streets and the need to construct an ethnic 'religious' Other to Islam. Once again, it was negative views about politicians and authority consistently that came through strongly (to put it mildly) in what people thought about Cameron's remarks on the Bible and Christianity as sources of Christian heritage. His remarks were as follows:

> [From] human rights and equality to our constitutional monarchy and parliamentary democracy ... the first forms of welfare provision ... language and culture ... The Judeo-Christian roots of the Bible also provide the foundations for protest and for the evolution of our freedom and democracy ... [They form] the irrepressible foundation for equality and human rights, a foundation that has seen the Bible at the forefront of the emergence of democracy, the abolition of slavery and the emancipation of women ... Responsibility, hard work, charity, compassion, humility, self-sacrifice, love, pride in working for the common good and honouring the social obligations we have to one another, to our families and our communities these are the values we treasure. Yes, they are Christian values. And we should not be afraid to acknowledge that. But they are also values that speak to us all – to people of every faith and none.[31]

'I think that's a load of bollocks' was the surprised response of one Leave voter when she heard it, whereas another Leave voter said in exasperation, 'I cannot see how it comes from the Bible at all. Bloody hell!' One Remain voter was also puzzled: 'He said that? He also said that they are the values of everyone? It doesn't make sense. How can they belong to everyone?' One Leave voter who denied Britain was a Christian country but said that Cameron's views tallied with his own experiences of Christians, suggested that Cameron's claim 'proves ... what a massive bellend he really is', with further comment on Cameron's end-of-slavery argument: 'what a fucking statement that is, CLOWN!'. A Remain voter in his forties similarly laughed in disbelief at Cameron's comments and again made the connection with a perceived hypocrisy of political behaviour. These comments might be colourful, but the sentiments were typical:

> What the fuck is he talking about? Ha ha. Fucking bullshit! Absolute bullshit! He can't even peddle it out himself or his party! Does it

include shagging a pig's head? Not very Christian of him! Not very Christian or nice the way they act in parliament when they are slagging each other off and generally being gobshites. Schoolkids at Alfs [Alfred Barrow, a lively secondary school which closed in 2009] showed more decorum than them!

What is also notable about these sentiments was the implicit understanding of Christianity (whether accepting of it or not) which also revealed standard assumptions about Christianity and the Bible which were not especially negative (e.g., politeness, sexual restraint, peace), as well as including more hostility towards politicians. This was not the only time Cameron's alleged behaviour was mentioned in relation to his idea about the Bible and Christianity. There was an implied allegation of hypocrisy in the nickname given to Cameron ('Oinkgobble') by one Remain voter, even if there was an agreement with some of Cameron's sentiments. One non-voter responded with 'That's just stupid. What's he on about? Isn't he into bombing countries? Where does that fit in? I don't think Jesus said much stuff like that … Hard work? What, thou shalt work hard? I don't remember that one!' However, some points like 'compassion' were conceded but even here it was suggested that 'it's not like only the English are compassionate for fuck's sake'. The already obvious suspicion came further to the fore: 'Is he just saying this stuff to sound like he's a nice bloke or something?' One non-voter claimed that Cameron was either confused or a hypocrite because 'the Bible talks about things that have nothing to do with democracy' while one retired Leave voter (who supported same-sex marriage) pointed out that same-sex marriage is not in the Bible. Such claims of Cameron being wrong in his view of the somewhat innocent Bible was a near-universal sentiment among interviewees, across different perspectives.

With perhaps some echoes of Storm's claims about Christianity and ethnic identity, occasional participants (all middle aged and up) responded by identifying with the Church of England, even though they did not attend a church and even though such identification presumably would not have been mentioned if such a question had not been raised. In response to one Leave voter in his sixties claiming to be 'Church of England', a (reluctant) Remain voter responded incredulously, 'He's not a bloody Christian! Since when has he ever gone to church or believed in any of that?' 'I would personally always say my religion is Church of England', said another Leave voter, whose immediate point of contrast was to say that 'I wouldn't say I was Catholic.' Nevertheless, there was still little support for Cameron's claim. 'I don't agree that they're all [the listed values] from the Bible', even though he believed that 'democracy and tolerance and everything else he said are part of our way of life'. Other responses probably reflected such sentiments by showing a lack of interest in discussing the Bible or Christianity. Indeed, it was striking that the question which caused consistent puzzlement, indifference, or incredulity was that which sought the interviewees' opinions about Cameron's claim about Britain, Christianity and the Bible.

A retired Leave voter thought Britain 'was a Christian country' but that it was changing and that 'Cameron's statement is far too general.' He added that 'when I was a kid it [the Bible] was taught' and that it was as 'a set of rules, good rules, but people are drifting away from it'. It should be added that there was no indication that this was an especially good or bad thing and he ended his point with another sentiment that would turn up on a number of occasions: 'I don't mind people being religious but as long as they don't make me religious.' The idea of a Christian past came up occasionally. After a long pause, one retired Remain voter gave the short answer, 'No', before she added after another pause, 'he's not right' and that 'when you were young, well, you just put "Christian" when you were asked to but no one in my family really believed in anything'. One non-voter casually claimed that 'I suppose we were a Christian country ages ago, maybe even in the 1950s or something, but I don't know anyone who goes to church and look around here and there's just abandoned churches. It's been like that for ages.' One Remain voter in her thirties simply did not believe that 'we're a Christian country' anymore and said that 'it is divisive to say we're a Christian country'. Rather, she claimed, 'we're a secular country' and she only knew 'one or two Christians'.

There were virtually no overtly longed-for, sentimental, nostalgic views of a Christian past, despite suggestions that the past might once have been 'Christian' and despite regular enough claims of a country that once was better.[32] Whenever such issues were raised, they were dealt with matter-of-factly, as if part of some great historical process. Perhaps tied in with such sentiments were those views which avoided the part of the question mentioning 'Christian' and the 'Bible' and proceeded to talk only about issues relating to British values. Another response by a Remain voter to the question about the Bible and Christianity (at most perhaps implying that Cameron's interpretation belonged to a romantic vision) was simply to register her surprise that Cameron did not vote for Brexit, adding in a now familiar way that 'he's old fashioned and stuffy, narrow-minded Oxbridge boy'. Another Remain voter did not discuss the Bible as such but rather expressed her hope for the realisation of ideals ('to have compassion for others'), as well as implying a degree of deception in Cameron's views (e.g., some people like the monarchy and others do not and that slavery has not ended as 'modern day' slavery goes on behind closed doors).

Yet it was notable that numerous Facebook posts would promote or share ideas about issues which might be popularly categorised as 'religious'. Posts about guardian angels, personal angels, fairies, ghosts, weddings, heaven, or the supernatural were easy to find and perhaps we might classify the very occasional Jesus meme alongside these. But the infrequent Jesus or overtly Christian memes I encountered on Facebook were different from posts about various supernatural beings like ghosts or guardian angels or statements about pets joining their owners in heaven in that they were militaristic and more akin to the anti-Islamic or anti-ISIS (depending on the user) memes about Christian crusaders fighting terror (memes which also occasionally occurred among Facebook users in Barrow). Beyond Barrovian networks, I saw non-militaristic Jesus memes on Facebook, from fairly conventional devotionals through comedy to something that might be perceived as 'New Age' or 'spiritual' and no doubt there would have been some of this on Barrovian Facebook pages. I did not, however, come across any in this sample.

In this respect, a comparison with discussions of Furness Abbey – a local heritage site on the outskirts of Barrow – is perhaps more instructive. Furness Abbey was a Cistercian monastery founded in the twelfth century. It became a ruin in the English Reformation and went into romantic memory thanks in no small part to figures like Wordsworth and Turner (and the reception of such figures and their work).[33] It also became associated with ghost sightings, medieval festivals, local walks, glue-sniffing in the 1980s, and a more refined location for discreet outdoor sexual encounters than (say) the docks. Recently, there was an attempt to get permission to build 'executive' housing on the Manor Lane entrance to the Abbey which, by the end of May 2016, had successfully been prevented by a local group after a two-year campaign. The public Facebook group, 'Stop development of green field sites around Furness Abbey', attracted a lot of activity and, given the object under discussion, might have been a rare occasion where issues relating to religion could get a public airing. By 20 July 2016 the page had 1,250 likes (including, for full disclosure, one by me) and there were over 200 posts with regular comments between 22 January 2014 and 26 May 2016, culminating in the victory for the protesters.[34] There were repetitive reasons given by commenters (whether part of the official case or not) for opposing the building of the new houses. Most common were those relating to local heritage, animal and wildlife conservation, and aesthetics, and, as ever, it was regularly presented as standing up to the distant, uncaring authorities. But, despite the building being an abbey, there were only very occasional references to anything that might just be popularly classified as 'religious' or 'theological', and, even then, it was not easy to differentiate such comments from 'aesthetic' reasons (e.g., ideas about being engulfed by quietness and calm, a special place, sense of awe). Perhaps the most explicit example was from one of the key players in the victory, Gill Jepson, who reported the news on her blog (also made available on the Facebook group), suggesting, with a popular allusion to Acts of the Apostles 9.18 (intentional or not), that the inspector 'cannot have failed to understand the historic importance of our amazing abbey and appreciated that to build a housing estate – however high status and beautiful – would detract from the reverence and spirituality of the approach. In short *the scales fell from his eyes*' (my italics).[35] But all these were, at most, isolated and occasional examples.

Not (always) doing God

What can we say about such Barrovian understandings of Christianity and the Bible? Whenever an obvious reference to the Bible turned up (e.g., 'Hard work? What, thou shalt work hard?', 'David and Goliath', 'scapegoat', 'scales fell from his eyes') it held a low-level nostalgic power with an ironic distance from what was an occasional cultural resource, much like Furness Abbey but probably not as popular. In this sense, they were minor examples of David Crystal's argument about the cultural survival of the language of the Bible (partly) through a witty use of idioms and a draining of anything perceived to be too 'religious' (Crystal was referring to the language of the King James Bible but the point stands).[36] This, as I have argued elsewhere, is evidence of an understanding of the Bible without context or content, deprived of any malignant properties as it continues to survive (and only just in this sample from Barrow) in Western cultural contexts, striving to come to terms with secularism, nationalism and global capitalism.[37] As a physical cultural artefact in a place like Barrow, the Bible was most likely to be received as a gift at christenings (one of the rare occasions where the Bible and Christianity might openly feature in public life) before being consigned to a life of gathering dust on the shelf.

As Barrovian sentiments revealed different subjective class assumptions so they revealed a blunt disjunction between a quasi-official Bible of the ruling class (or at least its politically authoritative interpreters) and the Barrovian sample (recall sentiments such as 'a load of bollocks', 'bullshitting', 'absolute bullshit', 'stupid', 'what?', 'eh?', 'he said that?', 'debateable', 'I don't think he knows what he is talking about', 'hypocrite', 'do they really relate that to the Bible?'), with all the accompanying puzzled looks, laughs, and untypically long pauses. One Leave voter who clearly had no such sentimental attachment to Christianity and the Bible, asked (as did others) whether Cameron got 'a lot of hassle for that?'. With such examples in mind, which appeared to be in line with national trends, Alastair Campbell's fears may not have been unfounded when he shut down an interview with Tony Blair using the famous phrase, 'we don't do God'. The British electorate, he also claimed, do not 'want their politicians banging the Bible all the time. They hated it, I was sure of that.'[38] It might be an understatement to claim that Campbell's view would resonate among at least some of the Barrovian electorate. As one Remain voter put it, she did not 'appreciate politicians using religion to sell us something'.

Such views would not, therefore, have been restricted to Barrow and they would have resonated well beyond. An important point of comparison here is Matthew Engelke's ethnography of the Bible Society between 2006 and 2009 with reference to Swindon and Greater Manchester. As he showed, the Bible Society, who were well read in academic literature on religious affiliation and beliefs in the UK, increasingly viewed the problem of 'credibility' in promoting an ever-more marginalised Bible from the 1990s onward. In their creative output (posters, pamphlets, promotions, etc.), they became acutely aware of issues about embarrassment of being a Christian in public, people thinking the Bible was about guidance rather than (say) Jesus, that posters about Jesus or the cross or church might be a turnoff, and how trying to tell people how to live their lives was not likely to be popular. It is striking that their output involved, for instance, trying to tap into the popularity of angels by providing angelic Christmas decorations for a shopping centre in Swindon at Christmas or running an advertising campaign in Greater Manchester featuring riddles based on tabloid headlines which just-so-happened to be biblically grounded. Engelke's reading of the situation would make equal sense if contextualised in Barrow and no doubt applied well beyond:

> ... as far as the Bible Society was concerned, in many ways the most significant challenge to public religion came not from those with something to say about God but from those who didn't bother to say anything at all. It was apathy, not antipathy, that really exercised the staff ... much of what they thought about was the general public, for whom God was understood to be irrelevant in terms of not only public life but life itself.[39]

Indeed, Engelke's feedback on the use of the Bible in Greater Manchester could likewise have come from Barrow and beyond (e.g., old-fashioned, a bit irrelevant, possibly helpful at times).[40]

Set against this backdrop, the tentative approach to religion and the Bible in the national media (typically vague, centrist, occasional criticisms, hostility to 'extremism') was, from the perspective of sales, an expected position.[41] A number of figures working in or close to the national media and parliamentary politics repeatedly suggested to me that it was something like a fashionable 'North London' atheism that drove a reluctance on the part of politicians to embrace overtly 'religious' rhetoric, as if the rest of the country were crying out for spiritual leadership from the capital, though to be fair plenty of people in media and political circles in London are quick to accuse people who hold differing views as being trendy (North) London. We should be suspicious of such reasoning given the evidence we have seen, as well as the long-term trend in declining church attendance, affiliations and self-identifications. Nevertheless, there were areas which bucked national trends and one partly helps explain why London-based figures may have thought that there was a taste for more religious rhetoric. For instance, the BSA 2015 revealed that Inner London had the lowest national level for those identifying with 'No Religion' (31 per cent) but also the highest national level for those identifying with non-Christian religions (28 per cent), a statistic which reflected tendencies particular to a city as diverse as London in recent years.[42] To get a flavour of this, we could point to Daniel Nilsson DeHanas' recent work which reveals some of the complexities that arose from civic society, social interaction, political activism, and affiliation to the mosque or the church, and related theological concepts, in the East End and Brixton among a younger generation with immigrant parents.[43] And, of course, there are other places unlike Barrow, Swindon, or parts of Greater Manchester where party-political views on religion and even the Bible might have resonated, whether producing admiration, harmony, discord, or an uneasy coexistence.[44]

From the perspective of the politician wanting to use the Bible or claim religion for the national interest, there was a fine line between inviting ridicule and appeasing interested parties. Campbell was worried about what the media would do with a Bible-wielding politician. Indeed, those like Tony Blair, Steve Webb and Tim Farron all had a bad press for expressing their views on Christianity and the Bible. But the consistent use of the Bible by politicians like Cameron and in official narratives did not necessarily have to be understood as a naive blunder, even if Barrovians thought him ridiculous for using it. PR-savvy figures like Cameron were perfectly aware of the need to tread carefully. Moreover, it was clear that no one had heard about Cameron's use of the Bible which might even suggest that Cameron's PR team were doing their job properly, or at worst got lucky. As we have seen, there are various reasons for the use of religion in political discourse. It certainly provided an authority that was not widely despised in and of itself, and it certainly spoke to respective political traditions historically tied up with different denominations (e.g., Tory Anglicanism, Liberal Nonconformity, Labour Nonconformity and Catholicism), and if worded carefully and deemed credible, it might just have gained a politician a favourable headline. But it also spoke to those with ears to hear. Like a vague biblical allusion, the use of the Bible or Christianity in political discourse might have bypassed those with no interest but not necessarily those who did, and such references could be found easily online or under specific headlines for those willing to look. Indeed, Christian media outlets almost always picked up on mainstream political uses of the Bible (and often favourably so). There may not have been a significant 'Christian vote' in the UK, or at least in England, but as stressed in the Introduction there was equally no need for a politician to alienate such voters nor indeed Christian lobbyists.

It is possible that a vague notion of the Bible and Christianity as moral resources might have had some purchase among those I interviewed, viewed and discussed.[45] Though there was plenty of scepticism about whether the Bible was really the source of Anglicised tolerance and democracy, for some the Bible produced some useful moral rules (even if its time was thought to have passed). And some, as we saw, clearly worked with the implicit assumption that there was a purer form of biblical morality which was abused by people like Cameron and even Donald Trump (e.g., the idea that warmongering and certain creative sexual activities were not the sorts of things promoted by the Bible). In this respect, it may be that notions of 'not passing by on the other side' from the Parable of the Good Samaritan (probably the most common contemporary use of the Bible in political discourse, we might recall) would hold sway as it is one of those biblical-sounding phrases that survived in cultural discourses and fits in with a vague notion of 'doing good' rather than elaborate claims about democracy, slavery, or freedom.[46] Corbyn (as we have seen, a regular user of the Good Samaritan) was the one politician who was commonly deemed to be a morally upright or decent person and yet in the Barrovian sample was not openly understood in terms popularly deemed 'religious', contrary to some dominant representations in mainstream political and media discourses.[47] There was no persistent discussion (positive or negative) of 'Saint Jeremy', 'JC', 'Messiah', 'Christ-like', 'religious fervour', 'revivalist meetings', 'sects', 'cults', or any of the other related language found in other political and media discourses. Perhaps one exception was a *Star Wars* meme shared on Facebook which compared Jeremy Corbyn with Obi-Wan Kenobi (a theme that would later be popular in the 2017 General Election) and which found its way to Barrovian Facebook networks. Certainly, anyone wishing to categorise this as 'religious' might recall the 2001 Census process where there was an attempt to get 'Jedi' recognised as an official religion and, fitting in with the common emphasis, it once again reflected the theme of fighting an evil authority (in this case, Kenobi/Corbyn versus the Empire). But it was equally telling that it was another isolated example.

Concluding remarks

In addition to a northern 'Leave town' having a diverse range of views on Brexit, we can now see what kinds of perceptions about religion and related terms were present among this sample of Barrovians and how they fitted with dominant political assumptions about, and constructions of, religion. There were hints that Christianity could be used as a kind of ethnic marker, with little concern for a nostalgic view of a

Christian past, a collection of moral guidelines, or church attendance. But, overall, there was minimal interest in Christianity, perhaps partly because immigration was not the same in Barrow as it was elsewhere. However, the views of these Barrovians in this instance cannot be fully understood aside from the post-Referendum context. Throughout these snapshots of Brexit Barrow, we have seen a consistent disdain for politicians and established authorities – and perhaps unsurprising for a town which faced sharp industrial decline since Thatcher. Indeed, it cannot be overstated how strong the anti-authority feeling was; it was near universal among those interviewed. A number of people who were a little nervous about what they were saying when interviewed were insistent that I publish their views on how much they dislike the political and economic elite. This theme ran through not only issues of voting in the EU Referendum itself but also notions of Englishness, Britishness, the Bible, Christianity and religion. Christianity and the Bible held minimal authority among those Barrovians I looked at and this may also have been partly why they were often viewed with such indifference but rarely with disdain.

Of course, discussions in real time can provide different results. We saw how Theresa May and the renewal of Trident brought a degree of positivity towards a new authority, a positivity only previously seen in political figures deemed anti-authority or victims of authority, such as Nigel Farage and especially Jeremy Corbyn. Similarly, had interviews taken place in one of the rare public outings of the Bible and Christianity (e.g., christenings, weddings and funerals) we might have witnessed some different understandings and an acceptance that certain contexts were their correct social location. Likewise, a more interventionist approach of recent ethnographic work (e.g., questionnaires, observed readings of biblical passages) on British Bible reading would no doubt have provoked new insights into the reading process of those who otherwise showed little interest in the Bible. Nevertheless, my snapshots of Barrow do seem to be in line with some of the results about shifting self-identifications in other (though certainly not all) parts of the UK, particularly those relating to Christianity.

The anti-authority theme also stretched to some understandings of issues related to religion among this group of Barrovians. In addition to a clear dislike for Cameron's use of the Bible as a source of authority for, and compatibility with, 'British values', there was another source of authority associated with discourses about religion which came out negatively, and the most obvious flipside of Christianity as a kind of ethnic marker: Islam as a source of intolerant authority. In this respect, Barrow reflected the views found in other Brexit towns, though the key difference was that immigration and people identifying as Muslim was minimal in Barrow. And while some may have been expressing solidarity with other towns in the UK, it would not have been difficult to turn this narrative about authority on its head in the case of the tiny minority of Muslims in Barrow, none of whom I was able to interview. Who, after all, held most power in this context? Perhaps not the 0.2 per cent of those who identified as Muslim. Furthermore, understanding post-industrial Britain and its hatred of political authority helps us understand why plenty of Barrovians could, in some cases, welcome Conservative authority with open arms (even among people who identified as Labour voters and were critical of authorities): they might just bring the perceived employment power of Trident. For when it comes to the possibility of stable employment, more working hours and bonus pay, do not be surprised to find plenty of Barrovians happy to accept the authority of one who is prepared to kill – as George Kerevan put it to Theresa May – '100,000 innocent men, women and children'.[48]

But the expected Conservative victory in Barrow did not happen. At 4.40 am, 9 June 2017, it was announced that Barrow and Furness once again voted Labour (just), with swings to Conservatives and Labour from UKIP, roughly following the national pattern. Even in the home of Trident, Corbyn was still not as problematic as expected, or at least the unexpected levels of support for Corbyn applied in Barrow as it did elsewhere, including among younger voters. To give some indication of younger (and upcoming) voters, a mock poll of 182 Barrow Sixth Form College students was carried out with 132 (73 per cent) voting Labour and, in a distant second, 23 (13 per cent) voting Conservatives. And it came to pass that a week after the General Election result, John Woodcock apologised to local Labour members. He stood by his strong views on Trident but added that 'the truth is that just as we could not have won without the people inspired to vote Labour by Jeremy's surge … we would not have got over the line without the way Jeremy Corbyn inspired young people and some former non-voters to get active and vote Labour'.[49] This might seem miraculous enough but there were already indications of potential support among those I interviewed in 2016 who were also not people used for focus groups, interviewed by 'embedded' journalists, or targeted for 'on the doorstep' chats by politicians and then reported in the media. Indeed, it was the role of the media that was integral to presenting Corbyn as unpopular and unelectable and it is to the portrayal of Corbyn in the national media, and the accompanying constructions of religious language, that we now turn.

5

Manufacturing Dissent from the Centre: Cults, Corbyn and the *Guardian*

Introduction

The emergence of Jeremy Corbyn as leader of the Labour Party in September 2015, and his second victory a year later, collectively made up one of the most unpredictable events in contemporary English political history. The shock was registered and heavily represented in the traditional national news outlets (e.g., *Daily Mail, Sun, Star, Telegraph, Guardian, Independent, Mirror, The Times, Express, BBC, Sky News*). Part of the reason why the Corbyn victory was such a shock to the traditional media (and indeed almost everyone else) was that the left of the Labour Party was deemed to have long faded into irrelevance as the neoliberal Thatcher-Blair settlement broadly understood had become embedded across the political spectrum in the national news outlets. Among the numerous reactions to the rise of Corbyn up to the 2017 General Election was a pejorative labelling of him and his supporters in terms conventionally associated with 'religion', whether the term 'religious' itself or more sinister labels still, most notably 'cult'. To look at the reasons why such terms came into prominent use in contemporary English political discourse, and the ideological positions at play, I will utilise and reapply Edward Herman and Noam Chomsky's analysis of the mass media, particularly the ways in which the media manufacture consent and sideline and manage unpalatable positions. What is particularly useful about their approach is that they often focused on the significance of the more liberal-left end of the media as an ideological barometer of what is acceptable. Obviously, Brexit, Farage and Trump represented distinctive changes in contemporary political discourse, and related figures too have been described in what might be deemed 'religious' language (e.g., 'Brexit zealots'). But even though Trump threw open the nature of political consensus in the American media, Farage and UKIP (and even Trump) had already been accommodated by some parts of the right-wing, English-based media. In the case of Corbyn, however, we had a figure who represented a challenge to the leftist end of acceptability. This issue contributed to the construction of 'religious' labelling, provided an indication of the ways in which such ideas were understood, and even indicated changes in the construction of the leftist end of the political consensus after Corbyn's relative successes at the 2017 General Election.

Herman and Chomsky's approach to the media is not only integral to my argument but it is also an approach which has regularly been misunderstood. I want to take some time explaining its analytical importance and the ways it can be adapted, before moving on to show how and why the language of 'religion' was important in the *Guardian*'s manufacturing of political consent. The *Guardian* is an especially important example to use because it was a staple of the Left in English political discourse, it had a significant international reach (particularly through its online presence), and it was a major platform for Labour and leftist politicians, journalists and thinkers. It also happened to publish many articles on Corbyn. It should also be remembered throughout this chapter that the main point is not to defend, attack or assess Corbyn's leadership, or indeed (with some exceptions) the validity of the media criticisms of Corbyn, but rather to evaluate the ideological tendencies involved in the reporting on Corbyn and the significance of these for constructing politicised discourses relating to assumptions about 'religion' on the Centre-Left (and beyond). And a reapplication of Herman and Chomsky's Propaganda Model of the media is ideal for carrying out such a task.

The Propaganda Model and Jeremy Corbyn

From his emergence as a most likely winner of the Labour leadership in the summer of 2015 to the General Election two years later, Corbyn did not receive a good press. To provide some flavour of the sorts of responses, we were informed by press headlines of the following:

> Revealed: How Jeremy Corbyn welcomed the prospect of an asteroid 'wiping out' humanity, attacked 'pigeon prejudice' and demanded a ban on Action Man toys. (*Daily Mail*)
>
> Corbyn: Abolish the Army: New leader's potty plan for world peace. (*Sun*)

Jeremy Corbyn's plan to turn Britain into Zimbabwe. (*Telegraph*)

Revealed: The evil monster haunting Jeremy Corbyn's past. (*Daily Express*)

Is this really the day to audition for Strictly, Jeremy? Corbyn appears to dance a jig at the Cenotaph as he waits for the Remembrance Day parade. (*Mail Online*)

Jeremy Corbyn dances his way down Downing Street as he attends Remembrance Sunday. (*Sun*)

As we saw with the claim of Corbyn cancelling Christmas (Chapter 2), these examples – among plenty of others – did not have an especially close connection to what Corbyn said or did. The claim about dancing a jig was eventually removed from both websites after it became clear that Corbyn was in fact walking and discussing with a Second World War veteran who had been edited out of the photograph. But none of this kind of manipulation was surprising because of the sort of political position Corbyn represented. The main reason for the hostility from the start of his leadership should be clear: throughout the neoliberal era, the British media attacked and misrepresented culturally prominent (or even non-prominent) figures deemed to be remotely left-of-centre (e.g., Tony Benn, Michael Foot, Bernie Grant, Neil Kinnock, Ed Miliband, Diane Abbott). Given the broad acceptance of the neoliberal settlement by Labour (especially through Blair and the New Labour project), the return after a long absence of anything ideologically close to pre-Blair figures on the Left to frontline parliamentary politics was always going to lead to such responses. Indeed, Greg Philo, research director of Glasgow University Media Unit and veteran analyst of media representations of controversial political topics, showed how the consistent anti-Corbyn bias, distortion and negative labelling was part of the long anti-leftist treatment of such figures since the 1970s.[1]

The media pressure on Corbyn was part of a wider system of propaganda. And by 'propaganda', I am using the term as developed by Herman and Chomsky who famously argued that traditional media discussions of politics generally reflect various elite discourses and corporate interests, irrespective of whether elite opinions are in agreement over details or not.[2] Individual journalists may think differently and sometimes may publish differently but, broadly speaking, traditional media outlets foreground certain issues, ignore others, and ridicule those which are deemed beyond the bounds of acceptability in order to help manufacture consent and the agreed assumptions of debate in liberal capitalist democracies. In terms of the applicability of Herman and Chomsky to the British media, we might refer in particular to the work carried out by Media Lens (David Edwards and David Cromwell), both in their ongoing online presence and in various publications.[3]

The idea that Corbyn signified a difference from such consent gains support from empirical studies carried out on representations of him in the traditional media. The Media Reform Coalition looked at press reporting on Corbyn in eight British newspapers after his 2015 victory and prior to negative poll ratings. Looking at 494 news, comment and editorial pieces, 60 per cent were negative and 13 per cent positive.[4] A study carried out by analysts from Birkbeck, University of London, in association with the Media Reform Coalition, looked at broadcast and online coverage of the Labour leadership contest in 2016. In the main evening bulletins, for instance, twice as much airtime was given to voices critical of Corbyn and a 'huge imbalance' towards issues raised by Corbyn's critics. They also noted that the BBC bulletins regularly used pejorative language of Corbyn, irrespective of whether his ideas were popular with the public, while Corbyn's opponents were cast in the more benign language of, for example, 'moderates'.[5] Similarly, in close readings of the representation of Corbyn in 812 pieces in eight British newspapers from 1 September 2015 to 1 November 2015, Bart Cammaerts, Brooks DeCillia, João Magalhães and César Jimenez-Martínez (London School of Economics) pointed out that 50 per cent of basic news reporting was 'critical or blatantly antagonistic', that there was a 'very blurred' distinction between comment, conjecture and fact, and that 70 per cent of opinion pieces and editorials were 'critical or antagonistic and delegitimising'. But what they also added was that while the left-leaning media had less focus on Corbyn on a personal level than the right-leaning media, the hostilities persisted (e.g., 'unelectable', 'unrealistic').[6] And the significance of left-leaning hostility to Corbyn can be highlighted with reference to probably the most influential news outlet from this perspective: the *Guardian*.

The role of the Guardian

So how did the *Guardian* initially react once it became clear that some of the otherwise tolerated critiques found among its most leftist commentators might become a political force with Corbyn? Despite individual articles of support, over 20 anti-Corbyn articles were published in one week once Corbyn took the lead in the summer of 2015, followed by a range of polemical articles and opinion pieces, some of which will be discussed below.[7] The *Guardian* did take some note of numerous criticisms. In his response to readers angered by the *Guardian's* reporting, the then readers' editor Chris Elliott looked at 43 pieces about Corbyn (37 of which were articles, the others were videos or cartoons), published between 21 and 30 July 2015. He claimed that 16 'broadly reflected opposition to the Corbyn candidacy', 17 'struck me as neutral' (e.g., news stories), and 10 'could broadly be described as either being comment pieces in favour of Corbyn or news stories reporting positively about him'.[8] Elliott gave no reference to which articles these might have been. Media Lens asked but Elliott replied that he was unable to provide the details because of a lack of time and resources. Moreover, after sifting through the *Guardian* articles, Media Lens further argued there was a disproportionate amount of negative criticism aimed at Corbyn in comparison with the occasional negative comments about the other leadership candidates.[9]

Journalists on the Left certainly predicted intense media hostility at the time Corbyn became favourite to win the Labour leadership, but it is striking what was absent from such analyses. Owen Jones, for instance, claimed in August 2015 that, if elected, Corbyn would face a vicious onslaught from the establishment media because he was a challenge to the political consensus.[10] When Jones later published a series of controversial critical questions to Corbyn and his followers as the coup against Corbyn had got underway in the summer of 2016, and when other leftist *Guardian* journalists were having similar anxieties, he referred back to his prediction and said that it was not prophetic but 'entirely obvious'. But Jones did not then mention the role of his own employer, the *Guardian*. Given this, it is worth observing what happened once Jones effectively gave up on Corbyn by February 2017. In an interview with the *Evening Standard*, Jones admitted not only that 'the Left has failed badly' but that he would 'find it hard to vote for Corbyn' in a Labour leadership election. While acknowledging the difficult situation Corbyn faced over Brexit, Jones cited reasons for his final change of heart, such as 'a lack of strategy, communication, vision' in getting the message across.[11] These views were effectively repeated on the BBC's *Daily Politics* on 21 February 2017, and then written up for the *Guardian* (1 March 2017) where he repeated his line that 'Britain's press is owned by an aggressively rightwing cabal who demonise anyone who even vaguely challenges the status quo' but again no mention was made of the liberal-left media opposition to Corbyn from the start. Jones restressed that 'there needs to be a sophisticated strategy to deal with such entrenched opposition' which has 'been sorely lacking'. But while Jones was personally self-critical, no suggestion at this time was given about how such a strategy might incorporate a critique of anything left of the 'rightwing cabal'.[12] Indeed, in response to questions on Twitter about the structural role of the *Guardian*, Jones answered by shifting the emphasis to whether his intentions were sincere. He also cited an example of a *Guardian* journalist (Gary Younge) who spoke out against Corbyn's *parliamentary* critics though, crucially, this did not include the sustained criticisms of Corbyn made by the *Guardian* (2–3 March 2017, @owenjones84). In the case of Jones, we can begin to see the tacit limits of self-criticism on the liberal-left at this time, particularly when it came to the function of the press. Despite or because of this, the assumption of the free, autonomous, independent journalist remained dominant and unsurprisingly so in an age of neoliberalism.

Jones' explanations about Corbyn, weak polling, and the February 2017 by-elections in Copeland (which Labour lost to the Conservatives) and Stoke (which Labour won but not as strongly as some expected) were typical of those provided by *Guardian* writers who likewise did not address the *Guardian*'s role in explaining the problems facing the Left. The *Guardian* editorial gave local explanations such as Corbyn's dislike of nuclear power being a particular problem in Copeland and for the west Cumbrian economy, as well as a broader issue of Labour's credibility eroding and Corbyn not providing a proper answer for the purpose of the Labour Party.[13] John Harris looked at the 'deep, historic crisis that preceded the arrival of Jeremy Corbyn' but nevertheless claimed that it was 'immeasurably deepened' by his leadership with 'far too little to say to its alleged core vote'.[14] More polemical still were the views of four of its columnists (Gaby Hinsliff, Gary Younge, Polly Toynbee and Giles Fraser) solicited by the *Guardian*, and the explanations for the failure focused on Corbyn in particular. What is significant about these views was that two figures previously supportive of Corbyn and firmly on the Left of the *Guardian* – Younge and Fraser – now joined the criticism. For Younge, 'those who think the Labour leader, Jeremy Corbyn, has risen to those challenges were not being honest with themselves' and that Corbyn failed to present an anti-austerity message, adding that

'Corbyn supporters should not be putting lipstick on this pig.' Giles Fraser, who still gave lukewarm support in that he did not see who could replace Corbyn, wondered why Corbyn was not being self-critical, suggesting that 'Corbyn doesn't do emotionally layered or existentially complex'.[15] Whatever the validity (or not) of these explanations there were nevertheless limits to what counted as a valid explanation, even where the language of 'honesty' (etc.) was prominent. Even on the more radical end of the *Guardian*, no sustained self-criticism of the role of the leftist journalist or the leftist media was at this time forthcoming in these pieces, despite the *Guardian*'s consistent and high-profile criticism of Corbyn since 2015.

Some columnists did attempt to address issues potentially difficult for the *Guardian* in the light of the February 2017 by-elections. Long-time Corbyn critic and senior *Guardian* journalist, Jonathan Freedland, claimed that with its focus on Trump, 'the "mainstream media" has barely bothered with Corbyn' between the summer of 2016 and February 2017 and mentioned that he was one of the people who warned that 'Corbyn would be a disaster from the start'.[16] Even if this claim about relative media silence were accurate it did not engage with the possibility that a year of anti-Corbyn articles might potentially have had different types of long-term impact in moulding perceptions of Corbyn (from word of mouth to framing media narratives). Rafael Behr – who, incidentally, has a penchant for Christian analogies in his political journalism – gave familiar reasons for by-elections failings (e.g., Corbyn, his attitude to nuclear power, Labour's disconnect from its traditional vote) and more, but entertained alternative explanations such as 'perfidious parliamentarians' and 'a partisan press'. He acknowledged 'that some British newspapers write about politicians of the left with vindictive aggression'.[17] But note the phrase 'some British newspapers'; this presumably was not meant to imply that the *Guardian* was complicit in the 'vindictive aggression' as Behr shifted criticism elsewhere.

A few days after the February 2017 by-election post-mortem in the *Guardian*, film director Ken Loach did publish some criticisms of the *Guardian*'s treatment: 'But the papers that present themselves as radical have been revealed to be nothing of the sort. The Guardian and Mirror have become cheerleaders for the old Labour establishment. Column after column demands that Corbyn should go.'[18] In addition to his celebrity and popularity, which helped in getting such statements published, Loach controversially had previous critical remarks edited out by the *Guardian* (see below). Even so, a couple of sentences by Loach represented very little in the light of the previous 18 months of *Guardian* coverage, below-the-line commenters (who, if we read them as a collective, seemed to have mostly turned against Corbyn by the turn of 2017) and a series of anti-Corbyn articles after the by-election. Of course, occasional reported sentences aside, it was unlikely that the other *Guardian* writers would have engaged in extensive structural critique of the role of themselves and their employers. Would this not have been counterproductive for any employee? Probably so, but that is partly the point.

To push this point home, the structural pattern of avoiding complicity or perceived wrongdoing on the part of the *Guardian* continued in the run-up to the General Election as senior Labour figures (e.g., John McDonnell, Barry Gardiner, Emily Thornberry) made vocal complaints about the media and academics wrote letters to the *Guardian* to complain about the media coverage. In response, Gaby Hinsliff wrote about right-wing favouritism across the media, the Communist Party past of the *Morning Star*, Corbynite criticisms of the press, how much media criticism Trump received, the connections between voter interests and newspaper interests, potential BBC bias and online criticism it faced, and difficult questions all this might raise for journalists and standards of integrity.[19] But Hinsliff did not mention the *Guardian*'s sustained criticisms against Corbyn. The *Guardian*'s veteran media analyst and former editor, Peter Preston, tried to address criticisms in the letters more directly. He certainly noted the *Guardian*'s scepticism towards Corbyn but stressed the importance of the interests of readers and that no matter how much effort was put in there could never be 'perfect equality'. Though careful in qualifying that Trump and Corbyn were politically different, Preston did point to the hostility to Trump who nevertheless won the presidency and so 'ordinary voters' (Preston's term) were the ones who ultimately factor in the credibility of the leader.[20] Preston certainly had a point on the complexity of the relationship between newspapers and voting intentions, though the comparison between the American media and the British media, and their audiences, probably needed nuancing. But, for our purposes, it is notable that the arguments were again functioning in favour of the *Guardian*'s innocence (or the normality of the cut and thrust of political journalism) and Preston only highlighted his argument with evidence from a serious-sounding editorial criticism of Corbyn about his credibility in the eyes of voters. This is not the same as comparing, in varying degrees, Corbyn and Corbynism to ISIS, fundamentalism, Charles Manson, puritanism, sects, cults, totalitarianism, zealots, and so on as the *Guardian* continually did (see below). Claiming that perfect equality does not exist and pushing the onus on voters effectively permitted an unmentioned hard inequality of reporting in the *Guardian* and conceded that sustained caricatures were part of the media game. It was the combination of the mentioned (serious editorial on voter interests) and unmentioned (sustained polemics) which once again avoided too much *Guardian* complicity in popular negative receptions of politicians from the Left.

While hardly without merit, an Owen Jones-style critique of the media was therefore limited because he did not focus on how the liberal-left played a crucial role in constructing one extremity of the political and economic consensus. Jones implicitly attempted to counter this by pointing out that the *Guardian* 'have never gagged me', a part of his individualised response to a structural question that Jones would repeat in his focus on personal sincerity.[21] But this is precisely the point: there were always unspoken constraints whether people knew it or liked it or not, and we should not have expected the *Guardian* to be so heavy-handed as to gag journalists. Having said that, and while we should not read too much into occasional examples, we should also note that David Graeber tweeted (@davidgraeber, 5 July 2016) that the *Guardian* removed the following section from his article on Corbyn and Momentum:[22]

80% of sitting MPs backing a vote of no confidence, but constituent Labour Parties have broken in almost exactly the opposite direction. (Angela Eagle's own CLP for instance put out a statement of confidence in Corbyn signed by 40 of its 44 delegates.) The Guardian, Mirror, Independent, and virtually all left-leaning news venues instantly called for Corbyn's resignation, but the heads of virtually every single major trades union put out an immediate statement of support.

It is not clear how many would have been as bold as Graeber or how many had such comments removed. Loach certainly was as bold, and his letter sent to the *Guardian* (where there was typically more freedom to be critical) was edited so that the introduction and conclusion were removed. The removed words were: 'Does your determination to undermine Jeremy Corbyn know no bounds? ... The Guardian is fast becoming the mouthpiece for this bunch of political losers who are intent on the destruction of the Labour Party they cannot control.'[23] This is not to say, of course, that the *Guardian* carefully edited all critical comments from its writers and it was unlikely to be a problem anyway given that there were not many in the *Guardian* known to be as radical as Loach or Graeber, at least not publicly so.

Indeed, one *Guardian* employee told me that they were inclined to support Corbyn in 2015 but they were reluctant to do so openly, not because there was an official editorial line and not because they would be told to believe otherwise, but because they felt that there was just too much of an anti-Corbyn atmosphere among influential *Guardian* journalists. There seems to be a similar logic of peer pressure rather than explicit top-down diktat behind Rhiannon Lucy Cosslett's piece during the 2017 Election as the *Guardian* was becoming more supportive of Corbyn. Cosslett claimed that she kept quiet after voting for Corbyn in the second leadership election, that she felt embarrassed and self-doubting after the framing of an incompetent 'doddery old fool whose politics belonged in the 70s or 80s'. Most tellingly, Cosslett revealed that she became so used to 'political commentators' criticising her for being a champagne socialist, loony lefty, and so on for admiring Corbyn's principle that she 'began to sort of believe it'.[24] Cosslett did not criticise the *Guardian* but the general air of conformity to a particular position seems clear enough. This was a harbinger for what would happen from the night of the General Election to the reflections on a hung Parliament when it turned out that Corbyn had performed far better than almost everyone at the *Guardian* predicted. A number of *Guardian* journalists (e.g., Toynbee, Freedland, Behr, Jones, White, Harris) admitted on Twitter and in the *Guardian* that they were wrong about the electoral appeal of Corbyn and that the result was changing the ways media analysts think about electoral politics. Owen Jones gave a 'heartfelt apology' to Corbyn and his circle, saying he was 'totally wrong' and even admitting that the *Guardian* was among the mistaken. His apology went further in implying (I put it no stronger than that) what he did not do previously. He observed that there might have been structural issues at play with the *Guardian* when he further explained that being in both the Labour movement and 'the mainstream media undoubtedly left me more susceptible to their groupthink'.[25]

Clearly, then, we have some direct evidence for the obvious: anti-Corbyn peer pressure contributed to journalistic consensus-making. But the situation was more complex still. Certainly, some of the misreporting about Corbyn looked deliberate and there were instances where little effort was made to represent him fairly. However, deliberate or even careless manipulation hardly explains all journalism. To illustrate the point, we might turn to Chris Elliott's response to readers' concerns about loaded labels like 'moderniser'. Elliott referred to his colleague, the *Guardian* political blogger Andrew Sparrow, and his explanation that labels were typically inadequate but were sometimes needed to make a point and could do so precisely because they were widely understood. Elliott added that Sparrow 'also put in a plea for readers not to imagine that everything written with which they disagree is motivated by bad faith or bias. A fair point, I think.'[26] This is both right and wrong. Being a regular reader of Sparrow for some time, it remains clear to me that he is a dedicated journalist, and I have never doubted his sincerity. Indeed, it is not difficult to sympathise with a political journalist, sometimes reporting by the minute, needing instant labels to communicate ideas quickly. But uses of such loaded language, even if meaningful, still perpetuated certain ideological positions irrespective of intentions, honesty or sincerity. The culturally shared connotations of 'moderniser' remained regardless of what the reporter may have been thinking, just like the structural role of the *Guardian* in constructing the boundaries of political and economic debate remained.

Caricatures of Herman and Chomsky's Propaganda Model would have it that they claimed journalists are almost robotically controlled from upon high and told to believe x, y and z, but this is not what Herman and Chomsky were suggesting, as Chomsky's interview with Andrew Marr in 1996 memorably highlighted.[27] Rather, as with plenty of other social groups, acceptable and unacceptable ideas are (often unintentionally) constructed and influenced by a range of social, cultural and historical factors. Such factors might involve the kinds of professionals who have close working connections with the more traditionally mainstream politicians and who are answerable to management working at the highest corporate level and thus engage with various financial and high political issues. In terms of the *Guardian*, advertising played a significant role in its revenue and the *Guardian* itself was (and is) run by the Scott Trust Limited. In other words, and to state what should be the obvious, the *Guardian* was part of the corporate world just like any other corporate media outlet. As Edwards and Cromwell put it, 'media performance is largely shaped by market forces, by the bottom-line goals of media corporations operating within state-capitalist society' with at least 75 per cent of progressive British broadsheets recently dependent on advertising revenue, though that now looks to be in decline.[28] And so, with his particular views on economics, was it ever likely that a figure like Corbyn would receive any significant and widespread support from the leftist end of the traditional media, even if there were exceptions?

We should also nuance the extent of the influence of the *Guardian* and other media outlets in a world where news consumption was becoming increasingly fragmented. Newspapers were not selling in the numbers they once did, digital media offered a range of alternative news outlets, and social media could often mean news tailored to reflect personal preferences. However, the *Guardian* and others from the traditional national press still played a role on what was brought to the fore in, for instance, television evening news and thus had some impact on what constituted 'the news'. There were other areas of political discourse where the *Guardian* could have had an influential role. Alex Nunns noted that, during the summer of 2015, nearly a quarter (perhaps more) of the *Guardian*'s core readership had a vote in the 2015 Labour leadership election, and the Labour establishment (e.g., David Miliband, Alan Johnson, Peter Hain, Tony Blair) saw the *Guardian* as a significant vehicle for communicating with the membership and wrote in the newspaper during the 2015 Election.[29] In other words, the *Guardian* was an influential venue for establishing what was deemed acceptable on the contemporary Left, Centre-Left, and in the Labour Party.

Indeed, a certain radicalism was tolerated (including the work of Owen Jones) which was perhaps necessary to maintain the *Guardian*'s leftist credentials.[30] Crucially, though, radicalism was regularly commodified which not only shows its compatibility with the neoliberal settlement but also kept anything potentially too extreme at a safe enough distance. At least some people at the *Guardian* knew that there was such a market among its readership, plenty of whom (if letters and comments were anything to go by) were more critical of the Thatcher-Blair economic consensus than the *Guardian* as a whole or than many (most?) *Guardian* writers. In terms of Corbyn as representative of such a tendency, Chris Elliott referred to a poll of 630 members of the *Guardian*'s 'core readership in the UK' carried out by the *Guardian*'s 'consumer insight team' where 51 per cent said Corbyn was their preferred choice with rivals each below 10 per cent.[31] Such readers were obviously important for the *Guardian* and any regular visitor to the website over the past few years will have noticed advertisements presumably aimed at them, including the anti-New Labour t-shirts ('Labour: I prefer their old work') which could even be found on anti-Corbyn articles online. Another t-shirt (and mug) with the polemical words of Nye Bevan in the shape of a rat – 'That is why no amount of cajolery, and no attempts at ethical or social seduction, can eradicate from my heart a deep burning hatred for the Tory Party that inflicted those bitter experiences on me. So far as I am concerned they are lower than vermin' – were likewise advertised by the *Guardian*. Unaware of just how far his newspaper had been trying to appeal to such an audience in less challenging times, Jonathan Freedland expressed surprised concern when this was pointed out to him. This was just after he tweeted from the Labour Party Conference 2016, 'Troubled by the "Tories are lower than vermin" mug. Dehumanising your opponents rarely ends well' (@Freedland, 25 September 2016), unintentionally implying that there were indeed views present at the *Guardian* willing to commodify a less centralist position.

As these examples suggest, in normal circumstances it would have been relatively easy for the *Guardian* to keep more leftist readers calm enough. Similarly, the *Guardian* was able to publish qualifying statements about having to hold your nose and vote for Labour over Conservative, or even include articles critical of neoliberalism, though the signs were there of a more controversial centrist direction when they suggested voting Liberal Democrat in 2010, of which readers regularly reminded them. But circumstances changed, and the emergence of the Corbyn movement showed the limits of what the leftish end of the media could accept and how the *Guardian* was involved in the manufacturing of consent. Polly Toynbee even implicitly admitted this in her claim that, in an ideal world, she would be even more radical than Corbyn but, in this world, it was necessary to be a more centrist pragmatist.[32] Irrespective of her intentions and whether she would have liked it or not, did this pragmatism not have the same impact and maintain a position which was more about managing the neoliberal status quo rather than challenging its foundations? Put another way, if the example of Andrew Sparrow above was reminiscent of Marx's classic formulation of ideology ('they do not know it, but they do it'), then Toynbee was more reminiscent of Slavoj Žižek's reformulation of Marx for a postmodern age: 'they know very well what they are doing, but still they are doing it'.[33]

Corbyn's policy suggestions could have been classified as a Keynesian critique of the Thatcher-Blair economic consensus which only further highlights how narrow and how far towards economic neoliberalism the press had moved. In order to highlight the potentiality of Corbyn as a signifier of the neoliberal Other, we might turn to *Guardian* pieces which manufactured a past by constructing the ultimate symbol of what neoliberalism tried to vanquish – 1970s-style, union-dominated nation-alisation – and the idea that Corbyn was a return to the quintessentially bad 1970s and 1980s Labour Party (outside the more liked Kinnock leadership). For Tom Baldwin, a former Labour Party Director of Com-munications and Strategy, 'Corbyn is trapped in the 1970s'.[34] According to Toynbee, 'Corbyn is a 1983 man, a relic of the election that brought him to parliament when Labour was destroyed by its out-of-Nato, anti-EU, renationalise-everything suicide note.'[35] One headline in the *Guardian*'s sister paper, the *Observer*, even claimed that 'Jeremy Corbyn suggests he would bring back Labour's nationalising clause IV', despite, as Nunns noted, the first line of the same article being 'Labour leadership candidate Jeremy Corbyn has denied that he would reinstate clause IV of the Labour party constitution'.[36] What was not often recalled in the criticisms of Corbyn was what he actually said (which in turn belonged to a long-standing view of public ownership in the Bennite tradition), which I flag up as a point of contrast with some of the criticisms:

I believe in public ownership, but I have never favoured the remote nationalised model that prevailed in the post-war era. Like a majority of the population and a majority of even Tory voters, I want the railways back in public ownership. But public control should mean just that, not simply state control: so we should have passengers, rail workers and government too, co-operatively running the railways to ensure they are run in our interests and not for private profit.[37]

In sum, all detail and complexity of history and ideas was masked over in the manufacturing of ideological consent and construction of history. It remains clear that Corbyn functioned in a way which challenged this consent in the traditional media and among journalists' public personas in a way that selling a radical t-shirt or publishing a few articles on the evils of neoliberalism did not. Now it mattered.

However, the General Election 2017 showed that the boundaries of consent could change. While the national media outlets did not stop attacking Corbyn, there was more scope for him to get the Labour Manifesto across and more scope for Theresa May to make mistakes that could be seen. There was also a return to the dominance of two-party politics as voters typically rallied behind either Labour or Conservative. The polling was changeable but some polling (e.g., YouGov) had Labour closing the gap and coming to within a couple of points of the Conservatives and a significant lead for Corbyn among younger voters. The *Guardian* accordingly became less hostile and even supportive. Indeed, we should not underestimate the possibility that these Corbyn voters could also have been seen as potential *Guardian* punters. Various journalists appeared to have had a change of mind, though, as expected, Owen Jones and Giles Fraser were firmly behind Corbyn's Labour. Rhiannon Lucy Cosslett's article epitomised the shifting interests at the *Guardian*: 'I used to be a shy Corbynite but I'm over that now'.[38]

But what was especially striking was the change of heart by some who had been polemical in their opposition. Gary Younge, who had started off as a Corbyn supporter but, as we saw, would claim that some Corbyn supporters were being dishonest with themselves to the point that they 'should not be putting lipstick on this pig', was a few months later critiquing those who argued that Corbyn was 'unelectable'. He now claimed that those who had supported Corbyn were treated like climate change deniers and that it was the political and media elites who had been promoting their own interests and prejudices.[39] Polly Toynbee, who as we just saw claimed that Corbyn was a '1983 man' and a 'relic', called the leaked Labour Manifesto a 'cornucopia of delights' that was 'not a repeat … of the 1983 manifesto' after all. Toynbee, while still being critical of Corbyn himself, warned us of the inevitable 'blowback from the Tories and their bully press' who would blare that 'it will "take us back to the 70s"'.[40] While not uncritical, the *Guardian* editorial endorsed Corbyn and claimed that he 'is on to something resonant, something common, something good'.[41] A month earlier, Jonathan Freedland, one of its most senior journalists, was scathing of Corbyn's chances, mocking proposals like extra bank holidays, noting that focus groups showed how unpopular Corbyn was and that a new leader could make a serious challenge to the Conservatives.[42] Whatever the long-term impact of Corbyn and the 2017 Election, what we can see is that the Corbyn moment showed that there was potential to open up the political consensus post-2008, even to the point of (and probably the necessity of) writers appearing to contradict themselves.

Religion and manufacturing dissent

If the traditional media would inevitably have been hostile, what alternatives were there for the Corbyn movement? One was social media where Corbyn's team were particularly effective, even if social media influence was limited and could not dictate media narratives and reporting in the way the traditional media could. We have also seen that being credibly connected to a certain tradition of Christianity, as Corbyn sometimes was and he himself was quick to make such a connection, provided a degree of protection in, or from, the traditional media. While there were exceptions among niche opinion writers, issues relating to Christianity and the Bible were treated positively by the British press and were broadly and vaguely understood to be a Good Thing and part of the British cultural heritage. In two studies Jackie Harrison and I carried out on the press reporting of Pope Benedict XVI's UK visit in 2010, we found that the dominant assumption of the British Press was that whatever 'religion' may be it was largely deemed benign (with a small minority of hostile voices) because it was perceived to be compatible with liberal democracy, with any problematic Otherness ignored, and that deviations from this were typically explained away as a perversion or distortion (e.g., terror) with one exception discussed in Chapter 3 – Islam.[43]

In this respect, it is notable that in another study I argued that one of the precursors to Corbyn – the political interventions of Russell Brand – was ridiculed in the press, particularly when Brand mentioned discourses assumed to be 'religious' or 'spiritual' of a more problematic variety (e.g., meditation, Hare Krishna, pantheism, transcendentalism, etc.).[44] Christianity and the Bible were almost always *not* ridiculed and, if not deemed a false Christian, Brand was even cast as an opponent of Christianity despite openly identifying with its traditions. Yet, while Brand's use of the Bible and Christianity may have been deemed inauthentic and his Christ-Che image deemed too flippant in the press, there was little in the way of attacks on anything constructed as authentically Christian in what he has written, said or performed. Nevertheless, Brand's form of 'religion' was too alien and too foreign for acceptability in the political pages of the traditional press. While Brand may not have been thought culturally credible, Corbyn was less easy to attack on such issues, given that he long had connections with nostalgic discourses associated with radical Nonconformist Christianity, particularly through Tony Benn, and to which even some (small 'c') conservatives warmed (e.g., Peter

Hitchens, Peter Oborne). Corbyn could be variously described, often ironically, as a kind of Messiah or Jesus-figure, as well as someone like Obi-Wan Kenobi who had a similar cultural role as a saintly wise-man (and picked up in a different way by the *Guardian* cartoonist Steve Bell).

But, crucially for Corbyn after some of the criticisms he received on the issue of patriotism, this was a construction of an *English* or *British* sage. For Giles Fraser, the *Guardian*'s regular Church of England commentator who would have his doubts as we saw, Corbyn and Momentum were a mild version of the Bible on the topic of wealth yet still Corbyn was 'the only one who even approximates to Christian teaching' on this matter. Indeed, given that Christianity was the official state religion, 'you'd think that the Queen would be cheering on Corbyn, encouraging his bold redistributive instincts, and dismissing the Blairites for their fondness for Mammon'.[45] As I suggested, connecting Corbyn with a more revered tradition was one aspect of the reporting of Corbyn in 2015 that some of the hostile articles had to try and reject or use ironically, such was its embeddedness. As we saw in Chapter 1, this tradition of radical Christianity and radical biblical interpretation long had associations not only with socialism in different guises, but also with culturally and politically credible anti-totalitarian English or British traditions, with an emphasis on liberty and freedom of conscience and with reference to discourses about helping the poor and, more specifically, the founding of the National Health Service. This was not a tradition likely to be treated with sustained overt disdain in the media or by opposing politicians.

A sect is for other people

These understandings of religion afforded only limited protection for Corbyn, however. Establishing Corbyn in terms of Jesus, a Messiah, or radical Christianity helped enable a discourse about him in terms of religious language and this shed more light on the manufacturing of consent and dissent in the English-based media. One of the problems for Corbyn was that he was perceived to believe, *really believe*, in his socialism rather than the apparent practical necessity of politicians to be 'ideology-lite' in contemporary political discourse. Building on what was argued earlier about Christmas (and again in somewhat Žižekian terms), we might say that a perceived lack of hard ideological commitment was a typical move in postmodernity in that it masked what actually was a hard-ideological commitment to neoliberal capitalism, with political differences emerging over technocratic details. In this respect, it is notable that the language of, for instance, 'cult', 'sect', 'puritan' and 'fundamentalist' was repeated when trying to ostracise Corbyn and his followers rhetorically, whether in the media or by hostile politicians presumably hoping such terms denoting deviation would catch on.

For instance, Suzanne Moore (12 August 2015) staked a claim to represent a socialist tradition in tension with Corbyn's 'asceticism', suggesting that Corbynism represented a 'kind of purity' which 'always shades into puritanism, an unbecoming exercise in self-flagellation'. Moore lamented that 'champagne socialist' was now an insult and that while austerity was very real for some, it was puzzling that 'middle-class people pretend to live austere lives', whether in terms of green or healthy lifestyles. Rather than reduce everything to the 'economy or inequality', Moore looked to a socialist tradition of sharing more of life's pleasures, whether clothes, buildings or music.[46] Moore was further supported by Toynbee on Twitter who, despite elsewhere claiming that 'the vitriol of the press has been shocking' in their treatment of Corbyn,[47] tweeted: 'Brilliant Suzanne Moore on dourness of Corbyn puritanism' (@pollytoynbee, 13 August 2015). Moore gave no indication about whether Corbyn would promote his personal drinking habits or promote the gastronomical and cultural habits of Corbyn supporters to the nation, and nor was there reference to any studies about how something like Corbynism became an exercise in self-flagellation. We might note that a month after Moore's article, Corbyn went to a pub packed full of supporters to celebrate his victory while #Cans4Corbyn and 'big bag of cans' became a popular drinking refrain of Corbyn supporters.

But in one sense this is not really the point. Instead, Moore's piece functioned not only to discredit what Corbyn represented but also to promote a preferable ideological position, presumably in constructing a 'puritanism' in implied opposition to a (once) normative broad church. In this respect, it is worth noting that a Peter Mandelson article was given the following headline, 'Labour is a broad church – Jeremy Corbyn is turning it into a narrow sect bound for the abyss'. Yet what is significant about the contents of Mandelson's article was that unlike the classic Labour language of 'broad church', the word 'sect' did not occur. This addition was presumably due to *Guardian* editing, and perhaps not unreasonably as 'sect' was used to describe Corbyn's followers by others, including the Mandelson ally and now former Labour MP, Tristram Hunt, as reported the previous month in the *Guardian*.[48] Put another way, this binary of closed in-group versus 'broad church' was hardly alien to the *Guardian* and the thinking of figures like Mandelson. But there was more to this dichotomy. Mandelson's article fired at controlling 'hard-left' groups and Trotskyites who functioned as a kind of Communist, totalitarian, and anti-capitalist fringe to the Labour Party's normative, inclusive, democratic, 'historical mainstream' dedicated to its 'traditional values of equality and internationalism'.

A similar ideological binary was at work in Moore's article. While not disputing her intentions nor the socialist credentials of the tradition she invoked, the way this tradition was presented in her article had obvious resonance in discourses of individualistic neoliberalism, much as in Owen Jones' responses to criticisms of the *Guardian*. Moore's conclusion to her promotion of a more bountiful socialism was, strikingly, applied not communally (as it was with the example of Nye Bevan she cited) but instead to herself. As she concluded (with reference to *Withnail & I*): 'So you have your Bennite tea, I shall continue to demand the finest wines known to humanity.' It might even be said that this assumption of personal affluence dovetailed neatly into one implied audience who might approve of the regular advertising for luxury holidays in the *Guardian*. Whatever else 'puritanism' might have signified in this discourse, here it was cast as the opposite of material comforts which realistically remained available to those who could afford them and who had the right kinds of tastes. Here we might compare Tristram Hunt's use of 'sect' which was part of a speech delivered to Cambridge University's Labour club. For Hunt, a small group of elites from the educational establishment assuming leadership presumably did not represent a 'sect' because they were deemed the right kinds of people: 'You are the top 1%. The Labour party is in the shit. It is your job and your responsibility to take leadership going forward.'[49]

In light of reactions on Twitter, Moore wondered what might be next: 'Really sorry Corbyn supporters that I pointed out another long and honourable strand of left-wing thought. You could ban me? That works ...' (@suzanne_moore, 13 August 2015). This hinted at another, related line of attack on Corbynism that was also present in Mandelson's critique: a potential totalitarianism or strict thought control. In this sense, the label 'fundamentalism' was useful for Michael White (30 July 2015), then assistant editor and former political editor at the *Guardian*. White appeared to imply that there was a comparison of type to be made between the Corbyn movement and ISIS ('a different version of populist fundamentalism on offer') when Corbyn looked likely to win the Labour leadership election.[50] A social historian of Britain, Iraq or Syria might point out that there were no obvious sociological or typological parallels (loose or otherwise) between, on the one hand, Corbyn supporters (with an interest in anti-austerity politics, non-renewal of Trident, and establishing a politics, arts, culture and community festival at the Labour Party conference) and, on the other, ISIS (with an interest in beheadings, a fulfilment of prophecy, enslaving women, and the establishment of a caliphate), both with very different and complex histories and ideological genealogies. However, this would, as ever, be beside the point because from the perspective of the mainstream political consensus in 2015, anti-austerity politics were still more to the fringes, something tolerated at the leftist end of the *Guardian*, union activists, or direct-action groups. Anything seriously challenging, or substantially deviating from, the Thatcher-Blair settlement in the mainstream might, by this definition, be constructed as 'fundamentalism'.

Implicit paralleling with Islamic 'fundamentalism' occurred again in the *Guardian* but the next example was from another issue that emerged as a point of similarity to, and thus near-disqualification of, Corbyn and his followers: Marxism, Communism and the Soviet Union. Not for the last time in the *Guardian*, one writer looked at the emergence of Corbyn in the light of their own abandoned Communist past – in this case the art critic Jonathan Jones' youthful toying with Soviet Russia (8 August 2015). Even contemporary leftist critiques of capitalism which were not necessarily 'Marxist' were effectively disqualified by Jones, as terms such as 'the one per cent' (developed by, for instance, the anarchist David Graeber and the economist Joseph Stiglitz) and 'austerity' (used across the political spectrum) were now deemed 'neo-Marxist'. Marx himself may have been gentle, claimed Jones, but his ideas 'would lead to human suffering almost unequalled in the history of the world' and 'dreamed up in the fevered minds of zealous thinkers'. The 'terrifying reality of Marxism in power' may have been a thing of the past, and Corbyn 'is no Stalin, or Lenin, or Mao Zedong'. Indeed, Jones even refused to label Corbyn 'Marxist'. Nevertheless, he added, Marxist ideas had a spectral presence around Corbyn and his followers, not least through Corbyn's praise of Marx himself as someone from whom we can learn. And so it was now necessary to remember what was done 'in the name of an extreme version of socialism in the 20th century'. Why? Because of the emergence of such a 'radical socialist conscience' and because such 'fervour, enthusiasm and optimism ... refuses to see that it drags behind it the chains of a brutal history'. This 'fervour, enthusiasm and optimism' was significant for its leftish Other represented by Jones: 'moderate, reasoning, and sceptical' and the hallmarks of a reformed capitalism. Indeed, from this perspective, it is little surprise that for Jones part of the appeal of 'Islamic fundamentalism' was that it has filled the gap left by Marxism.

Jones elsewhere constructed irrational sympathies for the Russian Revolution and the Soviet Union in terms typical of popular understandings of 'religion' and then contrasted with a more positive construction of capitalism.[51] A more sustained connection of the Soviet Union, Stalin, Communism, and so on, with the construction of a dangerously irrational 'religion' was carried out by another *Guardian* writer with a Communist past, Martin Kettle, effectively representing the minority of journalists who were critical of religion per se. Here, Kettle (22 January 2016) reflected on David Aaronovitch's recent book about his Communist upbringing and his claim that 'The Party was a church ... Its strength was that it was about belief and faith as much as about intellect.' 'Nothing,' claimed Kettle, 'is harder for an atheist than to be told they are, in fact, religious.' He referred to Eric Hobsbawm's suggestion that the Cold War was a war of religion but that, in the 1950s, 'the claim that communism was a religion would have been both insulting and laughable to my parents ... Marxism was scientific'.[52] Already, then, we can see some assumptions about what 'religion' was deemed to be and from the rest of the article we learn that it was understood to be about certainty, true believers, faith over intellect, internal debates, dismissive of alternative views and sceptics, and so on. This is not, of course, to deny that Kettle's parents thought in the terms he described but rather the point remains as ever: to look at the rhetorical and ideological tendencies at work in the use of the term 'religion'.

The idea of 'religion' (and thus Corbyn) as an anti-capitalist signifier through Communist associations was especially relevant in Kettle's constructions, even if the construction of 'church' was more negative than other uses in the press:

we do without doubt have a revived left in Britain, which has dusted off some of the same ambitions, some of the same political ideas, some of the same historic dreams and some of the same deep flaws, foolishness and even intellectual turpitude that made British communism unsustainable. If politics is 'an act of faith' then its opposite is 'a programme and a willingness to change and adapt to new times' ... This left of today looks to me suspiciously as if it is developing into another church. This left too is marked by a reluctance to ask necessary but difficult questions about its plans for the world beyond the church walls. This left too seems happiest as a fellowship of true believers, squabbling among itself, dismissive of all those who remain sceptics or whose beliefs the elders find unacceptable. Just as the communists knew things deep down that they should have faced up to, so too does this left ... There is nothing inherently wrong with having a politics that is essentially a religion, providing that you recognise it for what it is, something personal between you and your friends. But I've been there and done that. If politics is an act of faith ... it will fail, as communism did. That's fine for those for whom belief in socialist principles matters more than anything else, just as it was for the communists. But it won't work. And in the end people will hate it too.

As ever, playing around with terms like 'church' and 'religion' can show how ideologically malleable such uses were. We might think of those groups who may typically be designated 'religious'. Let us take the Church of England. It seems to be one national myth (whether right or wrong I leave to one side) that the Church of England is about compromise, pragmatism and willingness to doubt. Does this mean they are not a 'religion' according to Kettle's definition? In this respect, it is probably significant that there was no mention by name in the quotation from Kettle of Corbyn or Corbynism, or any potential policy in detail, because the implicit analogy had to be sufficiently decontextualised and generalised to work, in much the same way the cliche of 'science is just another religion' works. Clearly, there were specific interests at play in this game of defining what religion really is and the decision about its meaning was grounded in the vague authority of personal experience. For this analogy to work, Corbynism was not only paralleled with Communism but further discredited with a constructed association with Stalinism and mass murder, for whom, as Kettle put it, 'the faith still seemed plausible, providing you overlooked Stalin's trials and purges, the invasion of Hungary, the ban on Boris Pasternak and the rest'. The logic of this argument was one which was long typical of classic liberal propaganda: *Beware! Look what happens when capitalism is undermined too much from the Left!*

The *Guardian* included other variants on the 'fundamentalism' theme. Anne Perkins claimed that the Corbynite wing of the Labour Party represented 'an apocalyptic tendency' which again obviously functioned as a means of contrasting an overenthusiastic Corbyn with a perceived norm. This 'apocalyptic tendency' represented a 'party of protest, not a party of government' and 'Labour is a party of government' which meant it had 'to shape and articulate the beliefs and aspirations of a majority of its citizens'.[53] In solicited assessments of Corbyn in the *Observer*, Tom Holland used the old anti-Jewish slur 'pharisaical'. While Holland clearly did not use the term with any anti-Jewish connotations, and was surely unaware of this background, it is worth pointing out that 'pharisaical' has been challenged over the past few decades (and presumably ineffectively) by biblical scholars because the term grew out of, and functioned as, a stereotyping of the group representing Jews as legalistic, petty, harsh, unloving, and so on, over against loving Christians (or their precursors). While Holland perpetuated the label as a derogatory one, its function was now to describe Corbyn as someone close to being the antithesis of 'the very fabric of our parliamentary democracy'. For Holland, Corbyn not stepping down was such a threat and implied a degree of irrationality, 'because – like the zealot he is – he believes in a higher cause'. Furthermore, there was an unintentional challenge to the argument that the media might have contributed to misrepresenting Corbyn, and perhaps even a hint of Corbyn-as-Marxist representing an anti-capitalist threat, in Holland's related suggestion that British voters would not elect 'a sympathiser with the IRA': 'Corbyn himself can blame this on false consciousness all he likes'.[54]

If Corbyn was said to inspire faith or the like, it follows that other related language could be used, and typically to denote irrational enthusiasm. According to Freedland, the Labour MP Cat Smith was a 'Jeremy Corbyn disciple' in light of her perceived absurdity in defending the scale of Labour's defeat in the Copeland by-election.[55] Toynbee, an openly atheist critic of religion, likewise constructed a more sinister image of such a leader whose 'Machiavellian back-room manoeuvring is out of keeping with his benign, almost devotional image'. She also recalled how she could not properly communicate with 'Corbyn believers' who were marked by 'no compromise, blocked ears, total denial of electoral facts, a post-truth conviction'. They only thought Corbyn could be the next prime minister because 'conviction moves mountains' (cf. Mark 11.23; Matthew 17.21; 21.21; 1 Corinthians 13.2) and, despite being 'likeable people', they were still beyond rationality and scepticism: 'I envy their certainty – the way you can envy the religious their delusions.'[56] By the time of the Copeland and Stoke by-elections of February 2017, ideas about Corbyn or Corbyn's supporters as a somewhat irrational fringe in contrast to a rational political settlement could simply be assumed by Behr when he imagined the thought processes of such people: 'If Corbyn's supporters dig really deep into their faith', he claimed, then they could refer to the 'unreliable witnesses' (cf. Mark 14.56–59) of Labour MPs and bring up 'the option of blaming a partisan press for the non-contagion of Corbyn's message'.[57]

In the summer of 2015, one term with especially sinister and irrational implications began to be used of Corbyn's followers: 'cult'. Former Labour Party Chief Press Secretary and Official Spokesman and Director of Communications and Strategy, Alastair Campbell, tweeted, 'CyberCorbs at various points today suggesting that Neil Kinnock and Gordon Brown not really Labour. The zeal of the cult. Cult I said' (@campbellclaret, 16 August 2015). Former Labour Party member and then *Telegraph* columnist, Dan Hodges, likewise tweeted the term (which he used elsewhere): 'Corbyn Cultists: "You're all evil Tories". Me: "OK. You're a bunch of unwashed Trots". Corbyn Cultists: "You can't speak to us like that"' (@DPJHodges, 17 August 2015). This language became normative enough in the *Guardian*, and across the traditional media and beyond. According to Moore, the 'personality cult around Corbyn is just damn weird'.[58] Comparing the Corbyn movement with Trump, Hadley Freeman claimed that both 'have become cults of personality, ones it is forbidden to criticise' and which 'demonise' opponents. People 'still want to believe and belong – to something, anything, whatever the personal cost' but, she categorised, 'movements that demand devotion and prompt vilification are not grassroots democracies – they're cults'. As this suggests, Freeman legitimised the rhetoric in the direction of a kind of academic sociology of religion and pushed further still with the claim that 'cults rarely survive – they combust from their own internal pressures', using an even more sinister cultic disqualifier as her example: the Manson murders and the end of the 60s dream.[59] More light-hearted reporting of Corbyn and his supporters by Simon Hattenstone could still casually refer to 'the cult of Corbyn', with Corbyn himself as a 'seer' and even interpreted people moving aside in related language, with crowds 'split down the middle like the

Red Sea to allow him through'.[60] In his distancing from Corbyn, it is especially striking that Owen Jones, who had been critical of the ways in which Corbyn's followers were treated in the media, embraced the language of 'cult' to criticise certain supporters of Corbyn: 'The idea of witch-hunting people who dare to criticise your leader looks cult-like and doesn't attract anyone.'[61]

Obviously not applicable to the writer's own preferred ideological position and in-group, 'cult' was perhaps the most sustained example of constructing the Centre and the extreme, with an implied 'church' or 'religion' deemed more normative. This was clear in the comments by Labour MP Michael Dugher (and reported in the *Observer*) who claimed in similar terms to Mandelson that Labour leaders should 'recognise that the Labour party is a broad church, not a religious cult'.[62] The importance of the language of 'cult' to describe Corbyn and his followers was particularly shown in its use in debates among MPs and those connected with party politics, whether in attack or denial. But one example gave more detail to the construction. During the leadership contest of 2015, the Labour MP John Woodcock wrote an article in *Progress* about the 'cult logic' of Corbyn's followers which was described by the *Guardian* as a 'blistering intervention' in the leadership race.[63]

For Woodcock, such cult logic entailed despising Conservative voters and claiming that those who want to win them over to Labour were 'actively wicked'. This definition of 'cult' allowed Woodcock to develop a continuous, stable and legitimate Labour orthodoxy as its opposite, most notably in the use of the Attlee government of 1945 and the creation of the National Health Service which was perhaps the most significant moment in Labour Party mythology. Moreover, Woodcock claimed that the 'true guardians of the spirit of 1945 are those who seek to understand how fast the world is changing and change their ideas to meet the new challenges'. Woodcock's choice of highlighted figures from that administration was telling: 'Messrs Attlee, Bevan, Bevin and Cripps, men who governed through the horror of war and went on to win the peace, would send packing those who espoused the fantasy politics that is seducing many in the aftermath of our latest defeat'. This list of constructed heroes, tied in with the powerful Second World War mythmaking, provided both a source of legitimacy and a connection with the present. Yet a different reading of these figures might have revealed a more chaotic past and we might wonder how the Bevan who resigned over dental and spectacle charges would fit in. Or we might wonder what we do with the Bevan who was expelled from the Labour Party. Then there was the Bevan who, of course, thought Tories were lower than vermin. There could have been another problem for Woodcock's orthodox narrative: Labour's most celebrated government had much less successful elections in 1950 and 1951. Indeed, they were not as popular with Conservative voters, and Labour stayed out of power until 1964. And could not anyone in the Labour Party have picked out bits and pieces from Labour's history and made them their own to claim that Labour must behave likewise in the present? Obviously. But complicating history once again misses the point as creating a unified tradition was a way of coping with all the problematic contradictions. Woodcock stabilised this complex past by constructing an orthodox anti-Corbyn history held together by a unifying 'spirit'.[64]

Again, playing around with the term 'cult' highlights the point that a 'cult' typically denotes the behaviour of another group. After all, the same logic used against Corbyn and his followers could be reapplied to a group of like-minded journalists in a news outlet largely dedicated to promoting a given political position or to the 'on message' approach of Blairite New Labour. In fact, it could be used against rival factions in the Labour Party, and Blair even used the term of Gordon Brown and his circle, as well as the Labour Party more generally. In addition to the contrast with the more normative 'kirk', note the allusion to the conversion of St Paul (Acts 9.18):

> We had become separated from 'normal' people. For several decades, even before the eighteen years in the wilderness, Labour was more like a cult than a party. If you were to progress in it, you had to speak the language and press the right buttons ... The curse of Gordon was to make these people co-conspirators, not free-range thinkers. He and Ed Balls and others were like I had been back in the 1980s, until slowly the scales fell from my eyes and I realised it was more like a cult than a kirk.[65]

Clearly, then, we should not think of any of this labelling as having analytical or sociological use in trying to establish cultic, puritanical, or fundamentalist realities, particularly so if those trying to oust Corbyn could, by their own assumed definitions, be labelled as members of a 'cult' in order to establish the normality of the user of the label.

Fanaticism and anti-capitalism

The use of all this sort of language to help forge the boundaries of ideological acceptability and political consensus, as well as providing a stable and uncomplicated history of the assumed political and economic settlement, belonged to long established tropes about 'religion' and irrationality used to marginalise potentially anti-capitalist discourse in the context of liberal capitalism. This is made particularly clear in the light of one strand of Alberto Toscano's analysis of the history and uses of 'fanaticism' in his book of the same name.[66] If we look at some of the repetitive cliches about fanaticism discussed by Toscano throughout, we can see that none of the language used in the *Guardian* should now be a surprise. We might point to the construction of the fanatic who, like the religious person, could be deemed beyond tolerance, rationality, compromise and political debate, and demanded the removal of all rival views. This fanaticism could be seen to have a worrying abstract dedication to universalism and egalitarianism, though there was sometimes thought to be the possibility of longer-term progression towards moderation. The fanatical agent could be analysed as an ahistorical, monolithic threat, a political trope which regularly invoked analogy and similarity, and with formal likenesses privileged over political and historical context. Such fanaticism could represent the presence of *too much* religion, or the influence of an intensified form of religion on the secular public sphere. Some critics could ascribe political fanaticism to religious forms of behaviour while others could ascribe such behaviour to hubristic deviations from true, reasonable faith. Fanaticism was thought to be found in totalitarianism, whether understood as German Nazism or Soviet Communism, and functioning as 'political religion'. Similarly, revolutionary activity could be described in the language of religion. As fanaticism could also represent terror and the irrational opposition to the West, it could be applied to Islam as a particularly potent totalising fusion of religion and politics. Indeed, Soviet Communism and Islam have a history of being compared to one another as similar universalising phenomena. While the War on Terror could continue Cold War discourses in different ways, anti-totalitarian rhetoric against unconditional conviction and egalitarianism lingered. Thus, fanaticism could be seen as the construction of a liberal-capitalist Other.

With these examples from Toscano in mind, it is clear the *Guardian* was picking up on older ideas once again found useful in the aftermath of the post-crash crises and the first serious challenger to the existing neoliberal order in English political discourse. But it is notable in this respect that the more radical end of the mainstream Left overtly critical of neoliberalism could play the same game and, as Toscano did in his own qualified way, appropriate the language relating to such deviations from the perceived norm. Clive Lewis, a once and probably still Corbyn ally (and atheist), was reported to have detected 'an almost religious fervour' at some of the Corbyn events in the summer of 2015.[67] After the first Corbyn victory in 2015, George Monbiot argued that leftist movements should borrow ideas and survival methods from *evangelical* Christianity, even if he shared 'none of the core beliefs'.[68] And it is telling that when Monbiot gave up on Corbyn he claimed to have 'lost all faith' (@GeorgeMonbiot, 26 January 2017). Even in her lukewarm support of Labour in the 2017 Election, Toynbee quoted one of the most famous socialists in Labour's history (Bevan): 'the language of priorities is the religion of socialism'.[69] In light of what we have seen in previous chapters, it would not be a surprise to find some on the Left identifying with Perkins' claim of an 'apocalyptic tendency'. We might perhaps suggest that the fanatical slurs – analytically unhelpful though they typically are – might not have been entirely without merit in that such enthusiasm may indeed represent the lingering and threatening presence of an anti-capitalist force in English political discourse, despite every effort to remove it.

But the surprise General Election result showed ways in which this language was already shifting. It was, for instance, even possible to reverse the slurs. In his return to supporting Corbyn in the General Election, Younge invoked the ultimate anti-capitalist signifier, Marx, to show how ruling ideas were the ideas of the ruling elites but that the economic crash shifted the centre of political discourse and shifted the constructed borders of consent and brought excitement to the Election. And with this logic the centrists (traditionally understood) were 'high priests' who did not understand that centres change or even disappear.[70] A not dissimilar logic could be found with Owen Jones, who we recall had suggested that some of Corbyn's supporters were 'cult-like'. He now wanted an end to such language with Corbyn's victory as 'the mainstream commentariat, including in this newspaper' were 'wrong to vilify Corbyn supporters – from the day he stood – as delusional cultists'.[71] In other words, the shifting political consensus and electoral support meant that Corbyn had pushed his way and his agenda into the mainstream and so, from this perspective, could no longer be given the label deemed appropriate for political outsiders. This was clearer still in Jonathan Freedland's assessment as the supposed shifts in the levels of engagement of younger voters meant that it was 'not just indicative of a Milifandom-style cult limited to a narrow few'.[72] While this represented maintaining the language of 'cult' to describe the outsider, the language of religious enthusiasm could now even be embraced as a positive, as the repeated claim in the *Guardian* of 'hope' and 'inspiration' to describe Corbyn's performance might already imply. John Harris, for instance, described this new political realignment as a 'historic moral victory' and 'faintly miraculous'.[73] To foreshadow the discussion of 'political miracle' in Chapter 6, this unexpected irruption had shown that by mid-2017 there was potential for the seemingly immoveable political consensus (or Overton Window) to shift some way leftwards.

Conclusion

Throughout the pre-Election critiques of Corbyn, the more specific ideas that he mentioned – such as anti-austerity, collective rail ownership in distinction from the 1970s top-down models, housing, abandoning tuition fees, criticism of foreign policy relations (e.g., with Saudi Arabia) – tended not to be discussed in any thoroughgoing way. Some of his economic policies were compared (even in the *Guardian*) to present-day German and Scandinavian economic policies. But the consistent treatment of Corbyn and his followers in the *Guardian* revealed an exercise in setting the limits of acceptable political and economic beliefs. As of 2017, collectivisation of farms, killing dissidents, or inspirational similarities with ISIS or Charles Manson were not mentioned or implied by Corbyn. However, by implying such things about him, certain *Guardian* writers were making a curious move, and one that was to some degree reversed during the 2017 Election. They were implying (perhaps not always intentionally) that a chunk of the *Guardian* readership for whom Corbyn appealed, and some of its published articles in support of Corbyn, must be implicitly or potentially supportive of the Soviet Union, totalitarianism, and movements similar to ISIS and cults, a peculiar assumption in a newspaper that prided itself on its liberal heritage, and no doubt duly noted in light of potential new readers from a younger generation. How such parallels, which included militaristic states and organisations, matched up with another dominant (and not-entirely-accurate) construction of Corbyn and his followers as pacifists is unclear. But neither consistency nor accurate representation of readership were necessarily a problem from the perspective of propaganda or the perpetuation of the meaning of the cluster of derogatory terms associated with 'religion'.[74]

Repeated constructions of Corbyn in language relating to religion were circulated and repeated in the *Guardian*, thereby mystifying the specific views of Corbyn and the views of his followers and ensuring that they were not foregrounded. In doing so, they contributed to the development of broader media narratives about Corbyn and Corbynism. Whatever the actual insider views of Corbynism were, when using the language of religion media opponents regularly represented the movement as sufficiently vague and decontextualised in order to make sure that a sinister undercurrent could be maintained. The suitably malleable and ominous categories of 'cult', 'sect', 'fundamentalism', and so on, and even 'religion', with all the powerful cultural baggage of dominance, irrationality, deviation, weirdness and creepiness, were close at hand and could justify almost anything that was not deemed to be in line with the received political and economic settlement. Indeed, it was the emergence of Corbyn as refracted through the traditional media that brought such language about 'religion' to the fore in contemporary English political discourse. But it was also the emergence of Corbyn that showed the possibility for change in both the political consensus and the ways in which such language about 'religion' might be maintained by turning it against the (former?) accusers or rethinking it as part of the potentially new consensus as the old outsider language was now (to some degree) embraced more positively. How far this language could be embraced positively is the subject of the next chapter and particularly in the leftist support for Corbyn that came from northern Syria.

6

Red Apocalypticism on the Corbynite Left: Martyrdom, Rojava and the Bob Crow Brigade

Introduction

It was partly because of an overwhelmingly hostile national media that Jeremy Corbyn and his circle turned to social media. This was, of course, a time when technological advances in communication (e.g., mobile technology) now provided instant and ongoing access to wider or different audiences at almost any time, whether in leisure, politics, or work, or any combination of the three. Given pre-existing leftist networks, it was perhaps no surprise that social media and mobile technology were able to mobilise the Left but by the time of the 2017 General Election the received wisdom in the traditional media (and on parts of social media) was that Twitter and Facebook were 'echo chambers' and were not especially useful for reaching a wider audience or in helping swing the mythical Nuneaton and thereby securing election victory. To some extent this was understandable given that (put crudely) in the 2015 Election social media was often overestimated (remember #Milifandom?) and the traditional media often underestimated. But the 2016 American Election revealed how much money and effort was going in to targeted ads on social media, while a meme-based subculture (e.g., Trump as Pepe the Frog or, a little earlier, 'Bernie or Hillary?') became close to, or even part of, the mainstream. In the UK, Corbyn's team had utilised social media effectively in his rise to party leadership and, with newspaper sales in the UK having been in long-term decline and the rise of sympathetic alternative media venues (e.g., Novara, Canary), the possibilities were opening up for disseminating the message beyond the traditional media channels. By the time of the 2017 General Election, and building on the successes of the 2015 leadership campaign, Momentum, the Corbynite group linked with the Labour Party, were not only getting activists on the streets but taking advantage of social media, including #forthemany hashtags, countless memes, Corbyn videos, attack ads and WhatsApp cascades (estimated to have been received by 400,000 largely younger voters on polling day).[1]

To some extent this must have acted as counter to the overwhelmingly Conservative and anti-Corbyn national press and it would become clear that Labour benefitted from keeping hold of younger voters. While much had been made of sections of an older generation struggling under the crises of neoliberalism, a younger generation with its own issues (not least in the costs of education and precarious employment) was becoming increasingly observed as Election Day drew near, particularly how they might affect the widely anticipated Conservative landslide. While the Labour Manifesto must have appealed to some younger voters, Corbyn also had cultural capital which no other political leader could match, as was seen by the 'Oh Jeremy Corbyn' chant, various Corbyn t-shirts, Corbyn rallies, Acid Corbynism, and his popular post-Election appearances at Glastonbury. But the promotion of cultural Corbynism did not just come from official Momentum channels. Against the backdrop of numerous thriving leftist meme pages, a number of Facebook groups dedicated to pro-Corbyn memes and humour became particularly popular, with additional subcultural capital coming through the support of Grime artists like JME and Stormzy.

In this world, allegations thrown at Corbyn for being a terrorist sympathiser or a Communist of some stripe (e.g., Maoist, Stalinist) were ironically embraced. Corbyn and his supporters were, for instance, promoted in 'Jezbollah' t-shirts, and cast in kitsch Maoist- or Soviet-style memes or photoshopped images with rifle-toting, balaclava-clad radicals, as well as other provocative anti-May, pro-Corbyn memes (e.g., Red London, Grand Marshal Corbyn's Patriotic Meme Collective, June 8 Shitposting Social Club, Depressed Vegetarians for Corbyn), and all sitting comfortably alongside various gifs and videos of Corbyn (or Corbae) as (or better than) Jesus, Obi-Wan Kenobi and Stormzy. Opposition politicians (including those within the Labour Party) and opinion writers in newspapers were regularly mocked, whether being called out for half-truths, giving up on Corbyn, or having their appearances modified for comic effect. This was a subculture that was largely ignored, or occasionally dismissed, in mainstream political punditry before the Election result but these were groups with tens of thousands of followers bypassing or laughing at the conventional channels of political thought.

With this in mind, I want to focus on one particular group who were associated with Corbynism and Momentum who embraced this kind of subculture, particularly through the Marxist-Leninist Red London Facebook group (with about 50,000 followers at the time of writing): the Bob Crow Brigade (named after the late trade unionist – more on which below). A group of revolutionary socialists mostly from the British Isles, the Bob Crow Brigade were active in northern Syria between the summer of 2016 and the summer of 2017 (though some may have remained) both *against* ISIS and *for* revolutionary change in Rojava, a cause which continued to have plenty of support among such social media groups on the English Left. Their provocative, comedic and militarised images, hashtags, memes and one-liners, some of which were aimed at politicians, likewise helped them gain a wider audience than a group such as theirs previously would and they made their way to the fringes of mainstream English political discourse, including the Labour leadership debates of 2016.

To an even greater degree than Momentum (though with some overlaps both in terms of ideas and affiliations), such groups had the freedom to function outside the ideological constraints of Parliament and the Labour Party bureaucracy, and they formed part of the extra-parliamentary pull on Corbynism. The Bob Crow Brigade and Red London were children of their time, immersed in pop culture alongside, or rather embedded with, left-wing theories. Leftist or pseudo-leftist journalists, activists, trade unionists, politicians and thinkers who were mentioned (often satirically and often in strong agreement or strong dis-agreement) include Marx, Luxemburg, Lenin, Stalin, Gramsci, Trotsky, Mao, Žižek, Gerry Downing, Bob Crow (obviously), Eddie Dempsey, Black Panthers, Angela Nagle, Corbyn, Jon Lansman, Laurie Penny, Owen Jones and Ivana Hoffmann. These were clearly people who were part of leftist discourse (even if in rejection) and could be contextualised as such. However, precise sources of ideas were rarely given so what I will do instead is look at some (though only some) of the most important relevant trends in Marxist and leftist thought (particularly contempo-rary), as well as some historical and social contextualisation, which will not only illuminate the ideas of the Bob Crow Brigade but, most impor-tantly for my purposes, help explain their particular contribution to the ongoing construction of radical martyrdom and, more broadly, the use of 'religious' language in English radicalism associated with develop-ments related to supporters of the Corbynite Left. In addition to their published interviews and social media activity, the primary sources used in this chapter include an extensive anonymous interview I carried out with them at the end of 2016.

I stress again that I am not necessarily implying that these were conscious influences on them, and they were probably not in certain cases. Rather, I am viewing the Bob Crow Brigade as part of broad leftist debates, struggling with questions of capital and themselves directing the debates for subsequent interpreters, all of which has obvious relevance for the ongoing construction of English radicalism. It should be emphasised that my focus here is not confirming the veracity of reconstructions of the historical realities in northern Syria. Rather, my focus remains mostly at the level of discourses and contextualisation of these discourses, particularly in relation to the Bob Crow Brigade and their language associated with religion and martyrdom. I will look at how such language highlights some contemporary leftist thinking on revolutionary politics, the leftist pull on Corbynism, and an insight into a leftist generation radicalised since the financial crash.

Rojava and the Bob Crow Brigade

Some background detail on the political context of the Rojava revolution is perhaps required for readers unfamiliar with such developments. The Bob Crow Brigade belong to the International Freedom Battalion (IFB) fighting for, defending and developing the radical political changes in cantons of Rojava in the wider context of the Syrian Civil War. The IFB consists largely of such leftist foreign brigades fighting under the People's Protection Units (YPG) who, in 2012/13, developed out of what was then thousands of fighters among existing defence units for and of Syrian Kurds. The YPG began to run military training which included different social, ethnic and religious groups and they have since been at the frontline of defending and fighting against ISIS and Jabhat al-Nusra. The Women's Protection Units (YPJ) were formalised in 2013 and they fight alongside, and make decisions with, the YPG. The YPJ grew out of women's liberation in Rojava (and has in turn contributed its own challenges to patriarchy) and from women with fighting experience in, for instance, the Kurdistan Workers' Party (PKK). The YPG and YPJ are part of the multi-ethnic, secular-democratic alliance known as the Syrian Democratic Forces (SDF).

Emerging from the Arab Spring and the Syrian uprising, the revolution in Rojava (at least in representations among sections of the English Left) foregrounded issues about secularised cooperatives, confederal rule, democratic socialism, freedom of belief and equality, among the most prominent of which has been gender equality and feminism. A number of leftist views have been present in the mix in Rojava. Organisation has come from the leftist Democratic Union Party (PYD), a party associated with the PKK. By far the most prominent individual example of leftist politics associated with Rojava has been Abdullah Öcalan, founding member of the PKK. During his imprisonment by the Turkish government, Öcalan shifted (though parts are disputed) from Marxism-Leninism towards democratic confederalism, social ecology, self-sufficiency, feminism and libertarian socialism, with influences from Murray Bookchin. Marxism remained an important factor and it was the Turkish Marxist–Leninist Communist Party (MLKP) who were not only an important influence on the Bob Crow Brigade but were among the most instrumental groups in developing the IFB.[2]

The fighters in the Bob Crow Brigade were, it seems, represented by volunteers from England, Scotland, Ireland and Canada (though sometimes described as the 'British Isles' section of the IFB) in their mid–late twenties to early thirties. The form of neoliberalism intertwined with the 2007/8 crash, and the political crises that followed, left its mark on the reasoning of the volunteers among the Bob Crow Brigade. Certainly, there was some traditional socialist rhetoric present (e.g., trade unionism, leftist critiques of the EU) and, in the case of a Scottish volunteer, a socialist upbringing involving stories of the Spanish Civil War.[3] But, rather than close identification with shipyards or coalmines of yesteryear, the language was now marked by an era of declining unionisation, indebtedness, rising housing costs, zero-hour contracts, low pay and temporary employment (rather than careers, professions or jobs-for-life) that became normative for a generation, though one which became increasingly interconnected through, and proletarianised under, technological advancements in communication, which in turn provided potential for distinctive protest movements (even if fleeting) and a shared identity or even class consciousness.[4] In this sense, it is important to note that an English volunteer from the Bob Crow Brigade listed a sample of jobs, such as 'assembly line worker, railway track-worker, farm labourer, removals, classroom assistant, bike courier, and unemployed/ black economy'.[5] A Scottish volunteer, who identified as 'working class' from the 'British Isles' (not 'Great Britain', which was tellingly rejected), similarly came through an (alleged) employment enhancement opportunities scheme which, in reality, meant casual labour, gardening jobs, bar work, and so on, none of which provided the qualifications for industrial work.[6] And yet they pointed out that in the main cities of Rojava (e.g., Kobane and Qamişlo) they may have been celebrated and honoured but people also warmed to 'the fact that we're just normal guys who've left low paid, low level jobs to be with them'.[7]

From this perspective, it is easier to see why this background could be perceived to be an ideological opportunity or adventure, even if such concepts might have gone against the expectations of peers. Indeed, some of the volunteers became active leftists and revolutionaries since the financial crash and, at least in terms of the framing of one interview, this was tied in with claims about commitment to staying in Rojava partly because of the lack of employment, housing and educational opportunities in their home contexts.[8] A more isolationist form of working-class identity also meant that the Scottish volunteer felt out of place in radical political networks in Scotland which, unlike previous generations (including those of the volunteer's parents and grandparents), did not contain a sizeable contingent of what might still be labelled 'working class'. Rather, the Scottish volunteer noted, such meetings were dominated by middle-class students whose world was too alien (see also Red London's endorsement of Mark Fisher below).[9] The neoliberal British Isles provided a point of contrast with Rojava, at least according to the framing of one interview where the volunteer felt more at home in Rojava and was prepared to die for such a cause, even if he was going to try to avoid death if possible. Tellingly, given the prominence of martyrdom in their language, the neoliberal British Isles did not appear to be a vision worth dying for because, unlike revolutionary Rojava, it would involve a dreary existence of just growing old.[10]

Indeed, class was an integral part of the rhetoric of the Bob Crow Brigade, as signalled in the very name. Bob Crow was the leader of the Rail, Maritime and Transport Union (RMT) from 2002 until his death in 2014, aged 52, and was the most prominent left-wing union leader during the New Labour and Coalition years. We will look further at the significance of the choice of name below in relation to class, but Bob Crow was namechecked because he was thought to embody or represent a certain 'working-classness'. As the Bob Crow Brigade put it, he 'didn't mince his words', and 'he was a working-class guy, with working-class politics, delivered in a working-class style'. But we can hardly ignore the resonances this choice of name might have had in English political discourse because, they argued (and not unreasonably), this background was unacceptable to the British media who ridiculed and harassed him (contributing to his death, they added). Now the media were forced to use his name again 'for a cause they can't criticise',[11] which we might add allowed for a *potentially* more positive media presentation of a certain militant working-class persona. With issues of class in mind, we might note one response to the naming of the Bob Crow Brigade from a senior figure in the RMT who was reported to have claimed that Crow (a long-time anti-fascist) 'would have been honoured that young people from Britain would fight the forces of evil in his name', and that, as a 'great admirer of the international brigades that fought in Spain', would have 'drawn the parallels with the new international brigades fighting clerical fascism and defending Yazhidi, Muslim and Christian workers from slavery and persecution'.[12]

The politics of the Bob Crow Brigade

Precise political orientation of the volunteers connected with the Bob Crow Brigade was not always clear, though Red London has played around with the Marxist(-Leninist) tradition with a consistent anti-Trotskyite view (Alliance for Workers' Liberty and Trotskyites generally have been the butt of plenty of jokes with hopes of clearing such types out of Labour and Momentum), as well as supporting Lexit (a leftist take on Brexit broadly in the tradition of Tony Benn and Bob Crow). Anti-fascism and a revolutionary outlook appeared to have been unifying features of the Bob Crow Brigade. Some spent their more youthful days in 'that anti-capitalist smash-up-a-bank thing ... probably out of frustration at the Stop the War demonstrations' failure to stop the war'.[13] Bob Crow Brigade-style photographs can be seen on both Marxist and anarchist Facebook groups and they told me that the unity and solidarity among the fighters came through being revolutionaries, irrespective of otherwise identifying as 'Marxists, Anarchists, members of social democratic parties' or being active in 'insurrectionary circles' which is a view implied or interpreted elsewhere.[14] On other occasions, however, Bob Crow Brigade members stressed a more definitively Marxist outlook, including noting the importance of the MLKP in the development of an international brigade.[15] They also foregrounded arguments which became standard in contemporary Marxism. For instance, they told me that 'as Marxists' they emphasised that 'postmodernism is simply the ideological result to neo-liberalism', a view which does indeed owe much to a Marxist tradition associated with Fredric Jameson, David Harvey and Perry Anderson.

Here the name 'Bob Crow' took on further significance, particularly his openly Marxist persona (which was part of the intense media hostility). Crow identified as a 'Communist/socialist', had busts of Marx (until stolen) and Lenin in his office, named his Staffordshire bull terrier 'Castro', wanted the monarchy replaced with Tony Benn installed as President, and was an admirer of arguably the only union leader more famous and infamous in English political discourse over the past 40 years, Arthur Scargill, the socialist and former leader of the National Union of Mineworkers.[16] Rather than choosing a figure from the more distant past, the Bob Crow Brigade wanted a figure who reflected 'our politics today' and this involved his outspoken 'Marxist-Leninist politics' and 'refusal to accept Blairism and "social partnership" trade unionism'.[17] In English and British political discourse, Crow was distinctive for many reasons, from his pugnacious working-class persona to his media reputation as a 'dinosaur', an allegedly outdated figure from a time when unions held more power. However, against the 'dinosaur' allegation, we should rather see Crow as a figure who, along with other union figures elected around the same time, was very much of the present. Crow especially represented a reaction to the privatising agendas in the neoliberalism of Thatcher and Blair and was able to confront this head-on in a growing sector where gains for workers were possible. Indeed, Crow saw RMT membership grow after years of general union membership decline since Thatcher and membership pay rise after anti-union policy and legislation under both Conservatives and Labour, not to mention wage stagnation in the years before and after the 2007/8 crash.

Certain statements made by Bob Crow Brigade members pushed in a clear Marxist direction. They told Kevin Hoffmann that while acknowledging the hope that Rojava was a 'beacon of egalitarian politics and progressive policies', and that self-rule and independence (particularly for non-Kurdish areas) might not sound like 'outright Marxism', the revolution should be of interest to Marxists. This was because what was happening in Rojava was deemed to be the first step towards a democratic or bourgeois revolution and thus, according to this conventional Marxist understanding, this would be the requirement for a socialist revolution to then happen. They rejected the idea that Rojava had, or even claimed to have had, a full Communist revolution because while there had been some redistribution of land, some communes, some cooperatives, and so on, there had not been a 'mass expropriation of the local bourgeoisie' for that would involve thousands of small traders and, as an agricultural region, Rojava was reliant on cross-border trade. Sticking to a conventional Marxist line, the stage after the democratic/bourgeois revolution was the beginning of the class struggle within the revolution and this involved the creation of industry and a developed proletariat. Here, we get a critique of the 'ultra-left' who, they argued, were not concerned with developing a left-wing analysis. Instead, this group were worrying too much that ideas of 'direct democracy, autonomy, ecology and feminism' did not become 'infected with forbidden and unclean ideas, such as support for Parties, stages of revolution, national liberation, vanguards etc.'. By way of contrast, these volunteers 'welcome[d] this infection' as part of 'the reality of socialist struggle'.[18]

These volunteers were critical of what they saw as a sentimental understanding of the revolution they associated with, among others, certain libertarians and anarchists. It is notable (and normative in discourses associated with Rojava) that the Spanish Revolution was mentioned as an example of a revolution which appealed to this 'ultra-left'. Indeed, while similar disagreements between anarchism (or more libertarian forms of Marxism) and Marxism (particularly but not exclusively Marxism-Leninism) could, of course, be found from the disagreements between Marx and Bakunin onward, there is a leftist history of such disagreements in English and British political discourse with particular focus on what is to be done with such revolutions 'from below'. As I have argued elsewhere, competition between anarchism and Marxism over the legacies of the Spanish Civil War, 1968 and the English Civil War, has been present in English political discourse, including debates about naivety, degrees of radicalism, 'history from below', liberty, authority, gender, vanguardism, Bonapartism and Popular Frontism.[19] In the case of the tradition of the radical English Revolution/Civil War, the Bible and religion have played roles in such leftist constructions and in the legacy of influential readings by, for instance, George Orwell, Christopher Hill, Sheila Rowbotham and Tony Benn, and found in some of the most prominent figures on the contemporary Left, such as Corbyn, Lindsey German, John Rees and Owen Jones, as well as pamphleteering radical historians like Ian Brooke. For all the focus on Diggers and

Levellers, the constant discussions of Cromwell also meant that the question of authority and an authority figure – and whether this was a Good or Necessary Thing – lurked in this tradition.[20]

All these overlapping issues associated with both Marxism and anarchism, which are not easily disentangled, were regularly present in the thinking about the revolution in Rojava (including plenty of websites and in online debate). In this respect, the prominent presentations of Rojava from the Bob Crow Brigade through to the anarchist assessments by Zaher Baher (Haringey Solidarity Group) or David Graeber (London School of Economics) were the latest manifestations of a long-term debate in English political discourse on the Left when discussing the notion of a revolution from below. But one reason why the tensions between anarchism and Marxism, at least in certain forms, could have been more muted in the context of Rojava was because of overlapping interests and shared enemies, as well as solidarity with, and respect for, IFB anarchists such as the Revolutionary Union for Internationalist Solidarity (RUIS). We will return to various conceptions of overcoming a seemingly immovable common enemy but here we will turn to a particular one – fascism – because ISIS-as-fascism was associated with perhaps the most well-known discourses on 'religion' and concerning Syria. We will then look at concepts more obviously associated with radical understandings of certain biblical allusions that emerged in the language of the Bob Crow Brigade in overcoming the enemy – faith and miracle – before turning to the most central feature of their rhetoric: martyrdom.

ISIS, fascism and fundamentalism

The distinctive social media presence of the Bob Crow Brigade may have provided an alternative to the traditional media outlets and led them directly through to potential sympathisers, but it was also a playful way of getting into the *Daily Mail*, the *Independent*, *The Times*, and, less surprisingly, the *Morning Star*.[21] In particular, it was during Owen Smith's leadership challenge to Corbyn in the summer of 2016 that interventions from the Bob Crow Brigade provided their own take on the increasingly common blurring of social media and mainstream media in the generation of news stories. The catalyst for involvement of the Bob Crow Brigade in the Labour leadership election was an immediately controversial remark made by Smith in answer to a question about potential negotiations with ISIS: 'all solutions to these sorts of crises, these sorts of international crises, do come about through dialogue. So eventually if we are to try and solve this all of the actors do need to be involved.'[22] As well as criticising Owen Smith for betraying Corbyn, Bob Crow Brigade's tweeted responses, and the accompanying photographs, were what got them into the mainstream English media, in addition to tweets and photographs in solidarity with RMT guards striking against Southern Rail. Tweets were accompanied by pictures of Brigade members armed, masked and in front of the tweet written on the background wall (Figure 6.1):

.@owensmith2016 want to talk to ISIS? Tell that to the martyrs of Manbij #BobCrowBrigade (@bobcrowbrigade, 25 August 2016)

.@hilarybennmp banging on about the International Brigades one minute, then backing someone who would make deals with ISIS fascists the next (@bobcrowbrigade, 27 August 2016)

.@hilarybennmp from the actual international brigades fighting Daesh: when will you condemn your mate Owen's words? (@bobcrowbrigade, 27 August 2016)

The additional targeting of Hilary Benn is significant because of his role as the catalyst for the anti-Corbyn movement in the Parliamentary Labour Party. But it is also significant because, as we saw, Hilary Benn

Figure 6.1   Bob Crow Brigade's tweeted message for Labour leadership contender, Owen Smith
Permission: Bob Crow Brigade.

used the label 'fascist' for his take on the 'perversion of Islam' trope and, as these tweets obviously noted, this tied in his support for the bombing of Syria with the International Brigades in the Spanish Civil War.

Already, then, we see (as we did in Chapter 2) that the Bob Crow Brigade were involved in competing discourses about the nature of ISIS. The line of 'anti-fascism' was an important rhetorical move for the Bob Crow Brigade (and well beyond) because the revolution in Rojava relentlessly tapped into the mythology of the Spanish Civil War, with ISIS regularly cast as the fascists. This stood in sharp contrast to the popular discourses (fair or not) of the contemporary Left (especially Stop the War Coalition, Socialist Workers Party and Respect) as appeasers or accommodating of 'Islamofascism', 'Islamists' or the 'Islamic Right' (or whatever inevitably problematic term is chosen). These tensions were heightened after the ISIS-linked terror attacks in Paris, Nice and Brussels, particularly over issues of causality simplified in media reporting (with arguments along the lines of 'the Left are being PC for not blaming a perversion of Islam', 'the Charlie Hebdo attacks cannot possibly be linked to Western foreign policies', etc.), though this was a narrative challenged to some extent by Corbyn after the Manchester and London attacks in 2017. Of course, as also noted, the reality was much more complicated and an explanation that was serious about understanding such matters would need to address both issues of personal motivations in relation to understandings of 'religion' and the impact of Western foreign policy in the Middle East and North Africa, in addition to localised socio-economic issues, postcolonial migration, attitude shifts, and much, much more. Indeed, there were populist leftist presentations of the complexities in relation to Islam and terror, most famously perhaps Terry Eagleton's response to New Atheism in *Reason, Faith and Revolution*.[23] Nevertheless, at the level of the traditional media and political discourses, including social media venting, the binary of either Bad Islam or Foreign Policy, with plenty of accompanying polemic, remained common.

However, Rojava and the actuality of fighting ISIS provided an opportunity for those critics of 'religion' on the Left, if not to come to the fore, then at least to have a voice without compromising beliefs relating to a critique of Orientalism. Indeed, Meredith Tax – a prominent critic of leftist tolerance of those on the homophobic and misogynistic Islamic Right – later discovered to her pleasant surprise that in Rojava there were women collectively acting and fighting ISIS which functioned (for Tax) as an antidote for a poisoned Left.[24] Tax was careful not to essentialise Muslims and wrote about patriarchy in North Africa and the Middle East as a concept that covered a range of religious affiliations in the regions. She was critical of 'fundamentalism' and saw global fundamentalism partly as a reaction against the successes of the global women's movement. Rather than focus on, for instance, the significance of the labour of women for propping up neoliberalism, Tax argued that the Left (including some feminists) too often would support theocratic fundamentalists in the Middle East, cheer their representatives, endorse 'jihadis' in Iraq, and defend bodily subjugations of women. Nevertheless, feminists were still prominent in criticising religious fundamentalisms, not least, she noted, because women were often the ones being attacked. While Tax and her allies were formulating responses, so too were those involved in the revolution in Rojava in the face of ISIS and she concluded that 'they have shown the world new ways to dream about democracy, equality, and living together'.[25]

This was close to the logic of the Bob Crow Brigade who were especially vocal in challenging the cliche of the Left as sympathisers of illiberal Islam. As far as I am aware, there was little evidence of them pushing the line of distortion of a purer Islam that was ubiquitous in mainstream discussions of the issue from Left to Right, partly because of their firmer emphasis on ISIS-as-fascists. They acknowledged the struggle behind the problematic allegations of terror apologists, noting that Western leftists wanted 'to condemn Salafism and Jihadism whilst not writing off the material reasons behind resistance movements against imperialism like Hamas or Hezbollah'. Indeed, as we have seen, they tied this sort of position in with Corbyn by taking his view of 'a perversion of Islam' further in their SMASH ISIS, VOTE CORBYN picture (Figure 6.2). For the Bob Crow Brigade, the problem was narrowed to the influence of 'Salafi Jihadism' and, as such, terrorism should be understood better as a product of a 'tiny, tiny group from Saudi Arabia'.[26] There were potentially more practical ramifications of this shift. The Bob Crow Brigade were keen to see this as part of a movement which could simultaneously attack 'imperialism for creating refugee and migration crises through the impoverishment and destabilisation of the majority world' while 'championing the concerns of the working class in its own country, and trying to turn them against imperialism'. And this, they argued, would allow the Left to be put in a stronger position by being able to make the claim that 'we have sent volunteers to fight ISIS ... the left is the enemy of Jihadism ... It silences the critics, and emboldens the people.'[27]

Figure 6.2 Bob Crow Brigade's endorsement for the 2017 General Election
Permission: Bob Crow Brigade.

The political miracle of Rojava

Yet there were also hints that the Bob Crow Brigade (consciously or not) belonged to a history of leftist appropriations of the language of religion and the Bible for their own cause, as well as in their critique of ISIS. The Bob Crow Brigade gave me an example with striking and perhaps, given the context, necessary similarities to a notion of the political 'miracle' that made this possible:

> None of us had the gall to dream that in the heart of the Middle East there would one day be a triumphant, anti-Salafist, socialist, feminist movement, that was secular, driven by the people not a 'Westernising' imperialism. And one detail after another; each positive factor has a related story of liberation and victory, a chain of serendipitous developments brought on by this small nation's breakthrough.

The notion of the luck or surprise of the revolution carried close similarities to a long leftist history of the unexpectedness in the face of the revolutionary moment and the building of a post-revolutionary society against the odds and hence gets labelled as a political 'miracle'. The idea that the 'revolution is a miracle' for Lenin involved tension between, on the one hand, organisation (e.g., party structure, propaganda, military activities) and, on the other, the unexpected and spontaneous. As Roland Boer has shown, the reception of this tradition in subsequent Marxist thought in notions of ruptures, eschatological moments, Messianic time, and Events (e.g., Benjamin, Jameson, Agamben, Badiou, Žižek) typically stressed one-sided versions of this tension, that is, the spontaneous.[28]

That this implicit sort of thinking pre-existed the Bob Crow Brigade is significant enough for tracing the intellectual influences on them. But we might add that they also inherited such assumptions from other relevant revolutions from below, though (as ever) it is difficult to say whether this was conscious or not. Nevertheless, these ideas recur in thinking about similar issues, and so it is perhaps no surprise that they might recur in thinking about Rojava, including elsewhere in the output of the Bob Crow Brigade (see below). As an illustrative aside, we can briefly turn to two prominent examples of lauded 'revolutions from below'. First, in terms of English political discourse – and one of the centrepieces of the mythology of English radicalism noted by at least one member of the Bob Crow Brigade and figures close to Red London and the RMT – is its own revolution from below, the English Civil War, and its most influential interpreter on the English Left, Christopher Hill. Hill's understanding of the English revolution, where 'literally anything seemed possible',[29] foregrounded both sides of Boer's tension. Hill effectively constructed the views of his hero Gerrard Winstanley on the foundations of communal land use and economic democracy. Conceived 'in the cruel winter of 1648–9', this was 'so novel and so important that he attributed it to a divine command'. Obviously in the case of Hill's Winstanley we are dealing with something that was understood more 'supernaturally' than the standard Marxist miracle but the principle remained the same, and certainly for Hill. Moreover, in this same immediate context, Hill wrote that Winstanley had a vision which stressed the importance of working together, organising, and cultivating upon the common land.[30]

Second, arguably *the* great post-1917 revolution from below in Western leftist mythology was, of course, the Spanish Civil War which, as we have seen, was tied in with constructions of religion and Rojava in relation to understandings of fascism, and was an unsurprising radical reference point in the left-wing upbringing of a Scottish fighter in the Bob Crow Brigade. Given the overlapping anarchist and Marxist sympathies in and around Rojava and found in interviews with the Bob Crow Brigade, we might note the especially relevant example of something like the political miracle in the hands of one of the most famous leftist interpreters: Noam Chomsky. Chomsky, who repeatedly chastised irrelevant academic leftists and praised ongoing, day-to-day, and relevant hard work, likewise stressed the importance of organisation in leftist activism in relation to the Spanish Civil War, and if anything over the remarkableness of the revolution.[31] For Chomsky, the explosion and implementation of radical ideas in what he here called the Spanish *Revolution*, 'didn't just happen out of the blue', and he even took the emphasis away from the argument that it was 'spontaneous'. Instead, these things 'happened out of maybe fifty years of serious organizing and experimentation, and attempts to try it, and failures, and being smashed up by the army, and then trying again … it came from a lot of experience, and thinking, and working'. And so, once the mysterious 'revolutionary moment came', there was some idea about what to do on a mass scale.[32]

These are just two popular interpretations of what were, in leftist mythology at least, comparative revolutions from below where the combination of remarkable surprise and organisation were part of the ongoing ideological assumptions behind notions of the political miracle. That Rojava could be deemed a comparative revolution from below (with the Spanish Civil War in particular) with shared ideological assumptions was clear enough from Bob Crow Brigade interviews through to YPJ propaganda, and Rojava would almost inevitably be interpreted in light of such a heritage, consciously or otherwise. Yet this mythology was also potent because of the ongoing perception of an *absence* of an obvious Western revolution from below. Here, we can return to Boer's reading of the political miracle and his criticism of Western Marxist intellectual thought, particularly the lighter emphasis on organisation for the revolution and heavier emphasis on quietism, a move which would bring the Marxist-Leninist Boer in (curious) alignment with Chomsky. For Boer, this was due to the 'forlorn status of these largely Western Marxists' where the power of capitalism has been underestimated and a Communist revolution has never succeeded.[33] While such competing ideas were deeply embedded in Marxist discourses, they were undermined in *Western* Marxism in the past couple of years, and particularly in 2016, through the arguments of American Marxist academic and activist Jodi Dean, who emerged as a major voice in relation to Boer's tension in the unexpected recent challenges to the American neoliberal settlement, from Occupy to Bernie Sanders. Dean especially stressed the combination of the unpredictable spontaneity of the crowd and the hard work of involvement in, or building of, a party to bring about actual revolutionary change so alien to the contemporary Western Left.[34]

This, and the full-fat Leninist version of 'revolution-as-miracle', were part of the revolutionary logic of the Bob Crow Brigade who can be seen as having been active in what was understood to be a startlingly *new* revolutionary situation emerging at the same time as the prominent claims of Dean, with both thinking through their situations in similar ways. But, strikingly, the Bob Crow Brigade had to stress their physical move just outside the constructed boundaries of the West as a means of aiming their polemics at the inertia and quietism of contemporary Western leftism afraid of, and detached from, revolutions. From this position they pushed to change the situation through emphasising the importance of (revolutionary) organisation – whether on the shop floor or the battle-field – and made internationalist connections, both important features of the rhetoric of the Bob Crow Brigade.[35] But the Bob Crow Brigade more precisely contextualised the sort of quietism that needed rectifying and the target here was one very familiar to that of Dean by the time of the 2016 American Election (see further below): the contemporary (neo)liberal settlement and its cultural logic. For instance, they told me that 'we have all been kicked in the crotch by postmodernism, repeatedly, with ever greater force, since the mid-1980s' which, they argued, resulted in inertia that involves 'a need to discuss not before acting, but instead of acting. A need to discuss our discussions, and then discuss how we discuss, and if we have the right to discuss.'

Faith and fidelity

As part of engaging in a situation like Rojava, with physical and ideo-logical risks (what if we die? what if it is not a genuine revolution?), the Bob Crow Brigade suggested that actions such as theirs would reclaim a 'key value' for the Left: 'faith. Faith in itself to overcome individualism and cultural isolation to create meaningful internationalism and faith in itself to take action.'[36] Of course, in general terms, perceptions of loyalty to and faith in the perceived rightness of any given piece of historic leftist thinking has been an integral part of the logic behind any number of the cliched leftist schisms (which Red London frequently satirised, alongside calls for vigilance and correct lines). But there have been some important Marxist ideas developed in relation to such notions of faith. Probably the most significant contemporary Marxist take on such issues has been Alain Badiou's concept of fidelity to the revolutionary Event and the radical possibilities opened up by the Event, which in religious studies was most famously presented in his work on St Paul, and has elsewhere been enthusiastically developed by Žižek.[37] Fidelity still required thinking and rethinking in order to develop new ideas for new situations but these new ideas were to be developed in light of the significance of the Event, even if the radical possibilities opened up by the Event appeared to be abandoned or defeated. And it still required faith despite all the uncertainty in what might come next.

The Bob Crow Brigade's rhetoric of *reclaiming* a notion of faith is worth developing here because Rojava was also a new revolutionary situation for the post-2008 Left. While the Bob Crow Brigade might theoretically have appreciated Badiou's fidelity to 1968, it was fidelity in the face of the seeming victory of neoliberal and postmodern settlement which, as the late British critic Mark Fisher showed, was part of a cultural malaise where alternatives to capitalism were barely conceivable.[38] This all fed into a major issue on the Left, namely, the notion of 'left melancholia', a discourse which diagnosed the late twentieth- and early twenty-first-century Left as marked by failure and fracturing, though perhaps deemed reinvigorated post-2008, depending on the theorist.[39] In the contemporary UK, the importance of the rhetoric of *reclaiming* faith may also be seen against the backdrop of perceived failures of a comparably newer generation of Stop the War Coalition-inspired activists from 2003 onwards who (to paraphrase the Bob Crow Brigade) failed to stop the war. Moreover, the Stop the War Coalition had the organisational might of the Socialist Workers Party (an occasional satirical target of Red London), which since 2013 was in steep decline after their internal treatment of rape allegations. We might also locate the reclamation of faith in the context of those who saw little progress after the soon-dampened student uprisings against the Coalition's tuition fees, and it is notable that Red London and, to some extent, the Bob Crow Brigade were critical of a perceived feebleness of student politics. Given all this, it is significant that the Bob Crow Brigade and Red London allied themselves with what is widely regarded from Right to Left as a near-miraculous happening just after the demoralising Conservative victory in 2015: the Corbyn movement.

The dramatic revolutionary moment of Rojava also stood in sharp contrast to, or at least some tension with, an older generation of leftist thinking. We might think of the sort of cynical or even reluctant acceptance of the status quo (the attitude of 'nothing will change, I've seen it all before') or a lack of a developed concept of an alternative to neoliberalism, just as the old Marxists settled into their comfortable positions on the New Labour frontbench. As Fisher not unreasonably argued, the naturalisation of retrospection, erosion of the future, and an anticipated future that failed to arrive permeated twenty-first century popular culture.[40] But the Bob Crow Brigade's reclamation of faith also functioned as an implicit critique of an older generation of leftists who did not win, gave up, or who had to look to displaced notions of revolution. In terms of the latter, we might even think of the prominent work of Fredric Jameson on utopianism and the displacement of revolution to more vague possibilities otherwise constrained by late capitalism, from the ongoing explorations of the utopian impulse in Sci-Fi to – and with an interesting partial realisation of what was actually happening in Rojava – the playful idea of (re)nationalising a de-militarised army and using its collectivism as an alternative to neoliberalism.[41] There certainly remained hope of revolutionary change in Jameson's thinking but it is notable that, rightly or wrongly, a major representative of post-2008 Marxism like Jodi Dean could respond with the argument that Jameson's military utopianism effectively avoided engagement with present political struggles.[42]

For recent English leftist discourse (and, of course, plenty of others), the most haunting failure or nostalgia for a lost past was the twentieth century itself, from memories of an ascendant post-war Left to the victories of Thatcherism, accompanied by a fraying faith in the Russian Revolution after 1956 in particular (i.e., Khrushchev on Stalin, Soviet intervention in Hungary).[43] Even Eric Hobsbawm was aware that his lasting fidelity to the 1917 Revolution was tenuous in light of the seeming dominance of liberal capitalism in the West. That Hobsbawm was repeatedly asked until his dying days to explain why he remained a member of the Communist Party is indicative of the dominance of a Cold War and post-Cold War discourse about The God That Failed.[44] As Žižek argued (in 2009), it is easy to mock Francis Fukuyama's notion of the 'End of History' but in practice the acceptance of liberal democratic capitalism as the only realistic solution effectively became the default post-Cold War position, including among (especially among?) leftists.[45]

Yet against the backdrop of a failed twentieth century and of perceived false dawns of the Stop the War Coalition or student discontent, it was clear that there was an immediacy underpinning the reclamation of faith by the Bob Crow Brigade because Rojava was a revolution that was amazingly happening in the here and now! This partly helps us understand the 'apocalyptic' or 'eschatological' language – and indeed faith – in their discourse. The following example is from the Bob Crow Brigade's Instagram account (14 November 2016), with an accompanying photograph of a fighter in a damaged building, and is particularly striking for its use of the Bible:

> We are not in the least afraid of ruins. We are going to inherit the earth; there is not the slightest doubt about that. The bourgeoisie might blast and ruin its own world before it leaves the stage of history. We carry a new world here, in our hearts. That world is growing in this minute.

The allusion to the Beatitudes (Matthew 5.5) came from a quotation from one of the most famous anarchists of the Spanish Civil War, Buenaventura Durruti, in 1936 (a few months before his death). These words, only ever reported in English, were in response to Pierre van Passen of the *Toronto Star* who suggested to him that, if victorious, 'You will be sitting on a pile of ruins.'[46] This was at the hard-revolutionary end of 'apocalyptic' or 'eschatological' thinking that remained part of a shared heritage between the far left and Christian and Jewish traditions found regularly in English and British radical political discourses. That this sort of thinking might be seen as part of the construction of 'apocalyptic' or 'eschatological' thinking in leftist discourse was further confirmed by the Bob Crow Brigade in various comments made in interviews. 'Now more than ever', they argued, 'the struggle to go beyond capitalism and imperialism is a life and death struggle, for the survival of life on the planet itself, so the left must once again think in terms of life and death.'[47]

Revolutionary martyrdom in Rojava

There was one dominant feature of such 'apocalyptic' or 'eschatological' language used by the Bob Crow Brigade (and among countless other groups and on social media in Rojava) that made it distinctive in English political discourse even on the Left and highly problematic for mainstream political assumptions about language associated with religion: a thoroughgoing concept of martyrdom and martyrs as 'immortal' (e.g., @bobcrowbrigade, 9 September 2016). Certainly, a rhetorical emphasis on martyrdom was not entirely alien to English radical traditions and it had recognisable overlaps with the 'apocalyptic' or 'eschatological' emphasis on an egalitarian reconfiguring of the social order. But this was not some vague political metaphor or merely an affirming nod in the direction of historic and heroic martyrs from some distant socialist past. Rather, the deaths described by the Bob Crow Brigade were happening in northern Syria and were understood as deaths which would help inaugurate revolutionary change. To use Banu Bargu's words from the related left-wing martyr traditions in related Turkish Marxism, such activities are part of an 'eschatological passage from oppression to emancipation'.[48]

One of the primary reasons for initiating what the Bob Crow Brigade described to me as 'our project' was in 'honour of the socialist martyrs, ones who fought entirely out of sympathy with the Rojava project rather than any ethnic or regional tie to the Kurdish movement, who we felt had not received the attention their sacrifices demanded'. This foregrounding of martyrdom for the revolutionary cause rather than 'just' a local nationalist cause (a point shared in the propaganda of the IFB, YPG, YPJ, etc.) is crucial in understanding the ideological tendencies running throughout their output. This was not simply bringing 'attention' (as conventionally understood) to, for instance, the death of the 19-year-old German-born fighter and Communist Ivana Hoffmann in March 2015. The national media did mention her death, but the national media had its own interests and it was no surprise that they were labelled 'bourgeois' by the Bob Crow Brigade. Instead, they told me that the social media spectacle had a distinctive ideological function in that it drew a different kind of 'attention', with the intention of drawing people to be revolutionaries and emulate Hoffmann's struggle.

References to 'martyrdom', 'martyrs' and 'immortal martyrs' could be found regularly in Bob Crow Brigade tweets and in interviews, and provocatively so. While closely related language of leftist martyrdom could be found in areas of the online Left (e.g., Worker's Spatula, anti-fascist groups) to denote a fallen comrade, any reader at home in mainstream English political discourse should realise how odd the martyr language of the Bob Crow Brigade would have been. Martyrdom for a socialist or revolutionary cause, or indeed a Muslim, Jewish or Christian cause (should they be distinguished from 'political'), was not the sort of thing that was typically palatable for more liberal understandings of religion, or indeed liberal constructions of religion in the hands of mainstream politicians. Certainly, language with similarities to martyrdom itself was not unusual, as politicians and journalists could talk about soldiers making sacrifices for the country and the popularity of being able to sacrifice life for the family is not difficult to imagine. Indeed, the Bob Crow Brigade's foregrounding of martyrdom may have been a mimicking of the one place where prominent assumptions relating to martyrdom remained in liberal political discourse and certainly in mainstream English political discourse, namely, the military or those who die in the service of the liberal state.[49] As the Bob Crow Brigade told me, 'Bourgeois culture makes a martyr of every soldier and police officer who dies in their service, not just in official parades but in every film and book and "like" on a picture on Facebook.'

Even though there was relatively positive reporting of anti-ISIS fighters in Syria, worthy death (for Westerners, at least) was never likely to be thoroughgoingly cast in terms of 'martyrdom' in the traditional media. This point has been shown in grim fashion. It was announced that Ryan Lock from West Sussex died on 21 December 2016 while fighting ISIS around Raqqa. News reports foregrounded heart-breaking stories about how his death affected his family, friends and community. A BBC News report (3 January 2017) spoke about Lock as committed to 'the Kurdish cause' and tried to explain that while it was difficult for people to understand why people get involved in a foreign war, some do 'feel inspired by this Kurdish struggle against Islamic State'. The BBC News report presented the concept of martyrdom but as something deemed distinctly Other: on the one hand, it was pointed out that the British government may see fighters on whatever side as breaking British terror laws; on the other, 'in the Kurdish community many people will see it very differently' and 'they' will see Lock and 'many like him as martyrs' (my transcript). Among other examples, a more extreme distancing from martyrdom, and a certain kind of 'Anglicising' of death, could be found in the Murdoch paper, the *Sun*, which unsurprisingly presented the tragedy in the way it would the death of a British solider (2 January 2017). The headline to the original article was 'BRIT DIES A HERO: British chef, 20, dies fighting ISIS in Syria alongside Kurdish forces in battle to liberate extremists' capital Raqqa' and explained that he was an inspiration to his 'anti-extremist comrades'. The updated version of the article framed Lock as a James Bond figure and, with reference to his previous job, retitled the article with a typical tabloid play on words: 'HOGS OF WAR: Brit chef killed fighting ISIS served roasts for family firm just a week before jetting off to Syria'.

While not without nationalist overtones, martyrdom as understood by the Bob Crow Brigade and related leftist traditions was, of course, clearly a deviation from devotion to the home state and for contemporary liberalisms. Almost by default, the language of martyrdom associated with the Bob Crow Brigade and other fighters in northern Syria picked up on a range of figures and themes on the radical and revolutionary Left (e.g., James Connolly, Rosa Luxemburg, Fred Hampton), the most famous being Che Guevara, who, according to Raya Dunayevskaya's memorial shortly after his death, 'has joined the ranks of immortal martyrs'.[50] Additionally, the immortality of martyrs could have evoked a wide range of potential meanings, whether in Rojava, English political discourse, or beyond. The ubiquitous language of the immortal memory of inspirational martyrs would no doubt have had some resonance among those familiar with popular presentations of groups like ISIS and it was also, of course, a concept familiar to Islam and Christianity in the region. Martyrdom could also have been part of the vocabulary of international Christian fighters, or those familiar with radical Christian traditions like liberation theology (we might recall that in 2015 Pope Francis recognised one of the most high-profile liberation theologians, Oscar Romero, as a 'martyr'). The killing of IFB volunteer Michael Israel (a friend and comrade of Lock) by Turkish forces at the village of Arima on 24 November 2016 was, as expected, presented as a martyrdom but it is worth noting that his Christianity was mentioned as a motivating feature of his political radicalism, with one propaganda memorial/meme quoting John 15.13 ('No one has greater love than this, to lay down one's life for one's friends').[51] The Bob Crow Brigade, it should be added, were represented at his funeral.

Nevertheless, the language of 'immortal martyrs' as used by the Bob Crow Brigade was directly taken from the Kurdish idiom Şehid Namirin, a phrase in related regional variations that is often found in military and nationalistic contexts to denote the fallen. But there were, as might be expected, close interconnections with the concepts of martyrdom developing in light of deaths and self-destructive tactics in extra-parliamentary, revolutionary Turkish Marxism, concepts which managed to transcend the factionalism of the regional Left.[52] Such issues were known to the Bob Crow Brigade, though they stressed to me that in the case of Rojava, the death count was unprecedented for its type. The language of martyrdom also had more precise resonances in English radical discourses which they brought with them to Rojava.

One of the major points of reference for the English Left was the trade-unionism-in-the-making of the nineteenth-century Tolpuddle Martyrs, who had strong Methodist connections. There was a museum and monument erected in their name as well as an annual summer festival which featured luminaries of the Left, such as Tony Benn and Bob Crow himself. The Tolpuddle Martyrs Festival and Museum also issued a statement after Crow's death, memorialising him (and elsewhere Benn) firmly in the same tradition: 'He was a great fighter and leader who fought in the same spirit as the Tolpuddle Martyrs, and a great friend and frequent guest at our Festival.'[53]

Yet while the uses of martyrdom in the language of the Bob Crow Brigade may well have had resonances in internationalist, Turkish, Kurdish and English political discourses, they referenced one of the most famous socialist anthems (or indeed a 'parting hymn'), 'The Red Flag', fittingly penned by an Irish radical Republican who also worked in London, Jim Connell. In one IFB picture (Figure 6.3), the fighters are pictured on a roof with the graffiti: WITH THE BLOOD OF THE MARTYRS OUR FLAG IS RED. Picking up on the lyrics of 'The Red Flag' ('The people's flag is deepest red, It shrouded oft our martyred dead … Though cowards flinch and traitors sneer, We'll keep the red flag flying here'), Red London used the tagline, 'Though cowards flinch and traitors sneer we fight on, proud of our past and sure of our socialist future. With the blood of the martyrs, our flag is red.' To provide some further contextualisation, the hymn was famously held in disdain by New Labour but, true to form, Bob Crow owned a brick from the house of Jim Connell. On the brick were the immortal words, 'The people's flag is deepest red, It shrouded oft our martyred dead.'[54]

Unsurprisingly, then, the ideas of the death and immortality of these martyrs incorporated a cluster of recognisable radical and revolutionary positions. Though martyrdom was not prominent in mainstream presentations of the Left, its language was not entirely absent either. In 2016, anarchist street group Class War framed (through a meme) the handling of activist Jane Nicholl by the police in terms of perhaps the most famous martyrdom – the crucifixion of Jesus. Even so, the notion of police brutality was hardly an alien one to the far left (and certainly not to Class War) and in stark contrast to martyrdom in Turkish Marxism, the realities of actual death for The Cause had not been something prominent in English leftism and was more typically presented as a proud but distant memory of a glorious socialist past. This point was not lost on the Bob

Figure 6.3   IFB and the Red Flag
Permission: Bob Crow Brigade.

Crow Brigade ('martyrdom is a concept long forgotten by the Western left'[55]) who likewise saw the reclamation of martyrdom in contemporary Western leftism as something distinctive. Indeed, there was the implication that a certain Orientalism had been at play when they told me that the Western Left was dismissive of the language of martyrdom as 'a crude or simplistic way of dealing with deaths brought on by overly violent movements in uneducated lands'. However, they elsewhere said that it was essential to defeat 'the modern Western neo-liberal mindset of inertia and selfishness that says, "your life is far too important to sacrifice or even risk"'.[56] In this respect, one piece of promoted propaganda is striking in that it utilised famous words from subcultural memory. A picture of Mancunian anti-fascist graffiti, around the corner from one featuring Palestinian solidarity and another proclaiming the certainty of socialism, read: THERE IS A LIGHT AND IT NEVER GOES OUT (Figure 6.4). As readers will no doubt be aware, this referenced a popular – perhaps *the* most popular – song of the same name by the influential Manchester indie band The Smiths, which includes lyrics about dying by your side as a heavenly way to die. So there we have it: countercultural martyrdom with added subcultural capital.

There were, of course, more immediately brutal reasons for the use of martyrdom language. In answer to what might have seemed a somewhat dim-witted question about the prevalence of such language, the Bob Crow Brigade simply (and politely) told me that people were dying

Figure 6.4   A light that never goes out: IFB graffiti in northern Syria
Permission: Bob Crow Brigade.

regularly and there was no alternative term for someone who gave their life for a cause. It might be suggested that this was a means of coping and constructing a degree of political agency against the sheer enormity of the task at hand in the face of the might of the Turkish state and an organisation like ISIS, not to mention the repeated awareness among the fighters that the might of the American state could be around the next corner. The other, or interrelated, great oppositional and seemingly inde-structible force in this sort of thinking was, of course, capitalism. Here we might recall the eschatological claim that has become associated with Jameson and Žižek, namely, that it is easier to imagine the end of the world than it is to imagine the end of capitalism, its revolution-ary overthrowing, or even a more modest radical change in capitalism.[57] Monotonous repetition of the present was all that was imaginable and for Mark Fisher, the influential contemporary British representative of this sort of thinking, the use of this saying by both Jameson and Žižek encapsulated what he meant by 'capitalist realism', that is, capitalism assumed to be the only political and economic system with a coherent alternative impossible to imagine. In dystopian terms, this was a world of ironic postmodern detachment where even our anti-capitalism was performed for us (e.g., in film) and where dangerous hopes for a better future were instead traded in for the promise of protection from fanaticism.[58]

The claim of the prevalence of capitalist realism was a position shared with the Bob Crow Brigade and Red London. On 13 January 2017, it was announced that Fisher had died, and Red London provided a tribute. This tribute was accompanied by probably his most controversial article (from 2013) which particularly influenced Red London, and which was critical of so-called 'identity politics' that Fisher (like the Bob Crow Brigade and Red London) saw as dominating much of the academic and non-working-class Left (particularly on social media) and typical of capitalist realism. For Fisher, this trend involved an implicit (and sometimes explicit) hostility to class-based politics and thus functioned as a privileged 'bourgeois-liberal perversion and appropriation of the energy' of leftist movements by focusing on identity (other than class), individuals, individualism, guilt, and looking for niche victims.[59] Red London took seriously Fisher's call to exit the perceived sapping of this Vampire's Castle (Fisher's metaphor) and Red London's 'Gary Oak' took this logic one step further by joining the revolution in Rojava and forming the Bob Crow Brigade.

Nevertheless, even upon exiting Fisher's Vampire's Castle, if capitalism could still be perceived to be the seemingly unchanging and unchangeable eschaton, then how could such a powerful construct be overcome? Clearly, there was a revolutionary Marxist logic to this that was shared by the Bob Crow Brigade and here we could turn to any number of theorists on the necessity of revolutionary violence from the nineteenth century onwards to provide contextualisation, most obviously Lenin in *The State and Revolution*. In terms of our neoliberal era, we might think of the common leftist argument about the banality and de-centred nature of often-ignored violence, from poverty to the conditions of those producing iPhones and how 'blame' can get shifted away from the inevitabilities of capitalism to the immorality of bad perpetrators or, in trying to rectify a given problem, hope getting displaced to the morality of charitable campaigners. Against this ideological backdrop, so a materialist argument might go, violence would then be categorised in bourgeois thought, not as symptomatic of capitalism but more in a diversionary sense as a sudden act against the state, law and society (e.g., terrorism, knife crime).[60] According to this logic, of course, the violent rupture of revolution and forced liberation is necessary to destroy the pervasiveness of capitalist ideology.

This was the kind of violent revolutionary logic that was infused in the thinking of the Bob Crow Brigade, as has been seen in their treatment of Western neoliberalism and in their criticisms of the inertia of the contemporary Western Left. But it was perhaps clearer still, and certainly pushed further still, in their claims to me that martyrdom must be integral in the destruction of what is assumed to be capitalist power: 'it is so inherent to the socialist belief that we will one day achieve a society without structural violence that we see violent death in the service of this cause as part of this greater whole'. Yet there was more to the role of martyrdom and death among the Bob Crow Brigade and here we can turn to the social anthropologist of (among other things) death, Douglas Davies. Death may be an unavoidable part of human existence but, Davies argued, human beings construct 'words against death' as part of the affirmation of life and hope for the future. For Davies, this can provide the means for individual adaptation and social survival: 'having encountered and overcome this experience, both the individual and society are transformed and gain a sense of power which motivates ongoing life'.[61] Or, as members of the Bob Crow Brigade put it in one interview, 'the best kind of life is given meaning by a communal attitude and actions that serve others, either specifically, or generally, in building a better collective society'.[62]

Language, rhetoric, performance, ritual, and so on are all important ways in which transformation-through-death can be carried out and looking at the playful social media presence of the Bob Crow Brigade, along with social media sites of the IFB, YPG, YPJ, and so on, soon bears witness to this. But, Davies further argued, if the (live) human body can express social values then illness and death provide some kind of challenge to society.[63] Davies also built on the suggestion of Zygmunt Bauman that institutions hide the reality of death by implying that death is under control and that if this were not the case the full force of the reality of death might be devastating for social life.[64] As I have argued elsewhere, this angle of Davies' work can be taken in a different direction in reading leftist thought, in that death can be constructed as a mytho-logical vehicle for sweeping revolutionary political change and creations of new social orders. In this case, I argued that this comes through the residual Marxism in the narrative of American origins in Sergio Leone's westerns, a point that also applies even more so to a number of more overtly left-wing Italian westerns and Italian revolutionary politics where notions of violence and anti-imperialism remained as prominent as anywhere on the Western European Left.[65] Martyrdom among the Bob Crow Brigade, and the IFB more generally, may likewise be seen as an updated version of this kind of leftist and Marxist discourse of violence, with death-through-commemoration constructing a degree of social order in order to pursue revolutionary upheaval, but also by using the shock value of death with the intention of smashing the neoliberal consensus back home.

In this respect, Bargu's analysis of martyrdom and 'necroresistance' in revolutionary Turkish Marxism has a number of features which are unsurprisingly applicable to Rojava. In this sense, martyrdom may function as a form (a 'sacralised' form, if you prefer) of Marxist vanguardism or the anarchist 'propaganda of the deed' as a means to provide an example of, and attraction to, the revolution in Rojava, correctly understood.[66] As the Bob Crow Brigade suggested, martyrdom 'is the ultimate demonstration of this way of living life, and should be used to inspire people – not only to follow directly in the footsteps of the martyrs and join an armed struggle, which of course only a few people can do, but in day to day tasks, movement-building and ideological development'.[67] The benefits of vanguardist or inspirational martyrdom were required back home as, they told me, the 'bubble of social peace' in the West was being burst by the impoverishment of the lands where violent struggle takes place, and that any serious defence of any historical gains made by the Left will mean facing martyrdom. If the Left will not 'integrate the dead into our world-view', and more broadly promote the emulation of 'selflessness of the martyrs', then 'we will lose'.

Nevertheless, the sacrifice of martyrdom became a crucial means of perpetuating the cause of Rojava – indeed, the certainty of the rightness of the cause – and even potentially attracting international recruits, particularly when coupled with the extensive social media presence of groups related to the YPG. In terms of the Bob Crow Brigade, not only was martyrdom foregrounded in their social media presence and in interviews, but so too was the certainty of the victory. Prominent among a backdrop of graffitied walls on one picture were the words, SOCIALISM WILL WIN (Figure 6.4). Deaths of the martyrs effectively became memorialised and a source of revolutionary authority and agency for the living, as well as becoming part of the cultural assumptions and regular practices among the community or communities, as can be seen in the repeated mention, photos, videos, and evocation of martyrs on the relevant Facebook groups (e.g., Institute for the Unity and the Solidarity of the People (SYPG), International Freedom Battalion), and in civil society in Rojava (e.g., memorial days, funerals, graveyard minding, material and social support for families),[68] while the Bob Crow Brigade (in addition to their tweets about martyrs) could suggest that part of inspiring a revolutionary movement might involve 'every progressive' having 'pictures of people like Che Guevara and Ivana Hoffmann on their walls'.[69]

What Bargu noted of the interconnected Turkish Marxist martyrdom tradition may apply here. The Communist ideal was pushed to a mythical future as victory was continually deferred as a 'chain of revolutionary martyrs stretches endlessly from the depths of history to an imagined end point of final victory'. The ultimate reward was to be for those lucky enough to live in the ultimate end times, those who will benefit from 'the actions of those who sacrifice themselves and who will commemorate the martyrs as immortal'.[70] The Bob Crow Brigade could likewise talk of a 'long line' of martyrs which, crucially, would not be 'an infinite number' and who will 'one day' be seen as 'both a historical abnormality of an inhuman time, and heroes for fighting against the conditions that make our historical era so'. These martyrs would not be forgotten and would be remembered for the consequences of their actions and thus the Bob Crow Brigade concluded their interview with me with a claim made with 'complete sincerity': 'the martyrs are immortal'. Furthermore, Bargu's notion of necroresistance and the 'long line' of martyrs reveal how such ideas could also function as a challenge to more dominant discourses and histories. In terms of the representation of Rojava, this sort of thinking functioned as a counter narrative to the labelling of Kurdish and international fighters as 'terrorists' by the Turkish government, a label that may well be applied in Anglo-American media in the future, depending on American policy in Syria beyond the current (and sometimes uneasy and often pragmatic or realpolitik) alliances between America and the PYD.

Gender and martyrdom

The revolution in Rojava became sometimes known as a 'feminist revolution', a not unreasonable representation of the changes happening in political culture in Rojava,[71] and partly inspired the British volunteer Kimmie Taylor, as well as the internationalist solidarity messages from

Figure 6.5 'International Freedom Battalion in solidarity with our sisters in Ireland fighting to #repealthe8th' Permission: Bob Crow Brigade.

the Bob Crow Brigade (Figure 6.5). The promotion of the YPJ played a major role both in challenging local patriarchal assumptions and in fighting the ISIS enslavers and sex-enslavers. But this was a shared assumption with English-based media presentations of the Bob Crow Brigade, at least at the leftist end. According to a *Morning Star* report, the partner of one fighter in the Bob Crow Brigade talked about being 'very proud of my fiancé, he is brave and dedicated in fighting against all forms of fascism, including the misogynistic and oppressive Isis', that the 'Rojava revolution is a women-led struggle', and that as 'a feminist and a socialist, I understand the importance of the international volunteers and the support they provide to the revolutionary struggle'.[72]

This revolutionary feminism was also part of the ongoing construction of the sorts of socialist traditions discussed above. In a feminist take on the notion of the political miracle, the Bob Crow Brigade told me that the feminist aspect of the revolution in Rojava was 'really the stuff of dreams', at least from the perspective of the assumed Western leftist. 'What progressive,' they added, 'hasn't dreamed of women taking up arms against patriarchy? Who could have credibly scripted "the most misogynistic force in modern times will give rise to women taking up Kalashnikovs against it"?' In line with a certain leftist combination of miracle and hard work discussed above, they kept the stress on organisation alongside the unexpected. For instance, they contrasted the views of an over-idealisation among Western supporters and the 'crazy expectations' of 'American anarchists' about the abolition of the police and an economy of communes with 'the truth' that the police had been socialised, that there was a women's police force, that there was a women's court of law, and that this was a localised street policing system that endeavoured to avoid criminalising people. Nevertheless, they still concluded with a sentiment of the unexpected in the single word sentence: 'Amazing.'[73]

But it was radical feminism in relation to martyrdom that again provided the most sustained example of the development of radical 'apocalypticism' in the hands of the Bob Crow Brigade, as becomes clearer still when we look at some of the histories of the relevant discourses. In their immortalisation of the martyrs, the Bob Crow Brigade, Red London, and the social media output of the YPJ, YPG and the IFB foregrounded the immortal memory of women who became martyrs – whether in the face of ISIS and 'fascism' or as part of the social revolution of Rojava – and the various social media pages highlighted the deaths of a long line of women who fought. The martyrs of (/for) Rojava were also constructed (implicitly or explicitly) as part of an internationalist tradition of women as martyrs for the socialist cause. Among the most prominent was Rosa Luxemburg who was already being given the label shortly after she was executed in 1919, as Max Bedacht's title made quite clear (*In Memoriam. To Our Comrades Karl Liebknecht, 1871–1919, Rosa Luxemburg, 1871–1919: Martyrs to the German Revolution*).[74] Luxemburg's name was not difficult to find in the propaganda of Rojava and was openly designed to appeal to potential international fighters. For instance, one YPJ commander, Zin, spoke of the revolutionary society as a victory made with the 'blood of the martyrs' while also making connections with women explicitly identified as *European* models of resistance, with Clara Zetkin and even Joan of Arc mentioned in addition to Luxemburg.[75]

Another significant tradition for understanding the rhetoric of the Bob Crow Brigade (and, by implication, the revolutionary feminist take on martyrdom in particular) was, as ever, the Spanish Civil War. The iconic prominence of fighting women in photography, film and popular memory of the Spanish Civil War has long been part of the gendered ideology of such representations of the martyrs of Rojava. This was certainly present in the memorialising of the Spanish Civil War in English political discourse and was no doubt part of an assumed tradition inherited by the Bob Crow Brigade (see below). For instance, one of the most high-profile leftist (admittedly with Trotskyite tendencies) constructions of women, death and the Spanish Civil War in recent decades came from the popular (on the Left) Ken Loach film, *Land and Freedom* (1995), where the role of women in the militia in relation to revolutionary thought and practice is one of the major themes. Moreover, if there is a concept of martyrdom in the film it comes through the revolutionary Blanca (*spoiler alert*). On the death of her partner, Coogan, she does not apportion blame (other than to the fascists) and says it is likely to have happened to any of them. Her words are also central to the funerals in the film, including her own, where death becomes a means by which the certainty of the revolutionary future is imagined, despite present deaths and failures.

The construction of women-as-martyrs in relation to constructions of language associated with 'religion' is significant because of the predominance of the masculinisation of martyrdom and political violence in Western (and non-Western) patriarchal societies. Despite women as agents of political violence, terror, or martyrdom (or however we categorise) having a long history, there remains a tendency to see this as an unusual phenomenon (note how foregrounding *women* as martyrs is part of the distinctiveness of this chapter). Women carrying out political violence can be presented as an especially terrifying deviation, as madness, a manifestation of latent hatred or revenge, or as a means of masculinising the woman and de-masculinising men. This is partly because of deeply entrenched idealised stereotypes about women as passive, domestic, private, nonviolent, nurturers, and so on – cliches which can be played upon to deadly and theatrical effect by the perpetrators – coupled with a common neglect of an array of complex reasons for undertaking violent acts. Even in contexts where women have been seen as, for instance, both fighters and mothers, the conventional patriarchal assumptions about a women's place can return post-violence.[76]

These sorts of assumptions were hardly alien to English political discourse and one of the most infamous tabloid examples was Samantha Lewthwaite who was linked with al Qaeda, ISIS and international terror activities, and tellingly nicknamed 'the white widow' (she was married to a 7/7 bomber). Gendered media cliches included placing the remarkableness of her behaviour against the backdrop of an upbringing that could not ordinarily be assumed to produce a terrorist. We repeatedly heard or read that Lewthwaite was the daughter of a soldier who served in Northern Ireland fighting 'terror', a pleasant and happy girl, a quiet and shy (or a loud and popular) teen who lived in Buckinghamshire (of all places), someone who might be found in a shopping mall, and 'mother of four' (or 'mum of four'). And yet, so the narrative goes, she was someone who somehow – perhaps due to the divorce of her parents or associating with dubious religious types – became a terror mastermind and an alleged mentor to a crack team of all-women jihadi fighters.[77] Notions of familial and gender normativity are clear enough, but we might note throughout the implicit racialising in that a *white* woman brought up in the UK doing such things was a perverse aberration of the behaviours associated with whiteness. Indeed, was this not also a muted form of the racial slur that is sometimes levelled at anyone deemed even faintly Middle Eastern or Muslim: 'suicide bomber'?

But what can be done (and was done by the Bob Crow Brigade) with these broad assumptions of race and gender involved in political violence is to turn them upside down and, as might be expected from the perpetrators, see such violence as a tool to fight injustice (and by implication revolutionary martyrdom as a source of authority), as they were for some time in leftish Kurdish thinking. A commonly promoted and deliberately de-masculinising idea in relation to YPJ propaganda was the rumour that an ISIS fighter will not get to paradise if killed by a woman, a view which we might contextualise in light of the fight against ISIS's own brand of horror and misogyny. For the Bob Crow Brigade, inverting some of the stereotypes about gender, race and political violence was encapsulated in one of the most prominent deaths (certainly in Western media outlets) of an international fighter for the revolution in Rojava, that of Ivana Hoffmann. The case of Hoffmann is of particular interest because it was not only her gender that was foregrounded in IFB propaganda but her upbringing and internationalism too. Despite not personally knowing her, her martyrdom was a 'huge event' for the Bob Crow Brigade because she represented both an inspiration to fight and 'a major shift in the relation between the left in the West and the left in the majority world' (Hoffmann was born in Germany to a German mother and Togolese father), uniting values across the globe that should likewise be acted upon across the globe.[78]

These materialist and internationalist takes on class, race, gender and sexuality (she was a lesbian, as was occasionally pointed out) underpinned their implicit take on martyrdom and were found in their solidarity with gender campaigns elsewhere. But they were also entangled with some of the fiercer disputes in leftist political discourse, particularly those involving gender, representation, and so-called 'identity politics'. As with the Bob Crow Brigade's conception of martyrdom more generally, this interest in gender was partly to critique contemporary feminism in relation to postmodernity and neoliberal hegemony (see the Red London meme, Figure 6.6), with significant overlaps with the influential and (in leftist circles) much popularised work of Nancy Fraser, Jodi Dean and Angela Nagle, the latter explicitly promoted by Red London.[79] The dominance of neoliberalism, they told me, meant an attack on the materialist basis for 'all theories of emancipation, including feminism'. Individualism had been rampant throughout all forms of analysis and given 'a maddening, postmodern twist', that is, personal feelings can override proof for claims. This, they argued, led to an idealist logic of *liberation* (e.g., people who might identify with a different race to that attributed to them at birth) to be applied to 'communities of immaterial subjects' (e.g., people who identify as animals) and 'even more immaterial subjects' (e.g., people who identify as dragons). This was part of what they saw as a 'serious problem' for post-60s feminism and subjective experiences of 'the personal is the political'.

The postmodern and subjective 'gender studies' or 'gender issues' (in line with Nagle, a certain reception of Judith Butler was implied here) – the near-inevitable consequence of neoliberalism, they argued – had 'almost killed' the notion of feminism as 'a collection of theories of the patriarchal oppression, of male supremacist society, and theories of women's liberation'. They pushed this further and argued that 'gender issues' had not produced material gains for women but instead had seen the rise of the anti-abortion movement, pornography and prostitution defended by much of the Left, alongside the 'pink princess' gendering of girls and a related rise in eating disorders. Instead, they lauded

Figure 6.6 What a feminist looks like: a Red London meme
Permission: Red London.

the feminism of their parents' generation and looked to 'the women's movement' or 'women's lib' from the 1960s and 1970s and the need to challenge neoliberalism. Instead of endless discussion about how we discuss and who has the right to discuss, they wanted to promote 'a new, proud, uncompromising and unapologetic socialist identity'. Indeed, they saw the women's movement in Rojava as not 'new' but 'real' feminism which gave 'simple' answers to hard questions (e.g., quotas and positive discrimination, alternative employment for sex workers) in contrast to postmodern feminism which, they argued, gave 'even more complicated anti-answers'. As 'Gary Oak' put it on Red London (3 July 2016) before departing to Rojava: 'mass politics ... will be less identitarian, less sub-cultural, more counter cultural'.

Conclusion

The language of martyrdom used by the Bob Crow Brigade and ubiquitous in social media representations of Rojava is, then, something that can tell us about a range of contemporary leftist ideas on class, race and gender, and thus their contribution to socialist and revolutionary understandings of language associated with religion. The Bob Crow Brigade and related groups and individuals in English political discourse, particularly those associated with Momentum, represented an example of the extra-parliamentary pull on Corbyn (particularly on foreign policy and terror – Corbyn was, for instance, critical of Saudi Arabia and Turkey) and in competition with the more centrist discourses of the recent Labour Party and the Blairite legacy. In terms of the construction of religion and the Bible, and the history of radical Christianity in English political discourse, this pull belonged to both a contemporary and historic 'apocalyptic' or 'eschatological' understanding of leftist social change and upheaval, particularly as it was refracted through the 'miraculous' revolution in the here and now. But the Bob Crow Brigade's emphasis on martyrdom and dying for a *revolutionary* cause was distinctive (distinctive in the UK, not in Rojava), as we have seen by locating the Bob Crow Brigade among related leftist ideas about revolution and death. This was not building on the rubble of a recently completed apocalypse like the Second World War or pessimism for a terrifying future (e.g., the impending nuclear wasteland) but death as an active agent of revolutionary change in the present. The language of martyrdom was not alien to English leftist discourse but the actuality of dying for The Cause had long been muted. This distinctiveness was again due to Rojava being an Actually Existing Revolution (or at least widely perceived to be one) and the constant threat of death in a warzone. But it also belonged to a reaction against Anglicised neoliberalism, particularly after the 2007/8 financial crash, and an alternative way of conceptualising life in the face of the drudgery of insecure employment.

Through a creative use of social media, the Bob Crow Brigade managed to have their moments in mainstream political debates, most notably in the Labour leadership election in 2016. But, despite their notable social media presence, particularly through Red London, their main ideas remained something that was alien to positive liberal understandings of religious language in mainstream English political discourse, including contemporary constructions of religion and radicalism (we might imagine the reaction if Corbyn publicly endorsed concepts of martyrdom for the revolutionary cause). Presentation of those fighting ISIS in Syria and Iraq produced by the House of Commons Defence Committee mentioned attacks on Kobane and Peshmerga fighters assisting in Kobane, but, as Margaret Owen pointed out, even here there was no mention in this report of Rojava, no mention of the YPJ and YPG, and no mention of their dramatic involvement in rescuing people at Sinjar.[80] Rojava did find its way to the fringes of party politics, even if concepts of martyrdom were less likely to do so. For instance, Derek Wall, the international coordinator for the Green Party, was perhaps the most consistent vocal supporter of what has happened in Rojava closest to mainstream English political discourse. But his was a voice from the left wing of the Green Party and it remained that this was not a widely known revolution beyond pockets of leftist parties.

Indeed, it is notable that the central language of martyrdom could cause some discomfort on the Left (including in comments left on Red London's Facebook page where the language became applied to socialist deaths beyond Rojava). And the language used to describe such a problematic concept was similar to politically mainstream dismissals of Corbyn in terms of religious irrationality, though tied in with a more overt dislike of (what is assumed to be) religion outside parliamentary discourses. Such criticisms could be found in certain leftist traditions. For example, on the suggestions that Öcalan gave advice from prison and the acceptance of fighters lacking military experience, one voice from the Left claimed that this implied the PKK/PYD's strength 'derives as much from fanaticism (combined with a semi-religious acceptance of martyrdom) as from any rational political strategy. This, of course, sounds very much like ISIS, despite all the obvious differences between the two types of cult.'[81] Nevertheless, by rethinking the Left, and its fascist Other, as those on the frontline against ISIS clearly did, and with the increasing popularity of Red London, their involvement with the even more popular Momentum, and a wealth of material just a couple of clicks away from reports in the online press, there remains the potential for more mainstream sympathies. These may well be the means by which the revolution in Rojava, and even concepts of martyrdom, can become a remembered feature in the ongoing construction of an English radical tradition.

Epilogue

The 2007/8 crash to the General Election of 2017 was a period that inaugurated the biggest challenges to the neoliberal settlement to date and helped generate distinct shifts in ideological tendencies in mainstream English political discourse, with authorising language about religion and related terms shifting accordingly from, or intensifying, the Thatcher-Blair template of economic and social liberalism.

Influenced by one aspect of Brexit, Theresa May toyed with ethnonationalist and economically protectionist understandings of Christianity and religion in rhetorical contrast to David Cameron's attempts at a more inclusive version of Christian paternalism and intensification of Thatcherism grounded in his notion of Big Society (founded by Jesus, no less). May's move owed something not only to the right-wing press but also to the rise of a new(-ish) kind of far right which perpetuated racialised discourses through notions of Islam and Muslims as excessively religious, and thus the greatest threat to Englishness or Britishness, sometimes understood as ethnically Christian. Building on previous mainstream political discourse, May made a similar move while simultaneously distancing mainstream politics from the far right and any economic grievances they raised, as well as from potential complicity in terror through state foreign policy. She (like other leaders before her) did this through the typical political categorising of terror, violence and religious excess as a 'perversion of Islam' rather than 'Islam' per se.

On the back of a Left which had been gaining traction since 2008, Jeremy Corbyn stressed a socialist Christian heritage with the Bible as an implicit source for his take on welfarism and welcoming of refugees, as well as for the ongoing construction of an English or British socialist tradition. This was a tradition which seemed to have effectively ended when Tony Benn lost influence in his later parliamentary years and through the dominance of New Labour, but it now returned with the rhetoric of a socialist Jesus and socialist understandings of the Bible, particularly the example of the Good Samaritan. In terms of Islam, Corbyn also used the 'perversion of Islam' trope but not, for instance, as May, Blair and Cameron did when they focused on internal and external enemies.

Instead, Corbyn used this way of pushing groups like ISIS beyond the pale to suggest that foreign policy should involve cutting off financial support for state sources of terror rather than supporting them. This was an argument developed after attacks in Manchester and London shortly before the 2017 General Election and marked a significant shift in such political reactions which was near unthinkable among political leaders before Corbyn.

Whatever Tim Farron wanted to promote, he was ultimately significant in highlighting the ongoing influence of a certain kind of socially liberal understanding of religion, particularly involving questions of sexuality, which ultimately led to his downfall. Indeed, it was only on the maverick Right (notably, Jacob Rees-Mogg) that religion and the questioning of homosexual relationships had any significant mainstream support, though (probably like Farron) Rees-Mogg opposed certain relationships in terms of personal morality and church teaching and not on legal grounds where they were to be tolerated. Worries about a threat deemed more serious to this confused distinction between public and private understandings of religion meant that when the DUP were brought to the fore of English political discourse just after the General Election, it was on these and other issues of religion problematically understood (e.g., creationism) that they were immediately perceived to be an Americanised aberration of the norm. Unsurprisingly, these issues were emphatically not foregrounded by the Conservatives, such was the ongoing political importance of social liberalism.

As the case study of Barrow-in-Furness and beyond showed, these main tendencies were all found in a fragmentary way among voters but with a striking difference in places like Barrow: such voters did not want politicians invoking religion or interpreting the Bible. One reason for this was that, in line with the contemporary crises of capitalism and the common view that a managerial political class had abandoned voters, politicians were deemed to be almost entirely untrustworthy authorities. At best, religion was assumed to be a private matter and something that involved a basic morality (e.g., helping others) and, at worst, it meant that Islam and Muslims were a potentially dangerous future authority. This raises bigger questions about the future of religion, the Bible, Christianity, and so on, as a source of authority and cultural resource in English political discourse. Certainly, there was a presence of such language as of 2017, even in the seemingly most a-religious settings. But if church and Christian affiliations continue their decline, will these authorities be worth employing as a justification to future generations as older generations die out?

That Corbyn opened up the opportunity for political transformation from the Left, including nuances in the ways 'religious' language was used, was shown by the Centre/Centre-Left reactions to him. In the *Guardian*, for instance, the language of deviation from a normative 'religion' was used to denote Corbyn and Corbynism's overenthusiastic deviance from accepted neoliberal assumptions (largely accepted by the *Guardian*, with telling exceptions), capitalism, and even rationality itself. After the surprise 2017 General Election result, there was some evidence of a rethinking, modifying and reconceptualisation of such language as the constructions of the boundaries of political consent (or Overton window, if you prefer) began to shift.

On the Corbynite Left, this opening up of opportunities was seen among galvanised younger voters and various social media subcultures which had some influence on the Election. In terms of the construction of religion, this involved ironic application of devotional language and imagery to Corbyn and his key supporters but also engagement with probably the most significant revolution (crucially understood as a feminist one) for the post-2008 Left in Rojava, northern Syria. Through Rojava, ideas about politically miraculous transformations, anti-fascism (with fascism now assumed to include ISIS), and a renewed 'faith' in the leftist cause were being developed by, for instance, the Bob Crow Brigade and their London-based proxies and comrades associated with Corbynism and the Corbynite group, Momentum. More dramatically still, and in a move alien to liberal democratic assumptions about religion and the state in English political discourse, martyrdom in the sense of physically dying *for* the revolutionary cause, and *against* the neoliberal settlement, was also taken up and used more widely among anti-fascist groups.

We now await the longer-term consequences of this world turned upside down, or at least turned partially on its side. Just how wrong and surprised political pundits were between 2015 and 2017 ought to provide all the necessary warnings for anyone preaching predictive certainties. It is perhaps the wisest course, then, to point out from where some of the potential for developments in constructions of religion and related terms might come, with the qualification that there are still plenty of unknowns. Perhaps the most obvious prediction involves the assumptions about religion in its essential or most palatable form will continue to be understood as compatible with social liberalism, particularly as British social attitudes have been increasingly accepting of, for instance, homosexuality over the long term. Given the current high-profile discussions over trans-related issues, for instance, we might speculate that mainstream understandings of religion could follow suit, even if merely acknowledging the existence of such debates.

Brexit remained intertwined in political constructions of religion. Whatever the Conservative future may be beyond May, there is, of course, a 'hard' Brexit tendency within the party (e.g., David Davis, Boris Johnson, Michael Gove) which could perpetuate May's then distinctive nationalist line on Britain as Christian country in contrast to a tolerated ('Asian') Other, though figures like Johnson are flexible (and erratic) enough to shift political direction if need be. Indeed, toying with ethnocentric and even protectionist understandings of religion could be an ongoing line irrespective of a politician's personal views on Brexit. After all, Amber Rudd, a prominent figure in the Remain campaign, was still prepared to front the Brexit-inspired proposal that companies should identify non-British workers.[1] Yet, an antagonistic Right and the significance of leading Remain Tories and anti-Brexit voting interests should not be underestimated. Indeed, by Christmas 2017, and after one not-very-successful Election where nativist rhetoric was employed, May brought back Cameron's rhetoric she previously overturned when she spoke about such vague values being 'lived out every day in our country by people all faiths and none' and mentioned coming together 'this Christmas … confident and united in the values we share', 'whatever our faith'.[2] At the time of writing, these Brexit tensions over the very notions of what is 'religious' in relation to the nation can be found across May's speeches on Christmas and Easter and remain acute among the Conservatives.

Whether the Liberal Democrats might push a strong Remain construction of religion in relation to welcoming outsiders is certainly possible, likely even, but the apparent lack of an obvious Remain surge, or the fragmentation of Remain voters, may result in a reassessment of where to place the emphasis. After the fall of Farron, and therefore the removal of a figure problematic for contemporary notions of L/liberalism, Vince Cable turned to reclaiming voters from Corbyn's Labour, or at least trying not to lose more. Indeed, Cable's first Christmas message in 2017 was strikingly similar to Corbyn's Christmas messages by focusing solely on homelessness, non-secure housing and rough sleepers.[3] But while

Cable addressed the sort of audience who might be attracted to Corbyn, there were limits and there was no stress on broader societal transformation found with Corbyn. The Liberal Democrats are, after all, a party for whom the notion of a benign capitalism is ideologically integral.

Quite what happens to constructions of religion in the Labour Party remains uncertain because of the surprising transformation under Corbyn. Certainly, he ushered in the return of openly socialist understandings of religion into the political mainstream, but potential challenges remain – not least the divisiveness of Brexit, freedom of movement, migration and exploitation of labour – which have continued to be difficult topics among MPs, members and Labour supporters. While there was a shift in the rhetoric of Labour MPs who previously did not support him, the drip of Blairite antagonism has continued in the press and we cannot discount the influence of ongoing and accompanying neoliberal constructions of religion once associated with the Tony Blair Faith Foundation.[4] Other factions within Labour and with an interest in such language also hovered in the background to the rise of Corbyn and remain present, such as the concerns for mutualism and social conservatism, and critiques of both immigration and neoliberalism, associated with Blue Labour.

Nevertheless, after the 2017 General Election, Corbyn was undoubtedly in his strongest position to date in terms of influencing the future of the Labour Party. As his Christmas 2017 speech confirmed, and where previous leaders effectively assumed that there was no alternative to the neoliberal settlement and a few tweaks might make Labour better managers of the system than the Conservatives, Corbyn constructed Christianity and Christmas in terms of people bringing about a new kind of 'society, and world, we would like to live in'.[5] What was crucial to getting Corbyn into such a position – and presumably will continue to be – was the mobilisation of activists and the role of Momentum. Like Momentum, or because of Momentum, social media was integral to developing such constructions due to a degree of freedom from the constraints of party bureaucracy. Here, some of the creative and widely disseminated use of memes and videos allowed a range of leftist ideas outside Parliament (and even unpalatable for Parliament) to flourish in such influential leftist subcultures. These included recurring images of Corbyn and Corbyn allies in terms of kitsch religious radicalism (including, should we classify him so, Obi-Wan Kenobi) but with crucial ironic distance which helped imbue them with the necessary subcultural capital. If this continues, and if the traditional news press continues its decline in terms of print sales, we may see innovations in social media as central to future understandings of religion in English political discourse, and indeed beyond. Unlike America, and with some grudging admiration from the Conservatives, this is a stronghold of the Left for now. But the American example should perhaps be the biggest worry for the Left and Centre (and even parts of the Right) because if the online alt-right and its white supremacist arguments become mobilised in relation to mainstream English political discourse then they could be part of a new form of new far-right perceptions of religion with subcultural capital that the present Conservative-related attempts at memes simply do not have.

Notes

Websites last accessed 9 February 2018.

Introduction

1. Slavoj Žižek, *The Courage of Hopelessness: Chronicles of a Year of Acting Dangerously* (London: Allen Lane, 2017), pp. xi–xii.
2. In this sense, this work stands broadly in line with, for example, Russell T. McCutcheon, *Manufacturing Religion: The Discourse on Sui Generis Religion and the Politics of Nostalgia* (Oxford: Oxford University Press, 2003); Russell T. McCutcheon, *Religion and the Domestication of Dissent: or, How to Live in a Less than Perfect Nation* (London and Oakville: Equinox, 2005); Timothy Fitzgerald, *Discourse on Civility and Barbarity: A Critical History of Religion and Related Categories* (Oxford: Oxford University Press, 2007); Craig Martin, *Masking Hegemony: A Genealogy of Liberalism, Religion and the Private Sphere* (London and Oakville: Equinox, 2010); Craig Martin, *Capitalizing Religion: Ideology and the Opiate of the Bourgeoisie* (London: Bloomsbury, 2014); David Tyrer, *The Politics of Islamophobia: Race, Power and Fantasy* (London: Pluto Press, 2013); William Arnal and Russell T. McCutcheon, *The Sacred Is the Profane: The Political Nature of 'Religion'* (Oxford: Oxford University Press, 2014).
3. Martin H.M. Steven, *Christianity and Party Politics: Keeping the Faith* (Abingdon and New York: Routledge, 2011), pp. 36–64; Ben Clements, *Religion and Public Opinion in Britain: Continuity and Change* (Basingstoke: Palgrave Macmillan, 2015); James G. Crossley, *Harnessing Chaos: The Bible in English Political Discourse since 1968* (London: Bloomsbury/T&T Clark, 2014; updated edn, 2016), pp. 18–29, 43–7, 98–102, 277–82.
4. Erin Runions, *The Babylon Complex: Theopolitical Fantasies of War, Sex, and Sovereignty* (New York: Fordham University Press, 2014); James G. Crossley, 'We don't do Babylon: Erin Runions in English political discourse', *Bible and Critical Theory* 11 (2015), pp. 61–76.
5. For example, Yvonne Sherwood, 'Bush's Bible as a liberal Bible (strange though that might seem)', *Postscripts* 2 (2006), pp. 47–58; Jacques Berlinerblau, *Thumpin' It: The Use and Abuse of the Bible in Today's Presidential Politics* (Louisville: WJK, 2008); Nick Spencer, *Freedom and Order: History, Politics and the English Bible* (London: Hodder and Stoughton, 2011); Roland Boer, *Lenin, Religion, and Theology* (New York: Palgrave Macmillan, 2013); Matthew Engelke, *God's Agents: Biblical Publicity in Contemporary England* (Berkeley: University of California Press, 2013), pp. 97–161; Stuart McAnulla, 'Cameron's Conservatism: why God, why now?', *Political*

Quarterly 85 (2014), pp. 462–70; Crossley, *Harnessing Chaos*; Runions, *Babylon Complex*; Andrew S. Crines and Kevin Theakston, '"Doing God" in Number 10: British prime ministers, religion, and political rhetoric', *Politics and Religion* 8 (2015), pp. 155–77; Eliza Filby, *God and Mrs Thatcher: The Battle for Britain's Soul* (London: Biteback, 2015); Robert J. Myles, 'Winston Peters "puts his hand to the plow": the Bible in New Zealand political discourse', *Journal of the Bible and its Reception* 3 (2016), pp. 135–53; Ole Jacob Løland, 'Hugo Chávez's appropriation of the liberationist legacy in Latin America', *Relegere* 6 (2016), pp. 123–60.

6. Engelke, *God's Agents*, pp. 62–3.

1 Religion in English Political Discourse, 1979–2017: A Brief History

1. Especially James G. Crossley, *Harnessing Chaos: The Bible in English Political Discourse since 1968* (London: Bloomsbury/T&T Clark, 2014; updated edn, 2016).

2. Margaret Thatcher and Brian Walden, 'TV interview for London Weekend Television *Weekend World* (1980)', Margaret Thatcher Foundation, www. margaretthatcher.org/speeches/displaydocument.asp?docid=104210; Margaret Thatcher, 'Speech to the General Assembly of the Church of Scotland (1988)', Margaret Thatcher Foundation, www.margaretthatcher. org/document/107246.

3. Hugo Young, *One of Us: A Biography of Margaret Thatcher* (London: Macmillan, 1989), p. 422; Charles Moore, *Margaret Thatcher: The Authorized Biography, Volume One: Not for Turning* (London: Allen Lane, 2013), p. 137.

4. Margaret Thatcher, *Statecraft: Strategies for a Changing World* (London: HarperCollins, 2003), pp. 418–19.

5. Margaret Thatcher, *The Downing Street Years* (London: Harper Press, 1993), pp. 509–10.

6. Margaret Thatcher, 'I Believe: A Speech on Christianity and Politics (1978)', Margaret Thatcher Foundation, www.margaretthatcher.org/ document/103522.

7. Thatcher, *Statecraft*, p. 221.

8. Ibid., pp. 250–1.

9. On recent Greens see, for example, Natalie Bennett, 'A time for hope: Christmas message from Green Party leader Natalie Bennett', Green Party (23 December 2015), www.greenparty.org.uk/news/2015/12/23/a-time-for-hope-christmas-message-from-green-party-leader-natalie-bennett/; Jonathan Bartley and Caroline Lucas, 'Green Party Christmas message', Green Party (23 December 2016), www.greenparty.org.uk/news/2016/12/ 23/green-party-christmas-message/.

10. See also F.O. Wolf and Tony Benn, *The Levellers and the English Democratic Tradition* (Nottingham: Russell Press, 1976); Tony Benn, *Arguments for Socialism* (London: Jonathan Cape, 1979); Tony Benn, *Free Radical: New Century Essays* (New York and London: Continuum, 2003); Tony Benn, *Dare to Be a Daniel: Then and Now* (London: Arrow Books, 2004).

11. Tony Benn, 'The power of the Bible today', in *Sheffield Academic Press Occasional Papers: The Twelfth Annual Sheffield Academic Press Lecture, University of Sheffield, March 17, 1995* (Sheffield: Sheffield Academic Press, 1995), pp. 1–24.

12. Tony Blair, 'Full text: Tony Blair's speech (part one)', *Guardian* (2 October 2001); Tony Blair 'Full text: Tony Blair's speech (part two)', *Guardian* (2 October 2001).

13. 'Iraq', *Hansard* (18 March 2003), Volume 401, Columns 767–768, www.publications.parliament.uk/pa/cm200203/cmhansrd/vo030318/debtext/30318-07.htm.

14. Gordon Brown, 'Speech and Q&A at St Paul's Cathedral: transcript of speeches by the Prime Minister and Australian Prime Minister Kevin Rudd at St Paul's Cathedral' (31 March 2009), http://webarchive.nationalarchives.gov.uk/+/number10.gov.uk/news/speeches-and-transcripts/2009/03/pms-speech-at-st-pauls-cathedral-18858.

15. Tony Blair, 'Faith in Politics', Speech to the Christian Socialist Movement (London,2001),www.britishpoliticalspeech.org/speech-archive.htm?speech =280.

16. Johann Hari, 'A civil partnership: interview with Tony Blair', *Attitude* (8 April 2009), pp. 50–2.

17. 'Marriage (Same Sex Couples) Bill', *Hansard* (5 February 2013), Volume 558, Columns 125–230, www.publications.parliament.uk/pa/cm201213/cmhansrd/cm130205/debtext/130205-0001.htm.

18. Hari, 'Interview', p. 52.

19. Andrew Rawnsley, *The End of the Party: The Rise and Fall of New Labour* (London: Penguin, 2010), p. 44. Cf. Tony Blair, *A Journey* (London: Hutchinson, 2010), p. 347.

20. 'Iraq', *Hansard*.

21. James Ball and Tom Clark, 'Generation Self: what do young people really care about?', *Guardian* (11 March 2013); John Harris, 'Generation Y: why young voters are backing the Conservatives', *Guardian* (26 June 2013); Anonymous, 'Generation Boris', *The Economist* (1 June 2013); David Stuckler and Aaron Reeves, 'We are told Generation Y is hard-hearted, but it's a lie', *Guardian* (30 July 2013).

22. Jo Latham and Claire Mathys (eds), *Liberal Democrats Do God* (London: LDCF, 2013).

23. Steve Webb, 'Introduction', in Jo Latham and Claire Mathys (eds), *Liberal Democrats Do God* (London: LDCF, 2013), pp. 1–4.

24. Jonathan Raban, *God, Man and Mrs Thatcher: A Critique of Mrs Thatcher's Address to the General Assembly of the Church of Scotland* (London: Chatto and Windus, 1989), p. 33; Thatcher, 'Speech to the General Assembly of the Church of Scotland'.

25. Webb, 'Introduction', p. 2.

26. John Pugh, '"Doing God" in the Liberal Democrat Party', in Jo Latham and Claire Mathys (eds), *Liberal Democrats Do God* (London: LDCF, 2013), pp. 7–12.

27. David Cameron, 'Prime Minister's King James Bible Speech', *Gov.uk* (16 December 2010), www.gov.uk/government/news/prime-ministers-king-james-bible-speech.

28. David Cameron, 'Easter reception at Downing Street 2014', *Gov.uk* (9 April 2014), www.gov.uk/government/speeches/easter-reception-at-downing-street-2014.

29. David Cameron, 'Easter 2014: David Cameron's message', *Gov.uk* (16 April 2014), www.gov.uk/government/news/easter-2014-david-camerons-message.

30. Richard Seymour, *Corbyn: The Strange Rebirth of Radical Politics* (London: Verso, 2016); Alex Nunns, *The Candidate: Jeremy Corbyn's Improbable Path to Power* (New York and London: OR Books, 2016).

31. Dennis Skinner, *Sailing Close to the Wind: Reminiscences* (London: Quercus, 2014), p. 108.

32. Owen Jones, 'Sorry, David Cameron, but your British history is not mine', *Guardian* (15 June 2014).

33. Terry Eagleton, 'Occupy London are true followers of Jesus, even if they despise religion', *Guardian* (3 November 2011).

34. Russell Brand, 'We no longer have the luxury of tradition', *New Statesman* (24 October 2013); Russell Brand, *Revolution* (London: Century, 2014), p. 68.

35. Patrick Wintour and Nicholas Watt, 'The Corbyn earthquake – how Labour was shaken to its foundations', *Guardian* (25 September 2015).

36. Owen Bennett, 'Cat Smith talks Jeremy Corbyn, Jesus Christ and why socialism isn't "radical"', *Huffington Post* (25 August 2015).

37. For further details see, for example, Robert Ford and Matthew Goodwin, *Revolt on the Right: Explaining Support for the Radical Right in Britain* (New York: Routledge, 2014) and Simon Winlow, Steve Hall and James Treadwell, *The Rise of the Right: English Nationalism and the Transformation of Working-Class Politics* (Bristol: Policy Press, 2017).

38. Nigel Farage, 'Nigel Farage says Christmas is a Christian festival and we must defend who we are', *Sunday Mirror* (19 December 2015).

39. *Believe in Britain: UKIP Manifesto 2015* (Newton Abbot: UKIP, 2015), p. 31.

40. Cristina Odone, 'Nigel Farage: we must defend Christian heritage', *Telegraph* (1 November 2013).

2 Brexit Means Christmas, Christmas Means Socialism, and a Time for 'Homosexual Sex': Shifting Notions of Religion from the Frontbenches

1. Justin Welby, 'The Archbishop of Canterbury's Christmas Sermon', *Justin Welby, the Archbishop of Canterbury* (25 December 2016), www.archbishopofcanterbury.org/speaking-and-writing/sermons/archbishop-canterburys-christmas-sermon.

2. Mark Connelly, *Christmas: A History* (second edn, London and New York: I.B. Taurus, 2012); Christopher Deacy, *Christmas as Religion: Rethinking Santa, the Secular, and the Sacred* (Oxford: Oxford University Press, 2016); Martin Johnes, *Christmas and the British: A Modern History* (London: Bloomsbury, 2016).

3. Slavoj Žižek, *The Puppet and the Dwarf: The Perverse Core of Christianity* (Cambridge, MA: MIT Press, 2003), pp. 7–8.

4. Theresa May, 'Christmas 2016: Prime Minister's message', *Gov.uk* (25 December 2016), www.gov.uk/government/news/christmas-2016-prime-ministers-message.

5. Michael Stott and Leila Haddou, 'The making of May: her faith and father shaped British PM's core', *Financial Times* (1 October 2016); Eleanor Mills, 'The Interview: Theresa May', *Sunday Times* (27 November 2016); Rob Merrick, 'Theresa May reveals how her faith in God gives her confidence she is "doing the right thing"', *Independent* (27 November 2016).

6. James Crossley, *Harnessing Chaos: The Bible in English Political Discourse since 1968* (revised edn, London: T&T Clark/Bloomsbury, 2016), pp. 278–80.

7. I owe the point on gender to my colleague Chris Meredith.

8. Stott and Haddou, 'The making of May'.

9. David Maddox, 'Theresa May uses first Christmas message as PM to hail new role for Britain after Brexit', *Daily Express* (24 December 2016).

10. 'Oral Answers to Questions', *Hansard* (14 September 2016), Volume 614, Column 897–898, https://hansard.parliament.uk/commons/2016-09-14/debates/AAAAE948-7A3C-42C0-A08E-BA5D314368C2/Prime Minister.

11. Oliver Burkeman, 'The phoney war on Christmas', *Guardian* (8 December 2006); Oliver Burkeman, 'Mulled whine', *Guardian* (12 December 2006).

12. Crossley, *Harnessing Chaos*, pp. 286–7.

13. For example, Paul Nuttall, 'A Christmas message from UKIP Leader Paul Nuttall MEP', UKIP (24 December 2016) www.ukip.org/christmas_message_from_ukip_leader_paul_nuttall.

14. David Cameron, 'Christmas 2015: Prime Minister's message', *Gov.uk* (24 December 2015), www.gov.uk/government/news/christmas-2015-prime-ministers-message.

15. David Cameron, 'Christmas 2014: Prime Minister's message', *Gov.uk* (24 December 2014), www.gov.uk/government/news/christmas-2014-prime-ministers-message.

16. David Cameron, 'Prime Minister's King James Bible Speech', *Gov.uk* (16 December 2010), www.number10.gov.uk/news/king-james-bible/.

17. Slavoj Žižek, 'Multiculturalism, or, the cultural logic of multinational capitalism', *New Left Review* (1997), pp. 28–51.

18. 'Amber Rudd says "don't call me a racist" amid foreign workers row', *BBC News* (5 October 2015), www.bbc.co.uk/news/uk-politics-37561035.

19. 'Oral Answers to Questions', *Hansard* (30 November 2016), Volume 617, Column 1515, https://hansard.parliament.uk/commons/2016-11-30/

debates/9166FE05-E543-4446-9B94-37D3206E9409/OralAnswers
ToQuestions.

20. Crossley, *Harnessing Chaos*, pp. 70–91.

21. Heather Nunn, *Thatcher, Politics and Fantasy: The Political Culture of Gender and Nation* (London: Lawrence and Wishart, 2002), pp. 26–63; Eliza Filby, *God and Mrs Thatcher: The Battle for Britain's Soul* (London: Biteback, 2015), pp. 108–9.

22. Michael Hodges, 'Prime Minister Theresa May reveals what she'll be doing on Christmas Day', *Radio Times* (24 December 2016).

23. Theresa May, 'Easter 2017: Theresa May's message', *Gov.uk* (16 April 2017), www.gov.uk/government/news/easter-2017-theresa-mays-message.

24. 'Theresa May slams "ridiculous" decision not to include Easter in egg hunt title', *ITV News* (4 April 2017), www.itv.com/news/2017-04-04/cadbury-spitting-on-grave-of-religious-founder-by-not-having-easter-in-egg-hunt-title/; Jessica Elgot and Harriet Sherwood, 'Theresa May condemns National Trust for axing "Easter" from egg hunt', *Guardian* (4 April 2017).

25. Kim Sengupta, 'Last message left by Westminster attacker Khalid Masood uncovered by security agencies', *Independent* (27 April 2017).

26. Anthony Wells, 'Attitudes to Brexit: everything we know so far', *YouGov* (29 March 2017), https://yougov.co.uk/news/2017/03/29/attitudes-brexit-everything-we-know-so-far/.

27. *Forward, Together: Our Plan for a Stronger Britain and a Prosperous Future* (The Conservative and Unionist Party Manifesto, 2017), pp. 9, 16.

28. Jeremy Corbyn, 'Jeremy Corbyn's Mirror Christmas message: Christmas is the essence of socialism with solidarity for all', *Sunday Mirror* (19 December 2015).

29. Crossley, *Harnessing Chaos*, pp. 18–32.

30. Corbyn, 'Jeremy Corbyn's Mirror Christmas message'.

31. 'Jeremy Corbyn warns of "shocking rise in homelessness" in first Christmas message', *ITV News* (24 December 2016), www.itv.com/news/2016-12-24/jeremy-corbyn-warns-of-shocking-rise-in-homelessness-in-first-christmas-message/.

32. For example, Tony Benn, *Free Radical: New Century Essays* (New York and London: Continuum, 2003), p. 226.

33. 'Cameron, Miliband and Clegg release Christmas messages', *BBC News* (23 December 2014), www.bbc.co.uk/news/uk-politics-30586541.

34. Christopher Bryant (ed.), *Reclaiming the Ground: Christianity and Socialism* (London: Hodder and Stoughton, 1993). See further Crossley, *Harnessing Chaos*, pp. 26–9.

35. Owen Bennett, 'Cat Smith talks Jeremy Corbyn, Jesus Christ and why socialism isn't "radical"', *Huffington Post* (25 August 2015).

36. Crossley, *Harnessing Chaos*, pp. 267–9.

37. Labour Party, 'Jeremy Corbyn's first speech as Leader of the Labour Party', *YouTube* (12 September 2015), www.youtube.com/watch?v=xmgvhn13WPk#, at 16:00–16:20.

38. Margaret Thatcher and Brian Walden, 'TV Interview for London Weekend Television *Weekend World* (1980)', Margaret Thatcher Foundation, www. margaretthatcher.org/speeches/displaydocument.asp?docid=104210.

39. Crossley, *Harnessing Chaos*, pp. 315–17; James Crossley, 'We don't do Babylon: Erin Runions in English political Discourse', *Bible and Critical Theory* 11 (2015), pp. 61–76 (72–3).

40. Jeremy Corbyn, 'Speech by Jeremy Corbyn to Labour Party Annual Conference 2015', *Labour Press* (29 September 2015), www.policyforum. labour.org.uk/news/speech-by-jeremy-corbyn-to-labour-party-annual-conference-2015.

41. Anushka Asthana, 'Labour group urges party to do more to appeal to the English', *Guardian* (18 July 2017).

42. Tony Benn, *Against the Tide: Diaries 1973–76* (London: Hutchinson, 1989), pp. 50, 54, 568; F.O. Wolf and Tony Benn, *The Levellers and the English Democratic Tradition* (Nottingham: Russell Press, 1976), pp. 23–32, 114, 146; Tony Benn, *Arguments for Socialism* (London: Jonathan Cape, 1979); Tony Benn, *Arguments for Democracy* (London: Jonathan Cape, 1981), pp. 125, 175–6.

43. Daniel Boffey, 'Jeremy Corbyn's world: his friends, supporters, mentors and influences', *Observer* (15 August 2015).

44. Crossley, *Harnessing Chaos*, pp. 252–4.

45. Haydn Wheeler, 'Jeremy Corbyn MP speaking at John Lilburne 400 Conference', *YouTube* (23 July 2015), www.youtube.com/watch?v=75kMY xsAE_A.

46. Christopher Hope, 'Jeremy Corbyn "cancels Christmas" and refuses to issue festive message', *Telegraph* (23 December 2015).

47. 'Paris attacks: who were the attackers?', *BBC News* (27 April 2016), www. bbc.co.uk/news/world-europe-34832512.

48. Mac, 'MAC ON ... Europe's open borders', *Daily Mail* (17 November 2015); Ryan Grenoble, 'This Daily Mail anti-refugee cartoon is straight out of Nazi Germany', *Huffington Post* (17 November 2015).

49. Corbyn, 'Jeremy Corbyn's Mirror Christmas message'.

50. 'ISIL in Syria', *Hansard* (2 December 2015), Volume 603, Columns 484–485, www.publications.parliament.uk/pa/cm201516/cmhansrd/cm151202/ debtext/151202-0005.htm#1512031001687.

51. David Edwards, 'Manufacturing consensus – Hilary Benn's speech', *Media Lens*(8 December 2015),www.medialens.org/index.php/alerts/alert-archive/ 2015/807-manufacturing-consensus.html.

52. David Cameron, 'David Haines: David Cameron statement on killing', *BBC News* (14 September 2014), www.bbc.co.uk/news/uk-29198128.

53. 'ISIL in Syria', *Hansard*, Volume 603, Column 328, www.publications. parliament.uk/pa/cm201516/cmhansrd/cm151202/debtext/151202-0001. htm.

54. James G. Crossley, 'God and the state: the Bible and David Cameron's authority', in James G. Crossley and Jim West (eds), *History, Politics and*

the Bible from the Iron Age to the Media Age: Essays in Honour of Keith W. Whitelam (London: Bloomsbury/T&T Clark, 2017), pp. 146–62.

55. Cameron, 'Christmas 2015'.

56. 'Jeremy Corbyn warns of "shocking rise in homelessness" in first Christmas message'.

57. Lizzie Dearden, 'Jeremy Corbyn antisemitism speech in full: Labour leader vows to stamp out "hateful language or debate"', *Independent* (30 June 2016).

58. Lizzie Dearden, 'These British volunteers fighting against Isis in Syria want you to vote for Jeremy Corbyn', *Indy100* (3 June 2017).

59. Heather Stewart, 'Isis should get round the table with UK, says Owen Smith', *Guardian* (17 August 2016).

60. Tim Farron, 'Tim Farron's Christmas message', *Liberal Democrat Voice* (23 December 2016), www.libdemvoice.org/tim-farrons-christmas-message-2-52795.html.

61. Tim Farron, 'What is Christianity, do I need to take it seriously, and can I be a Liberal Democrat and a Christian?', in Jo Latham and Claire Mathys (eds), *Liberal Democrats Do God* (London: LDCF, 2013), pp. 13-20; Tom Brooks-Pollock, 'Tim Farron on gay sex: new Lib Dem leader declines to say if he considers it's a sin', *Independent* (18 July 2015); Crossley, *Harnessing Chaos*, p. 306.

62. Simon Hattenstone, 'The cult of Jeremy Corbyn, the great silverback mouse', *Guardian* (29 September 2015).

63. Ruth Gledhill, 'Gay sex "is not a sin" says Lib Dem leader Tim Farron, a committed Christian', *Christianity Today* (25 April 2017), www.christiantoday.com/article/gay.sex.is.not.a.sin.says.lib.dem.leader.tim.farron.a.committed.christian/107884.htm.

64. Farron, 'Tim Farron's Christmas message'.

65. New Forest Liberal Democrats, 'Tim Farron's Christmas Message 2015', *YouTube* (22 December 2015),www.youtube.com/watch?v=pAUYeXITU9w; Tim Farron, 'Lib Dem leader Tim Farron says we must focus on togetherness this Christmas', *Sunday Mirror* (19 December 2015).

66. 'Cameron, Miliband and Clegg release Christmas messages'.

67. 'Paddick quits Lib Dem frontbench over Tim Farron's "views"', *BBC News* (14 June 2017), www.bbc.co.uk/news/uk-politics-40277398.

68. 'Farron quits as Lib Dem leader over clash between faith and politics', *BBC News* (14 June 2017), www.bbc.co.uk/news/uk-politics-40281300.

69. Tim Farron, 'Why I had to choose between my Christianity or leading the Lib Dems', *Spectator* (14 June 2017), https://blogs.spectator.co.uk/2017/06/tim-farron-choose-christianity-leading-lib-dems/.

70. Good Morning Britain, 'Sir Vince Cable defends Tim Farron's controversial homosexuality remarks', *YouTube* (19 April 2017), www.youtube.com/watch?v=lH3kgwdJ360.

71. 'MP Jacob Rees-Mogg tells GMB he opposes gay marriage and abortion', *Good Morning Britain* (6 September 2017).

72. Peter Dominiczak, 'Pray consider: would God be a Lib Dem or a Somerset Tory?', *Telegraph* (25 August 2013). See also Madeleine Teahan, 'Jacob

Rees-Mogg: it is becoming more difficult to be both a Christian and an MP', *Catholic Herald* (3 February 2017).

73. Zoe Williams, 'Homophobia is back – it's no accident that nationalism is too', *Guardian* (2 July 2017).

74. Jack Blanchard, 'Coalition of crackpots: Theresa May's desperate deal with terror-linked DUP who oppose abortion and same sex marriage', *Mirror* (9 June 2017).

75. Lucy Pasha-Robinson, 'Tory-DUP deal: why are the Northern Irish unionists so controversial?', *Independent* (26 June 2017).

76. Chris York, 'DUP's record on abortion, creationism and LGBT rights', *Huffington Post* (11 June 2017).

77. For example, Malachi O'Doherty, 'The DUP was in trouble. Now it'll believe God's on its side', *Guardian* (9 June 2017).

78. Michael Hugh Walker, 'There's only one party who could save Theresa May in a hung parliament', *Independent* (31 May 2017).

79. Erasmus, 'The clerical roots of the Democratic Unionist Party', *The Economist* (9 June 2017).

80. Natalie Bennett, 'Christmas message from Green Party leader Natalie Bennett', Green Party (23 December 2014), www.greenparty.org.uk/news/2014/12/23/christmas-message-from-green-party-leader-natalie-bennett/.

3   Muslims, the 'Perversion of Islam', and Christian England on the (Far) Right

1. Gordon Burns and Margaret Thatcher, 'TV interview for Granada World in Action', Margaret Thatcher Foundation (27 January 1978), www.margaretthatcher.org/document/103485.

2. James G. Crossley, *Jesus in an Age of Terror: Projects for a New American Century* (London: Equinox, 2008).

3. The literature on the emergence of the EDL (etc.) is extensive. For a selection see, for example, Jamie Bartlett and Mark Littler, *Inside the EDL: Populist Politics in a Digital Age* (London: Demos, 2011); Matthew Goodwin, *The Roots of Extremism: The EDL and the Counter-Jihad Challenge* (London: Chatham House, 2013); Alexander Meleagrou-Hitchens and Hans Brun, *A Neo-Nationalist Network: The English Defence League and Europe's Counter-Jihad Movement* (London: The International Centre for the Study of Radicalisation and Political Violence, 2013); Daniel Trilling, *Bloody Nasty People: The Rise of Britain's Far Right* (London and New York: Verso, 2013); Alexander Oaten, 'The cult of the victim: an analysis of the collective identity of the English Defence League', *Patterns of Prejudice* 48 (2014), pp. 331–49; George Kassimeris and Leonie Jackson, 'The ideology and discourse of the English Defence League: not racist, not violent, just no longer silent', *British Journal of Politics and International Relations* 17 (2015), pp. 171–88; Joel Busher, *The Making of Anti-Muslim Protest: Grassroots Activism in the English Defence League* (London: Routledge,

2016); Hsiao-Hung Pai, *Angry White People: Coming Face-to-Face with the British Far Right* (London: Zed Books, 2016); Simon Winlow, Steve Hall and James Treadwell, *The Rise of the Right: English Nationalism and the Transformation of Working-Class Politics* (Bristol: Policy Press, 2017).

4. Jamie Cleland, Chris Anderson and Jack Aldridge-Deacon, 'Islamophobia, war and non-Muslims as victims: an analysis of online discourse on an English Defence League message board', *Ethnic and Racial Studies* (2017), pp. 1–17.

5. Ibid., pp. 12–13.

6. For example, James Treadwell and Jon Garland, 'Masculinity, marginalization and violence: a case study of the English Defence League', *British Journal of Criminology* 51 (2011), pp. 621–34; Matthew Taylor, 'English Defence League: new wave of extremists plotting summer of unrest', *Guardian* (28 May 2010); Busher, *Making of Anti-Muslim Protest*, pp. 118, 157–8.

7. Catarina Kinnvall, 'Borders and fear: insecurity, gender, and the far right in Europe', *Journal of Contemporary European Studies* 23 (2015), pp. 514–29 (515).

8. Enoch Powell, 'To the Annual General Meeting of the West Midlands Area Conservative Political Centre (Birmingham, 20 April 1968)', in *Reflections: Selected Writings and Speeches of Enoch Powell* (London: Bellew, 1992), pp. 161–9.

9. See also Winlow, Hall and Treadwell, *Rise of the Right*, p. 191.

10. Ingrid Storm, 'Ethnic nominalism and civic religiosity: Christianity and national identity in Britain', *The Sociological Review* 59 (2011), pp. 828–46; Ingrid Storm, '"Christianity is not just about religion": religious and national identities in a northern English town', *Secularism and Nonreligion* 2 (2013), pp. 21–38. See also Abby Day, *Believing in Belonging: Belief and Social Identity in the Modern World* (Oxford: Oxford University Press, 2011), pp. 50–6, 137–8, 179–88, 194–6; Clive D. Field, 'Christian country and other news', *British Religion in Numbers* (27 April 2014), www.brin.ac.uk/2014/christian-country-and-other-news/.

11. See now Joseph A. Massad, *Islam in Liberalism* (Chicago: University of Chicago Press, 2015). On the significance of this tradition for understanding the far right see, for example, Cleland, Anderson and Aldridge-Deacon, 'Islamophobia, war and non-Muslims as victims', pp. 10–11.

12. Yvonne Sherwood, 'Bush's Bible as a liberal Bible (strange though that might seem)', *Postscripts* 2 (2006), pp. 47–58.

13. Adam Withnall, 'Britain First "Christian Patrols" return to east London in wake of Charlie Hebdo shootings', *Independent* (19 January 2015). Cf. Sindre Bangstad, *Anders Breivik and the Rise of Islamophobia* (London: Zed Books, 2014); Hannah Strømmen, 'Christian terror in Europe? The Bible in Anders Behring Breivik's manifesto', *Journal of the Bible and its Reception* 4 (2017), pp. 147–69.

14. Robert Ford and Matthew Goodwin, *Revolt on the Right: Explaining Support for the Radical Right in Britain* (New York: Routledge, 2014).

15. Paul Baker, Costas Gabrielatos and Tony McEnery, *Discourse Analysis and Media Attitudes: The Representation of Islam in the British Press* (Cambridge: Cambridge University Press, 2013), pp. 1–2.

16. 'Ahmadi Muslims – perceptions of the caliphate', *ComRes* (23 May 2016), www.comresglobal.com/polls/ahmadiyya-perceptions-of-the-caliphate-polling/.

17. Baker, Gabrielatos and McEnery, *Discourse Analysis and Media Attitudes*.

18. Tom Parfitt, 'PC GONE MAD: top MP blasts chocolate firms for dropping "EASTER" from seasonal eggs', *Daily Express* (25 March 2016).

19. Liz Fekete, *A Suitable Enemy: Racism, Migration and Islamophobia in Europe* (London: Pluto Press, 2009), pp. 76–101; Kinnvall, 'Borders and fear', p. 523; Jorunn Økland, 'Death and the maiden: manifestos, gender and self-canonisation', in Yvonne Sherwood (ed.), *The Bible and Feminism: Remapping the Field* (Oxford: Oxford University Press, 2018), pp. 15–44.

20. Andrea S. Dauber, 'The increasing visibility of right-wing extremist women in contemporary Europe: is Great Britain an exception?', in Michaela Köttig, Renate Bitzan and Andrea Petö (eds), *Gender and Far Right Politics in Europe* (London and New York: Palgrave Macmillan, 2017), pp. 49–64 (53). Such figures are supported by related data. See, for example, Busher, *Making of Anti-Muslim Protest*, pp. 15, 17.

21. Bartlett and Littler, *Inside the EDL*, pp. 5, 16.

22. Cf. Meleagrou-Hitchens and Brun, *A Neo-Nationalist Network*, pp. 61–3.

23. Treadwell and Garland, 'Masculinity, marginalization and violence'. Cf. Bartlett and Littler, *Inside the EDL*, pp. 18, 21; Pai, *Angry White People*, pp. 23–4, 61–2.

24. Baker, Gabrielatos and McEnery, *Discourse Analysis and Media Attitudes*, pp. 197–229.

25. Jasbir Puar, *Terrorist Assemblages: Homonationalism in Queer Times* (Durham, NC: Duke University Press, 2007).

26. Alana Lentin and Gavan Titley, *The Crises of Multiculturalism: Racism in a Neoliberal Age* (London and New York: Zed Books, 2011), p. 38.

27. Peter Walker, 'UKIP under fire for choosing candidate who called Islam evil', *Guardian* (27 April 2017).

28. James G. Crossley, *Harnessing Chaos: The Bible in English Political Discourse since 1968* (second edn, London: Bloomsbury/T&T Clark, 2016).

29. 'London Attacks', *Hansard* (23 March 2017), Volume 623, Columns 927, 942, https://hansard.parliament.uk/commons/2017-03-23/debates/AF8D74DF-85B4-4BE6-9515-4E9A57EB2064/LondonAttacks.

30. Sam Jones, Ben Quinn and Conal Urquhart, 'Woolwich attack prompts fears of backlash against British Muslims', *Guardian* (23 May 2013).

31. Haroon Siddique and Sam Jones, 'Attacks on Muslims spike after Woolwich killing', *Guardian* (23 May 2013).

32. Crossley, *Harnessing Chaos*, pp. 293–4.

33. Tony Blair, 'Transcript of statement made by the Prime Minister Tony Blair', *Number 10.gov.uk* (7 July 2005), http://webarchive.nationalarchives.gov.uk/20060715135117/http://number10.gov.uk/page7858.

34. Tony Blair, 'Full text: Blair speech on terror', *BBC News* (16 July 2005), http://news.bbc.co.uk/1/hi/uk/4689363.stm.

35. Crossley, *Harnessing Chaos*, pp. 220–41.

36. David Cameron, 'David Haines: David Cameron statement on killing', *BBC News* (14 September 2014), www.bbc.co.uk/news/uk-29198128; David Cameron, 'Easter reception at Downing Street 2014', *Gov.uk* (9 April 2014), www.gov.uk/government/speeches/easter-reception-at-downing-street-2014.

37. David Cameron, 'Christmas 2015: Prime Minister's message', *Gov.uk* (24 December 2015), www.gov.uk/government/news/christmas-2015-prime-ministers-message.

38. Crossley, *Harnessing Chaos*, p. 295. Cf. David Tyrer, *The Politics of Islamophobia: Race, Power and Fantasy* (eBook, London: Pluto Press, 2013), for example, location 225.

39. Slavoj Žižek, 'Why we all love to hate Haider', *New Left Review* 2 (March–April 2000), pp. 37–45.

40. Arun Kundnani, *The Muslims Are Coming!* (London and New York: Verso, 2014), pp. 1–5.

41. David Cameron, 'Public Disorder', *Hansard* (11 August 2011), Volume 531, Column 1086, www.publications.parliament.uk/pa/cm201011/cmhansrd/cm110811/debtext/110811-0001.htm; Jessica Elgot, 'Tony Blair embroiled in Twitter spat with EDL's Tommy Robinson', *Huffington Post* (6 June 2013); Theresa May, 'English Defence League', *Hansard* (24 January 2011), Volume 522, Column 16, https://hansard.parliament.uk/Commons/2011-01-24/debates/1101248000029/EnglishDefenceLeague; Press Association, 'English Defence League not welcome in Birmingham, say city's political leaders', *Telegraph* (8 April 2017); Richard Littlejohn, 'If Britain votes to remain, we're all toast', *Daily Mail* (1 March 2016).

42. Winlow, Hall and Treadwell, *Rise of the Right*. See also Bartlett and Littler, *Inside the EDL*, p. 18; Treadwell and Garland, 'Masculinity, marginalization and violence'; Trilling, *Bloody Nasty People*, pp. 127–50; Pai, *Angry White People*.

43. For example, David Theo Goldberg, *The Threat of Race: Reflections on Racial Neoliberalism* (Oxford: Wiley-Blackwell, 2009).

44. Blair, 'The ideology behind Lee Rigby's murder'.

45. Kundnani, *The Muslims Are Coming!*, pp. 21–5.

46. See the discussion of 'post-racialism' in Lentin and Titley, *Crises of Multiculturalism*, pp. 67–70. On the nuances of Islamophobia, Muslims, race and racial discourses see, for example, Fekete, *A Suitable Enemy*, pp. 15–74; Tyrer, *Politics of Islamophobia*; Bangstad, *Anders Breivik*, pp. 16–25.

47. Patrick Wintour, 'David Cameron tells Muslim Britain: stop tolerating extremists', *Guardian* (5 February 2011); David Cameron, 'Full transcript: speech on radicalisation and Islamic extremism, Munich', *New Statesman* (5 February 2011); 'Muslim women's segregation in UK communities must end – Cameron', *BBC News* (18 January 2016); Tyrer, *Politics of Islamophobia*, location 1625–1633, 1694.

48. Hazel Blears, Bob Whalley, Tony Lord and Judith Lempriere, 'Examination of Witnesses (Questions 459–479)', *Select Committee on Home Affairs Minutes of Evidence* (1 March 2005), www.publications.parliament.uk/pa/cm200405/cmselect/cmhaff/165/5030102.htm.

49. Glen Owen, 'Tony Blair says murder of Lee Rigby PROVES "there is a problem within Islam"', *Mail on Sunday* (1 June 2013); Blair, 'The ideology behind Lee Rigby's murder'; Elgot, 'Tony Blair embroiled in Twitter spat'.

50. Kundnani, *The Muslims Are Coming!*, pp. 156–65.

51. While it needs updating after the emergence of ISIS, Michael Watts, 'Revolutionary Islam', in Derek Gregory and Allan Pred (eds), *Violent Geographies: Fear, Terror, and Political Violence* (New York and London: Routledge, 2007), pp. 175–203, remains an excellent survey in this respect.

52. Crossley, *Harnessing Chaos*, pp. 292–7.

53. Jones, Quinn and Urquhart, 'Woolwich attack prompts fears of backlash against British Muslims'.

54. Blair, 'Full text: Blair speech on terror'; Crossley, *Jesus in an Age of Terror*, p. 85.

55. I take and modify the phrase 'myth of innocence' from Burton L. Mack, *A Myth of Innocence: Mark and Christian Origins* (Minneapolis: Fortress Press, 1991).

56. Gethin Chamberlain, 'Apple's Chinese workers treated "inhumanely, like machines"', *Observer* (30 April 2011).

4   Brexit Barrow: Religion in Real Time
During a Summer of Political Chaos

1. An earlier version of this chapter was published in *Relegere* 6 (2016), pp. 19–60. I am grateful to Deane Galbraith for permissions.

2. BBC Newsnight, 'Burnley and Brexit: "We've done it!"', *YouTube* (24 June 2016), www.youtube.com/watch?v=Oq3qdX2TGps; Editorial, 'The Guardian view on political credibility: indispensable', *Guardian* (9 May 2017).

3. Graham Ruddick, 'Astute submarines keep Barrow and BAE Systems busy', *Telegraph* (31 August 2011).

4. 'EU Referendum: Local Results (B)', *BBC News*, www.bbc.co.uk/news/politics/eu_referendum/results/local/b; 'Election 2015 Results: Barrow and Furness', *BBC News*, www.bbc.co.uk/news/politics/constituencies/E14000543.

5. Helen Nugent, 'Census shows Barrow-in-Furness suffered steepest decline in population', *Guardian* (16 July 2012).

6. Russell Hotten, '600 more jobs to be axed at VSEL', *Independent* (1 March 1995); Ruddick, 'Astute submarines'; Graham Ruddick, 'BAE Systems wins £328m submarine contract', *Telegraph* (22 May 2012). In 2016, 8,000 or 26.7 per cent worked in manufacturing (compared with 9.9 per cent for the North West and 8.1 per cent for England): 'Labour Market

Profile – Barrow-in-Furness', NOMIS, www.nomisweb.co.uk/reports/lmp/la/1946157076/report.aspx#tabempunemp.

7. 'Labour Market Profile – Barrow-in-Furness'.

8. Kate Jackson, 'Barrow-in-Furness: the working-class capital of Britain', *Mirror* (28 January 2012); Caroline Davies, 'Barrow, capital of blue-collar Britain', *Guardian* (5 October 2008).

9. Murray Wardrop, 'Secret millionaire cash given back over Barrow-in-Furness smear', *Telegraph* (6 May 2009).

10. Chris Green, 'Brits happier than they've been in years, claims ONS', *Independent* (24 September 2014); Shield of Joy, 'Locals, town mayor and Hairy Biker unite in Barrow happy dance', *YouTube* (2 October 2014), www.youtube.com/watch?v=vA2ZcKxMq4M.

11. Sheena Moore, *Why We Voted Leave: Voices from Northern England*, Guerrera Films, https://vimeo.com/172932182; Mike Carter, 'I walked from Liverpool to London. Brexit was no surprise', *Guardian* (27 June 2016).

12. 'KS201EW – Ethnic group (Census 2011)', NOMIS, www.nomisweb.co.uk/census/2011/KS201EW/view/1946157076?cols=measures; 'KS006 – Ethnic group (Census 2001)', NOMIS, www.nomisweb.co.uk/census/2001/KS006/view/1946157076?cols=measures.

13. Paul Mason, 'Three new tribes of voters will dominate this election', *Guardian* (29 March 2015).

14. 'Election 2015 Results'.

15. '2014 Statistics for Mission', Church of England (January 2016), www.churchofengland.org/sites/default/files/2017-10/2016statisticsformission.pdf.

16. 'KS209EW – Religion (Census 2011)', NOMIS, www.nomisweb.co.uk/census/2011/KS209EW/view/1946157076?cols=measures; 'KS007 – Religion (Census 2001)', NOMIS, www.nomisweb.co.uk/census/2001/KS007/view/1946157076?cols=measures.

17. Those identifying as 'No Religion' were 19.8 per cent in the North West and 24.7 per cent in England. 'Religion Not Stated' was 6.4 per cent.

18. Ingrid Storm, 'Ethnic nominalism and civic religiosity: Christianity and national identity in Britain', *The Sociological Review* 59 (2011), pp. 828–46; Ingrid Storm, '"Christian nations"? Ethnic Christianity and anti-immigration attitudes in four Western European countries', *Nordic Journal of Religion and Society* 24 (2011), pp. 75–96; Stephen Bullivant, *Contemporary Catholicism in England and Wales: A Statistical Report Based on Recent British Social Attitudes Survey Data* (Twickenham, London: Benedict XVI Centre for Religion and Society, 2016). Further breakdown of the data for religious identification in England and Wales includes: 19.8 per cent 'Anglican' (20.4 per cent for the North West); 15.7 per cent 'Other Christian' (12.0 per cent for the North West); 8.3 per cent 'Catholic' (15.3 per cent for the North West); and 7.7 per cent 'Non-Christian Religion' (8.2 per cent for the North West).

19. Bullivant, *Contemporary Catholicism*, p. 7; Stephen Bullivant, *The 'No Religion' Population of Britain. Recent Data from the British Social Attitudes*

Survey (Twickenham, London: Benedict XVI Centre for Religion and Society, 2017), p. 7.

20. Bullivant (*Contemporary Catholicism*, pp. 11–13) also notes that 55.8 per cent of cradle Catholics still identified as Catholics by adulthood. However, there are notable regional variations for Catholic retention and in the North West the figure is 62.8 per cent with only the North East higher (64.3 per cent).

21. For example, Storm, 'Ethnic nominalism and civic religiosity'; Storm, '"Christian nations"?'; Abby Day, *Believing in Belonging: Belief and Social Identity in the Modern World* (Oxford: Oxford University Press, 2011), pp. 50–6, 137–8, 179–88, 194–6.

22. Day, *Believing in Belonging*, for example, pp. 29–31, 96–7, 174–9, 194–6.

23. For example, Callum G. Brown, 'The secularisation decade: what the 1960s have done to the study of religious history', in Hugh McLeod and Werner Ustorf (eds), *The Decline of Christendom in Western Europe* (Cambridge: Cambridge University Press, 2003), pp. 29–46; Callum G. Brown, *Religion and Society in Twentieth-Century Britain* (Harlow: Pearson, 2006), pp. 224–77; Callum G. Brown, *The Death of Christian Britain: Understanding Secularisation* (second edn, Abingdon: Routledge, 2009), pp. 175–233; Gerald Parsons, 'How the times they were a-changing: exploring the context of religious transformation in Britain in the 1960s', in John Wolffe (ed.), *Religion in History: Conflict, Conversion and Coexistence* (Manchester: Manchester University Press, 2004), pp. 161–89; David Voas and Alasdair Crockett, 'Religion in Britain: neither believing nor belonging', *Sociology* 39 (2005), pp. 11–28; Hugh McLeod, *The Religious Crisis of the 1960s* (Oxford: Oxford University Press, 2007); Diarmaid MacCulloch, *A History of Christianity: The First Three Thousand Years* (London: Allen Lane, 2009), pp. 985–9; Day, *Believing in Belonging*; Grace Davie, *Religion in Britain: A Persistent Paradox* (second edn, Oxford: Wiley Blackwell, 2015); Ben Clements, *Surveying Christian Beliefs and Religious Debates in Post-War Britain* (Basingstoke: Palgrave Macmillan, 2016); Bullivant, *The 'No Religion' Population of Britain*.

24. Corbyn also appeared to have come across comparatively well in Moore, *Why We Voted Leave: Voices from Northern England*.

25. For what it might be worth, the pro-Corbyn comments were by far those attracting the most 'likes' (occasionally as high as 40–50) whereas those supporting Woodcock rarely got 'likes' at all. It is worth noting that Woodcock's posts rarely attract more than ten comments. One exception was the opening of a new office in Ulverston (26 March 2016) which attracted 193 comments, but the points raised were again of a similar type and pattern as those in response to his video explaining why he voted to ask Corbyn to step down. Even his video on the Referendum result (24 June 2016) attracted more criticism, particularly on the Corbyn issue.

26. For instance, a Facebook post about how the Trident result was the 'proudest day' of his parliamentary life quickly amassed 160 'likes' and 'loves' and mostly positive comments. His announcement of the vote on Facebook got

over 200 'likes' and 'loves' but there were a number of critical comments, as there were with other posts close to the time of Trident, though they mostly appear to have been by people not from Barrow and tied in with national Labour Party battles.

27. Helena Horton, 'Glamour model Teresa May swamped by tweets from people thinking she is the next British Prime Minister', *Telegraph* (12 July 2016).

28. Compare also Ingrid Storm, '"Christianity is not just about religion": religious and national identities in a northern English town', *Secularism and Nonreligion* 2 (2013), pp. 21–38 (29–33).

29. Similar views emerged in Storm, '"Christianity is not just about religion"', pp. 34–5, where there was much more cultural diversity than Barrow.

30. 'Religion, 2011'; 'Religion, 2001'.

31. David Cameron, 'Prime Minister's King James Bible Speech (16 December 2010)', *Gov.uk*, www.gov.uk/government/news/prime-ministers-king-james-bible-speech.

32. Similarly, Storm, 'Ethnic nominalism and civic religiosity'.

33. C. Dade-Robertson, *Furness Abbey: Romance, Scholarship and Culture* (Lancaster: Centre for North-West Regional Studies, 2000).

34. Based on the 83 'likes' for the final post suggested a gender split of about two-thirds female. Age range was less clear.

35. Gill Jepson, 'Keyboard warriors, localisation and people power', *Out of Time* (26 May 2016), http://gilljep-outoftime.blogspot.co.uk/2016/05/keyboard-warriors-localisation-and.html. Jepson also referred to this as an underdog story of 'David and Goliath': Gill Jepson, 'Public consultations and planning – a tale told by an idiot, full of sound and fury, signifying nothing!', *Out of Time* (10 March 2016), http://gilljep-outoftime.blogspot.co.uk/2016/03/public-consultations-and-planning-tale.html.

36. David Crystal, *Begat: The King James Bible and the English Language* (Oxford: Oxford University Press, 2010).

37. R.S. Sugirtharajah, 'Loitering with intent: biblical texts in public places', *Biblical Interpretation* 11 (2003), pp. 567–78 (572–3); James G. Crossley, *Harnessing Chaos: The Bible in English Political Discourse since 1968* (second edn, London: Bloomsbury/T&T Clark, 2016), pp. 254–66.

38. Alastair Campbell, *The Blair Years* (Hutchinson: London, 2007), pp. 111–12; Alastair Campbell, 'Baroness Warsi misses point of "we don't do God", writes a pro faith atheist', *Alastair's Blog* (16 September 2010), www.alastaircampbell.org/blog/2010/09/16/baroness-warsi-misses-point-of-we-dont-do-god-writes-a-pro-faith-atheist/. On polling evidence see Clive D. Field, 'Is the Bible becoming a closed book? British opinion poll evidence', *Journal of Contemporary Religion* 29 (2014), pp. 503–28 (517).

39. Matthew Engelke, *God's Agents: Biblical Publicity in Contemporary England* (Berkeley: University of California Press, 2013), pp. 34–5.

40. Ibid., pp. 91–6.

41. James G. Crossley and Jackie Harrison, 'The mediation of the distinction of "religion" and "politics" by the UK press on the occasion of Pope Benedict XVI's state visit to the UK', *Political Theology* 14 (2015), pp. 329–45.

42. Davie, *Religion in Britain*, pp. 43–4, 52; Bullivant, *The 'No Religion' Population of Britain*, p. 7.

43. Daniel Nilsson DeHanas, *London Youth, Religion, and Politics: Engagement and Activism from Brixton to Brick Lane* (Oxford: Oxford University Press, 2016).

44. Compare, for example, Christian Karner and David Parker, 'Words and deed against exclusion: deprivation, activism and religiosity in inner-city Birmingham', in Mathew Guest and Martha Middlemiss Lé Mon (eds), *Death, Life and Laughter: Essays on Religion in Honour of Douglas Davies* (Abingdon and New York: Routledge, 2017), pp. 67–81.

45. See, for example, Storm, '"Christianity is not just about religion"', p. 27.

46. The significance of simplified ideas and generalised morality (e.g., 'do unto others', a modified version of the Ten Commandments) also comes through in Day, *Believing in Belonging*, pp. 132–3, 136–7, 156–62. On broader trends concerning understandings relating to the Bible see also Clements, *Surveying Christian Beliefs*, pp. 63–72; Clive D. Field, 'Christian country and other news', *British Religion in Numbers* (27 April 2014), www.brin. ac.uk/2014/christian-country-and-other-news/.

47. Crossley, *Harnessing Chaos*, pp. 306–18.

48. 'UK's Nuclear Deterrent', *Hansard* (18 July 2016), Volume 613, Column 559), https://hansard.parliament.uk/Commons/2016-07-18/debates/7B7A196 B-B37C-4787-99DC-098882B3EFA2/UKSNuclearDeterrent.

49. Amy Fenton, '"I'm sorry" – Barrow MP John Woodcock issues grovelling apology and admits he "misjudged" Labour leader Jeremy Corbyn', *Evening Mail* (16 June 2017).

5   *Manufacturing Dissent from the Centre:*
Cults, Corbyn and the Guardian

1. Greg Philo, 'Is Britain's media biased against the left?', *Open Democracy* (12 January 2016), www.opendemocracy.net/uk/greg-philo/is-britains-media-biased-against-left.

2. Edward S. Herman and Noam Chomsky, *Manufacturing Consent: The Political Economy of the Mass Media* (London: Vintage, 1988).

3. David Edwards and David Cromwell, *Guardians of Power: The Myth of the Liberal Media* (London: Pluto Press, 2005); David Edwards and David Cromwell, *Newspeak in the 21st Century* (London: Pluto Press, 2009); David Cromwell, *Why Are We the Good Guys?* (London: Zero Books, 2012).

4. Media Reform Coalition, 'The Media's attack on Corbyn: research shows barrage of negative coverage' (26 November 2015), www.mediareform.org. uk/press-ethics-and-regulation/the-medias-attack-on-corbyn-research-shows-barrage-of-negative-coverage; Des Freedman and Justin Schlosberg,

'Jeremy Corbyn, impartiality and media misrepresentation', *Open Democracy* (29 July 2016), www.opendemocracy.net/uk/des-freedman-justin-schlosberg/jeremy-corbyn-impartiality-and-media-misrepresentation.

5. Freedman and Schlosberg, 'Jeremy Corbyn'.

6. Bart Cammaerts, Brooks DeCillia, João Magalhães and César Jimenez-Martínez, 'When our watchdog becomes a bloodthirsty attackdog, be wary', *Open Democracy* (13 July 2016), www.opendemocracy.net/uk/bart-cammaerts-brooks-decillia-joa-o-magalha-es-and-ce-sar-jimenez-marti-nez/when-our-watchdog-be; Bart Cammaerts, Brooks DeCillia, João Magalhães and César Jimenez-Martínez, 'Journalistic representations of Jeremy Corbyn in the British press: from "watchdog" to "attackdog"', Media@ LSE Report (1 July 2016), www.lse.ac.uk/media-and-communications/research/research-projects/representations-of-jeremy-corbyn.

7. https://docs.google.com/document/d/1LoaTsGMHyxwEj7CErUDc IV2ydnJ9_AkfwLmfxhfHCT4/edit?pli=1.

8. Chris Elliott, 'Analysing the balance of our Jeremy Corbyn coverage', *Guardian* (3 August 2015).

9. 'Whitewash – the Guardian readers' editor responds on Jeremy Corbyn', *Media Lens* (8 August 2015), http://medialens.org/index.php/alerts/alert-archive/2015/798-the-guardian-readers-editor-responds-on-jeremy-corbyn.html.

10. Owen Jones, 'If Jeremy Corbyn wins, prepare for a firestorm', *New Statesman* (5 August 2015). See also Owen Jones, 'How can we have a more balanced debate about Jeremy Corbyn and Labour?', *Guardian* (15 December 2015).

11. Susannah Butter, 'Owen Jones: "I don't enjoy protesting – I do it because the stakes are so high"', *Evening Standard* (3 February 2017).

12. Owen Jones, 'Jeremy Corbyn says he's staying. That's not good enough', *Guardian* (1 March 2017).

13. Editorial, 'The Guardian view on byelections: as much about Labour as Brexit', *Guardian* (24 February 2017).

14. John Harris, 'This Copeland disaster shows just how big Labour's problems are', *Guardian* (24 February 2017).

15. Gaby Hinsliff, Gary Younge, Polly Toynbee and Giles Fraser, 'What next for Labour and Corbyn after the byelections?', *Guardian* (24 February 2017).

16. Jonathan Freedland, 'Copeland shows Corbyn must go. But only Labour's left can remove him', *Guardian* (25 February 2017).

17. Rafael Behr, 'Jeremy Corbyn, you broke it – now you must own it', *Guardian* (24 February 2017).

18. Ken Loach, 'Don't blame Corbyn for the sins of Blair, Brown and New Labour', *Guardian* (28 February 2017).

19. Gaby Hinsliff, 'Is Labour fighting "shocking" media bias or does it need to get its act together?', *Guardian* (20 May 2017).

20. Peter Preston, 'When it comes to Corbyn, does the media matter?', *Guardian* (21 May 2017).

21. Owen Jones, 'Questions all Jeremy Corbyn supporters need to answer', *Medium* (31 July 2016), https://medium.com/@OwenJones84/questions-all-jeremy-corbyn-supporters-need-to-answer-b3e82ace7ed3; Jones, 'Jeremy Corbyn says he's staying'; Owen Jones, 'Jeremy Corbyn must make a decision about his future as Labour leader', *YouTube* (1 March 2017), www.youtube.com/watch?v=lGhOTihjHlk&index=1&t=25s&list=PLTYmWuFco1_1xDo6DoYoBRnOX8mwBvoVb. Such individualised responses come through on the Twitter debates, 2–3 March 2017 (@owenjones84).

22. David Graeber, 'The elites hate Momentum and the Corbynites – and I'll tell you why', *Guardian* (5 July 2016).

23. Will Stone, 'Guardian edits out criticism from director Loach', *Morning Star* (29 December 2016).

24. Rhiannon Lucy Cosslett, 'I used to be a shy Corbynite but I'm over that now', *Guardian* (1 June 2017).

25. Owen Jones, 'Jeremy Corbyn has caused a sensation – he would make a fine prime minister', *Guardian* (9 June 2017).

26. Chris Elliott, 'In politics the meaning of "moderniser" is hard to pin down', *Guardian* (19 October 2015).

27. Andrew Marr, 'Interview with Noam Chomsky', *The Big Idea* (BBC2, 14 February 1996), available at www.youtube.com/watch?v=GjENnyQupow.

28. Edwards and Cromwell, *Guardians of Power*, pp. 5, 7.

29. Nunns, *The Candidate*, location 4219–4237.

30. Ibid., location 4451–4459.

31. Elliott, 'Analysing the balance of our Jeremy Corbyn coverage'.

32. Polly Toynbee, 'Free to dream, I'd be left of Jeremy Corbyn. But we can't gamble the future on him', *Guardian* (4 August 2015).

33. Slavoj Žižek, *The Sublime Object of Ideology* (London and New York: Verso, 1989), p. 29.

34. Tom Baldwin, 'Labour is trapped in the past – as is Corbyn. Can the party learn how to win again?', *Guardian* (24 September 2016).

35. Polly Toynbee, 'In Labour's leadership race, Yvette Cooper is the one to beat', *Guardian* (23 June 2015).

36. Frances Perraudin, 'Jeremy Corbyn suggests he would bring back Labour's nationalising clause IV', *Observer* (9 August 2015).

37. Quoted in Nigel Morris, 'Labour leadership race: rivals turn on Jeremy Corbyn in row over Clause IV', *Independent* (9 August 2015).

38. Cosslett, 'I used to be a shy Corbynite'.

39. Gary Younge, 'We were told Corbyn was "unelectable". His fightback shows he's anything but', *Guardian* (6 June 2017).

40. Polly Toynbee, 'Never mind who leaked it, this Labour manifesto is a cornucopia of delights', *Guardian* (11 May 2017).

41. 'The Guardian view on the election: it's Labour', *Guardian* (2 June 2017).

42. Jonathan Freedland, 'No more excuses: Jeremy Corbyn is to blame for this meltdown', *Guardian* (5 May 2017).

43. James Crossley and Jackie Harrison, 'The mediation of the distinction of "religion" and "politics" by the UK press on the occasion of Pope Benedict XVI's state visit to the UK', *Political Theology* 14 (2015), pp. 329–45; James Crossley and Jackie Harrison, 'Atheism, Christianity and the press: press coverage of Pope Benedict XVI's 2010 state visit to the UK', *Implicit Religion* 18 (2015), pp. 77–105.

44. James G. Crossley, *Harnessing Chaos: The Bible in English Political Discourse since 1968* (updated edn, London: Bloomsbury, 2016), pp. 297–305.

45. Giles Fraser, 'Corbyn is an atheist – but his ideas are true to the Bible', *Guardian* (29 September 2016).

46. Suzanne Moore, 'Where's the socialism that involves sharing life's joys?', *Guardian* (12 August 2015).

47. Polly Toynbee, 'Labour people are optimists, but this time I see no hope', *Guardian* (22 December 2015).

48. Peter Mandelson, 'Labour is a broad church – Jeremy Corbyn is turning it into a narrow sect bound for the abyss', *Guardian* (31 December 2015); Frances Perraudin, 'Labour risks turning into a sect, says Tristram Hunt', *Guardian* (2 November 2015).

49. Perraudin, 'Labour risks turning into a sect'.

50. Michael White, 'Jeremy Corbyn: is the world ready for his sandals and socks?', *Guardian* (30 July 2015).

51. Jonathan Jones, 'We cannot celebrate revolutionary Russian art – it is brutal propaganda', *Guardian* (1 February 2017).

52. Martin Kettle, 'How did my communist family get it so wrong? Because politics was their religion', *Guardian* (22 January 2016), with reference to David Aaronovitch, *Party Animals: My Family and Other Communists* (London: Jonathan Cape, 2016).

53. Anne Perkins, 'Labour Party members, please think before you vote for Jeremy Corbyn', *Guardian* (22 July 2015).

54. Alex Hacillo, Isabel Hardman, Kerry-Anne Mendoza, Tom Holland, Eliza Filby, Neil Kinnock, Dreda Say Mitchell, and Sue and Jennie, 'After Jeremy Corbyn's victory, what should Labour do now?', *Observer* (25 September 2016).

55. Freedland, 'Copeland shows Corbyn must go'.

56. Polly Toynbee, 'Why can't I get behind Corbyn, when we want the same things? Here's why', *Guardian* (27 September 2016).

57. Behr, 'Jeremy Corbyn, you broke it'.

58. Suzanne Moore, 'The bloodletting over Jeremy Corbyn is sad – the left is stuck in old binaries', *Guardian* (29 June 2016).

59. Hadley Freeman, 'From Labour's hard left to Donald Trump, it's been the summer of the personality cult', *Guardian* (30 July 2016).

60. Simon Hattenstone, 'The cult of Jeremy Corbyn, the great silverback mouse', *Guardian* (29 September 2015).

61. Butter, 'Owen Jones'.

62. Frances Perraudin, 'Jeremy Corbyn told Labour "a broad church, not a religious cult"', *Observer* (3 January 2016).

63. Rowena Mason, 'Gordon Brown to speak on Labour leadership as poll gives boost to Corbyn', *Guardian* (14 August 2015). For discussion of Woodcock on 'cults' see Crossley, *Harnessing Chaos*, pp. 308–11.

64. John Woodcock, 'Cult logic', *Progress* (14 August 2015), www.progressonline.org.uk/2015/08/14/we-are-the-true-guardians-of-the-spirit-of-1945/.

65. Tony Blair, *A Journey* (London: Hutchinson, 2010), pp. 89, 641.

66. Alberto Toscano, *Fanaticism: On the Uses of an Idea* (London and New York: Verso, 2010).

67. Patrick Wintour and Nicholas Watt, 'The Corbyn earthquake – how Labour was shaken to its foundations', *Guardian* (25 September 2015).

68. George Monbiot, 'The model for a leftwing resurgence? Evangelical Christianity', *Guardian* (15 September 2015).

69. Toynbee, 'Never mind who leaked it'.

70. Younge, 'We were told Corbyn was "unelectable"'.

71. Jones, 'Jeremy Corbyn has caused a sensation'.

72. Jonathan Freedland, 'Jeremy Corbyn didn't win – but he has rewritten all the rules', *Guardian* (10 June 2017).

73. John Harris, 'Britain is more divided than ever. Now Labour has a chance to unify it', *Guardian* (10 June 2017).

74. Cf. Philo, 'Is Britain's media biased against the left?'

6   Red Apocalypticism on the Corbynite Left: Martyrdom, Rojava and the Bob Crow Brigade

1. Robert Booth and Alex Hern, 'Labour won social media election, digital strategists say', *Guardian* (9 June 2017); 'Jeremy Corbyn: how Momentum HQ perfected social media outreach', *BBC News* (12 June 2017), www.bbc.co.uk/news/av/election-2017-40255298/jeremy-corbyn-how-momentum-hq-perfected-social-media-outreach. Cf. Richard Seymour, *Corbyn: The Strange Rebirth of Radical Politics* (London: Verso, 2016), pp. 18, 22–3.

2. For more detail on Rojava see, for example, Zaher Baher, *The Experiment of West Kurdistan: Feminism, Antisectarianism and Collectivism in the Syrian Revolution* (Huddersfield: Active Distribution, 2014); Eva Savelsberg, 'The Syrian-Kurdish movements: obstacles rather than driving forces for democratization', in David Romano and Mehmet Gurses (eds), *Conflict, Democratization, and the Kurds in the Middle East: Turkey, Iran, and Syria* (New York: Palgrave Macmillan, 2014), pp. 85–107; Michael Knapp, Anja Flach and Ercan Ayboga, *Revolution in Rojava: Democratic Autonomy and Women's Liberation in Syrian Kurdistan* (trans. Janet Biehl, London: Pluto Press, 2016); Meredith Tax, *A Road Unforeseen: Women Fight the Islamic State* (Kindle edn, New York: Bellevue Literary Press, 2016); Robin Yassin-Kassab and Leila al-Shami, *Burning Country: Syrians in Revolution and War* (London: Pluto Press, 2016), pp. 73–6, 88–9. Note too, Oso Sabio, *Rojava: An Alternative to Imperialism, Nationalism and Islamism in the Middle East* (Raleigh, NC: Lulu, 2015), for which a full-size version (which I reference)

is available at https://ososabiouk.files.wordpress.com/2015/04/rojava-an-alternative-to-imperialism-nationalism-and-islamism-full-size.pdf.

3. Gerardo Quercia and Laura Soldini, '"Se sputiamo tutti insieme, annegheremo quei bastardi": Bob Crow in Rojava', *Contropiano* (24 November 2016).

4. See, for example, Jodi Dean, *Crowds and Party* (London and New York: Verso, 2016), pp. 15–18. Cf. Paul Mason, *Why It's Kicking Off Everywhere: The New Global Revolutions* (London: Verso, 2011).

5. Norma Costello, 'Meet the Bob Crow Brigade: young British socialists fighting ISIS and patriarchy with the Kurds', *Vice* (14 October 2016).

6. Quercia and Soldini, '"Se sputiamo tutti insieme, annegheremo quei bastardy"'.

7. Kevin Hoffmann, 'Interview with the Bob Crow Brigade in Rojava', *Kevin Hoffmann* (1 November 2016), http://kevinhoffmann.blogsport.eu/2016/11/01/interview-with-the-bob-crow-brigade-in-rojava/.

8. Costello, 'Meet the Bob Crow Brigade'.

9. Quercia and Soldini, '"Se sputiamo tutti insieme, annegheremo quei bastardy"'.

10. Ibid. Cf. Costello, 'Meet the Bob Crow Brigade'.

11. Hoffmann, 'Interview with the Bob Crow Brigade in Rojava'.

12. Beth Pullman, 'Rojava International Brigaders honour the legendary Bob Crow', *Morning Star* (16 August 2016).

13. Costello, 'Meet the Bob Crow Brigade'.

14. Ibid.; Hoffmann, 'Interview with the Bob Crow Brigade in Rojava'. See also the interview with an IFB member in 'Weaponizing solidarity: an interview with the IFB', *subMedia.tv* (September 2016), https://sub.media/video/weaponizing-solidarity-an-interview-with-the-ifb/.

15. Hoffmann, 'Interview with the Bob Crow Brigade in Rojava'.

16. See, for example, Oliver Morgan, 'Arriving now, Comrade Bob', *Observer* (17 February 2002); Kevin Maguire, 'The Guardian profile: Bob Crow', *Guardian* (2 July 2004); BBC, 'Bob Crow: workers' friend?'. *BBC News* (5 September 2007), http://news.bbc.co.uk/1/hi/business/3850251.stm; Simon Hattenstone, 'If anybody says it is nice to be hated, they're lying', *Guardian* (20 June 2009); Bob Crow, 'Bob Crow: you ask the questions', *Independent on Sunday* (28 June 2009); Jim Pickard, 'Lunch with the FT: Bob Crow', *Financial Times* (25 March 2011); Agency, 'Bob Crow obituary: a working class hero who never shirked from industrial action', *Independent* (11 March 2014); Anonymous, 'Bob Crow – obituary', *Telegraph* (11 March 2014); George Eaton, 'What Bob Crow knew: better pay can't be won without a fight', *New Statesman* (11 March 2014); Matthew Holehouse and Padraic Flanagan, 'Bob Crow, leader of the RMT, dies', *Telegraph* (11 March 2014); Jon Kelly, 'Bob Crow: the union leader everyone had heard of', *BBC News Magazine* (11 March 2014), www.bbc.co.uk/news/magazine-26529781; Andy McSmith, 'Bob Crow: polarising but respected trade union leader who dedicated his career to improving pay and conditions for rail workers', *Independent* (11 March 2014); Carole Malone, 'Bob Crow:

bolshy, argumentative and unapologetic but a man you would want to fight your corner', *Mirror* (9 February 2015); Rob Williams, 'Bob Crow death: "Admired by his members, feared by employers" – tributes pour in for RMT union leader and "working class hero" Bob Crow', *Independent* (11 March 2014); Christian Wolmar, 'Bob Crow obituary', *Guardian* (11 March 2014); Katrin Bennhold, 'Bob Crow, firebrand at helm of British union, dies at 52', *New York Times* (13 March 2014); Anonymous, 'Bob Crow: the last walkout', *The Economist* (15 March 2014); Gregor Gall, *Bob Crow: Socialist, Leader, Fighter* (Manchester: Manchester University Press, 2017), pp. 122–3, 125–6, 146–80.

17. Hoffmann, 'Interview with the Bob Crow Brigade in Rojava'. See also Quercia and Soldini, '"Se sputiamo tutti insieme, annegheremo quei bastardy"'.

18. Hoffmann, 'Interview with the Bob Crow Brigade in Rojava'.

19. James Crossley, *Harnessing Chaos: The Bible in English Political Discourse since 1968* (second edn, London: T&T Clark/Bloomsbury, 2016), pp. 37–69, 140–52; James Crossley, 'George Orwell's Bible' (forthcoming).

20. George Orwell, 'What is socialism? (31 January 1946)', *The Complete Works of George Orwell: Vol. XVIII* (ed. Peter Davidson, London: Secker & Warburg, 2001), 2876, pp. 60–3; George Orwell, 'Introduction to *British Pamphleteers*, Volume I, edited by George Orwell and Reginald Reynolds (15 November 1948)', in *The Complete Works of George Orwell: Vol. XIX* (ed. Peter Davidson, London: Secker & Warburg, 1998), 3206, pp. 106–15 (108–9, 114); Sheila Rowbotham, *Women, Resistance and Revolution* (London: Penguin, 1972), pp. 15–34; Tony Benn, *The Levellers and the English Democratic Tradition* (Nottingham: Russell Press, 1976); Tony Benn, *Arguments for Socialism* (London: Jonathan Cape, 1979); Lindsey German and John Rees, *A People's History of London* (London: Verso, 2012); Owen Jones, 'Magna Carta: a striking example of useful myths', *New Statesman* (5 June 2015); Jason Cowley, 'Jeremy Corbyn: "I think we have to think in terms of the disillusioned who didn't vote"', *New Statesman* (29 July 2015); Ian Brooke, *England's Forgotten Revolution: 1641–1663* (Huddersfield: Rearguard Action, no date given).

21. Pullman, 'Rojava International Brigaders'; Beth Pullman, 'Owen Smith in bizarre row with anti-Isis fighters', *Morning Star* (27 August 2016); Robert Verkaik, 'Even the British fighters in Syria are on strike! Volunteers rename themselves the Bob Crow Brigade and break off from combating ISIS to support RMT union walkout', *Daily Mail* (26 August 2016); Lizzie Dearden, 'Syrian war: British volunteers in socialist "Bob Crow Brigade" prepared to die fighting Isis', *Independent* (16 September 2016); Hannah Lucinda Smith, 'Bob Crow Brigade go all-out for a strike ... on Isis', *The Times* (6 September 2016).

22. Joe Watts, 'Owen Smith says Isis should be "brought around the table" for Syria peace talks', *Independent* (17 August 2016).

23. Terry Eagleton, *Reason, Faith, and Revolution: Reflections on the God Debate* (New Haven and London: Yale University Press, 2009).

24. Meredith Tax, *Double Bind: The Muslim Right, the Anglo-American Left, and Universal Human Rights* (New York: Center for Secular Space, 2013); Tax, *A Road Unforeseen*.

25. Tax, *A Road Unforeseen*, location 485.

26. Lizzie Dearden, 'These British volunteers fighting against Isis in Syria want you to vote for Jeremy Corbyn', *Indy100* (3 June 2017).

27. Hoffmann, 'Interview with the Bob Crow Brigade in Rojava'.

28. Roland Boer, *Lenin, Religion, and Theology* (New York: Palgrave Macmillan, 2013), pp. 135–74. Some of these suggestions may be qualified, as Boer does. Žižek, for instance, can make arguments about Leninist organisation and institutionalisation. See, for example, Slavoj Žižek, *The Puppet and the Dwarf: The Perverse Core of Christianity* (Cambridge, MA: MIT Press, 2003), p. 9; Jodi Dean, *Žižek's Politics* (New York and Routledge: London, 2006), pp. 179–203. Cf. Žižek, *Violence: Six Sideways Reflections* (London: Profile Books, 2009), example, pp. 6–8, 213–17.

29. Christopher Hill, *The World Turned Upside Down: Radical Ideas during the English Revolution* (London: Penguin, 1972), p. 14.

30. Ibid., p. 129.

31. For example, Noam Chomsky, *Understanding Power* (ed. Peter R. Mitchell and John Schoeffel, New York: New Press, 2002), p. 238.

32. Ibid., p. 223. Cf. Noam Chomsky, *American Power and the New Mandarins* (New York: Pantheon Books, 1969), pp. 76–7.

33. Boer, *Lenin*, p. 157.

34. For example, Jodi Dean, *The Communist Horizon* (London and New York: Verso, 2012); Dean, *Crowds and Party*. She also discusses Žižek and miracle in *Žižek's Politics*, pp. 180–1.

35. For example, Costello, 'Meet the Bob Crow Brigade'.

36. Hoffmann, 'Interview with the Bob Crow Brigade in Rojava'.

37. For example, Alain Badiou, *Being and Event* (trans. Oliver Feltham, London: Continuum, 1988, reprinted in 2005), pp. 173–83, 201–11, 218–19, 232–9; Alain Badiou, *Saint Paul: The Foundation of Universalism* (trans. Ray Brassier, Stanford: Stanford University Press, 1997, reprinted in 2003); Žižek, *The Puppet and the Dwarf*; Slavoj Žižek, *Event* (London: Penguin, 2014).

38. Mark Fisher, *Capitalist Realism: Is There No Alternative?* (Winchester, UK, and Washington, DC: Zero Books, 2009).

39. For discussion see, for example, Wendy Brown, 'Resisting left melancholy', *boundary 2* 26 (1999), pp. 19–27; Jonathan Dean, 'Radicalism restored? Communism and the end of left melancholia', *Contemporary Political Theory* 14 (2015), pp. 234–55; Enzo Traverso, *Left-Wing Melancholia: Marxism, History, and Memory* (New York: Columbia University Press, 2017).

40. Mark Fisher, *Ghosts of My Life: Writings on Depression, Hauntology, and Lost Futures* (Winchester, UK, and Washington, DC: Zero Books, 2014), pp. 13–23.

41. Fredric Jameson, *Archaeologies of the Future: The Desire Called Utopia and Other Science Fictions* (Verso: London, 2005); Fredric Jameson, *An American*

Utopia: Dual Power and the Universal Army (ed. Slavoj Žižek, London: Verso, 2016).

42. Jodi Dean, 'Dual power redux', in Fredric Jameson, *An American Utopia: Dual Power and the Universal Army* (ed. Slavoj Žižek, London: Verso, 2016), pp. 105–32.

43. Francis Beckett, *Enemy Within: The Rise and Fall of the British Communist Party* (London, 1995), pp. 124–228; Evan Smith and Matthew Worley, 'The far left in Britain from 1956', in Evan Smith and Matthew Worley (eds), *Against the Grain: The British Far Left from 1956* (Manchester: Manchester University Press, 2014), pp. 1–22.

44. Eric Hobsbawm, *Interesting Times: A Twentieth Century Life* (London: Abacus, 2002), pp. 195, 217–18. See further Eric Hobsbawm with Antonio Polito, *The New Century* (London: Abacus, 2000), pp. 158–62.

45. Slavoj Žižek, *First as Tragedy, Then as Farce* (London and New York: Verso, 2009), p. 88.

46. Buenaventura Durruti and Pierre van Passen, 'Durruti's interview with Pierre van Paasen', *libcom* (5 August 2016), https://libcom.org/history/buenaventura-durruti-interview-pierre-van-paasen.

47. Hoffmann, 'Interview with the Bob Crow Brigade in Rojava'.

48. Banu Bargu, *Starve and Immolate: The Politics of Human Weapons* (New York: Columbia University Press, 2014), p. 258.

49. Cf. Talal Asad, *On Suicide Bombing* (New York: Columbia University Press, 2007), pp. 58–63, 88–9.

50. Raya Dunayevskaya, 'Che Guevara, revolutionary', *News & Letters* (November 1967), reprinted as 'The double tragedy of Che Guevara', *News & Letters* (December 1997), p. 4.

51. His friend David Roddy talked of 'his Christian beliefs' while the memorial on the Facebook page of the Democratic Socialists of America, Sacramento, added that he was 'motivated by his Christian ethics'. See Dana M. Nichols, 'Mother Lode native Michael Israel killed fighting in Syria', *Calaveras Enterprise* (1 December 2016), www.calaverasenterprise.com/news/article_6354972a-b7f5-11e6-b24f-5f61f4e3138a.html.

52. Bargu, *Starve and Immolate*, pp. 223–70.

53. David Bol, 'Bob Crow dies: Tolpuddle Martyrs Festival pays tribute to RMT union leader', *Blackmore Vale Magazine* (11 March 2014); Luke James, 'Trade unionists remember Crow and Benn at packed Tolpuddle', *Morning Star* (21 July 2014).

54. Hattenstone, 'If anybody says it is nice to be hated'.

55. Hoffmann, 'Interview with the Bob Crow Brigade in Rojava'.

56. Ibid.

57. Fredric Jameson, 'Future city', *New Left Review* 21 (May–June 2003), pp. 65–79 (76); Jameson, *An American Utopia*, p. 2; *Žižek!* (dir. Astra Taylor, 2007).

58. Fisher, *Capitalist Realism*. The reference to Žižek and Jameson is on p. 2.

59. Mark Fisher, 'Exiting the Vampire Castle', *The North Star* (22 November 2013), www.thenorthstar.info/?p=11299.

60. See, for example, Žižek, *Violence*.
61. Douglas J. Davies, *Death, Ritual and Belief* (second edn, London: Continuum, 2002), p. 1.
62. Hoffmann, 'Interview with the Bob Crow Brigade in Rojava'.
63. Davies, *Death, Ritual and Belief*, p. 10.
64. Ibid., pp. 16–17. Cf. Zygmunt Bauman, *Mortality, Immortality, and Other Life Strategies* (London: Polity Press, 1992).
65. James G. Crossley, '"Death, sometimes, has its price': how Douglas Davies and Sergio Leone cope with capitalism and change', in Mathew Guest and Martha Middlemiss Lé Mon (eds), *Death, Life and Laughter: Essays on Religion in Honour of Douglas Davies* (Abingdon and New York: Routledge, 2017), pp. 35–50. See also James G. Crossley, 'Once upon a time this West was full of radicals: Sergio Leone, revolution and religion', *Culture Matters* (19 June 2016), www.culturematters.org.uk/culture/item/2330-once-upon-a-time-this-west-was-full-of-radicals-sergio-leone-revolution-and-religion.html.
66. Bargu, *Starve and Immolate*, pp. 234–5, 239–40.
67. Hoffmann, 'Interview with the Bob Crow Brigade in Rojava'.
68. Knapp, Flach and Ayboga, *Revolution in Rojava*, pp. 128–9. Cf. Sabio, *Rojava*, pp. 462, 466, 674.
69. Hoffmann, 'Interview with the Bob Crow Brigade in Rojava'. Note also the commemoration of immortal martyrs in the subMedia interview, 'Weaponizing solidarity'.
70. Bargu, *Starve and Immolate*, pp. 240–1.
71. Knapp, Flach and Ayboga, *Revolution in Rojava*, pp. 61–83. Sabio, *Rojava*, pp. 418–21, 503–4, 516, 550.
72. Pullman, 'Rojava International Brigaders'.
73. Costello, 'Meet the Bob Crow Brigade'.
74. Max Bedacht, *In Memoriam. To Our Comrades Karl Liebknecht, 1871–1919, Rosa Luxemburg, 1871–1919: Martyrs to the German Revolution* (San Francisco: Socialist Party of San Francisco, 1919).
75. Ragihandina YPG, 'YPJ: women's defence units (women's protection units) English/Kurdi', *YouTube* (25 September 2016), www.youtube.com/watch?v=_OWQ-apZC78.
76. The literature on women and political violence is vast. For a snippet see, for example, Brigitte L. Nacos, 'The portrayal of female terrorists in the media: similar framing patterns in the news coverage of women in politics and in terrorism', *Studies in Conflict and Terrorism* 28 (2005), pp. 435–51; Rosemarie Skaine, *Female Suicide Bombers* (Jefferson, NC: McFarland, 2006); Mia Bloom, 'Female suicide bombers: a global trend', *Daedalus* 136 (2007), pp. 94–102; Laura Sjoberg and Caron E. Gentry, *Mothers, Monsters, Whores: Women's Violence in Global Politics* (London: Zed Books, 2007); Paige Whaley Eager, *From Freedom Fighters to Terrorists: Women and Political Violence* (London and New York: Routledge, 2008); Mia Bloom, 'Bombshells: women and terror', *Gender Issues* 28 (2011), pp. 1–21; V.G. Julie Rajan, *Women Suicide Bombers: Narratives of Violence* (New York: Routledge,

2011); Philip Seib and Dana M. Janbek, *Global Terrorism and New Media: The Post-Al Qaeda Generation* (London and New York: Routledge, 2011), pp. 75–88; Caitlin Ryan, *Bodies, Power and Resistance in the Middle East: Experiences of the Subjectification in the Occupied Palestinian Territories* (London and New York: Routledge, 2016).

77. See, for example, Damien Gayle and Simon Tomlinson, 'The shame of white widow's father who fought terrorism as British soldier in Northern Ireland and whose daughter has become world's most reviled terrorist', *Daily Mail* (25 September 2013); Tom Parry, 'White widow Samantha Lewthwaite's family torn apart by shame of terrorist link to Nairobi attack', *Mirror* (25 September 2013); Zoe Williams, 'The radicalisation of Samantha Lewthwaite, the Aylesbury schoolgirl who became the "white widow"', *Guardian* (27 June 2014); Oliver Wheaton, 'Wanted terrorist The White Widow is "spotted in north east England hotel"', *Metro* (4 January 2016); Julian Robinson, 'British white widow terror fugitive Samantha Lewthwaite "mentored all-female team of jihadists" who attacked Kenyan police station', *Mail Online* (15 September 2016).

78. Hoffmann, 'Interview with the Bob Crow Brigade in Rojava'.

79. Nancy Fraser, *Fortunes of Feminism: From State-Managed Capitalism to Neoliberal Crisis* (London: Verso, 2013); Nancy Fraser, 'How feminism became capitalism's handmaiden – and how to reclaim it', *Guardian* (14 October 2013); Jodi Dean, 'Not us, me', Verso Blog (26 November 2016), www.versobooks.com/blogs/2970-not-us-me; Angela Nagle, *Kill All Normies: Online Culture Wars from 4chan and Tumblr to Trump and the Alt-Right* (Alresford: Zero Books, 2017). See also Jen Izaakson's review of the launch of Nagle's book at the Marx Memorial Library promoted by Red London, 'Kill all normies: street fights of Tumblr liberals and the alt-right', *Morning Star* (1 July 2017).

80. Rory Stewart et al, 'The Situation in Iraq and Syria and the Response to al-Dawla al-Islamiya fi al-Iraq al-Sham (DAESH)', *House of Commons Defence Committee: Seventh Report of Session 2014–15* (27 January 2015), www.publications.parliament.uk/pa/cm201415/cmselect/cmdfence/690/690.pdf; Kurdish Question, 'Victory in Kobane: what next in the Rojava revolution? Part 2', *YouTube* (1 March 2015), www.youtube.com/watch?v=J4PVYxa28eE.

81. Anti War, 'On David Graeber: "victory in Kobane. What next in the Rojava revolution?"', *libcom* (5 March 2015), https://libcom.org/library/david-graeber-'victory-kobane-what-next-rojava-revolution'.

Epilogue

1. 'Amber Rudd says "don't call me a racist" amid foreign workers row', *BBC News* (5 October 2015), www.bbc.co.uk/news/uk-politics-37561035.

2. Theresa May, 'Prime Minister Theresa May's Christmas message 2017', *Gov.uk* (24 December 2017), www.gov.uk/government/news/prime-minister-theresa-mays-christmas-message-2017.

3. Vince Cable, 'Christmas Message 2017', Liberal Democrats (20 December 2017), www.libdems.org.uk/cable-christmas-2017.

4. James G. Crossley, *Harnessing Chaos: The Bible in English Political Discourse since 1968* (London: Bloomsbury/T&T Clark, 2014; updated edn, 2016), pp. 217–39.

5. Jeremy Corbyn, 'Think of the lonely and vulnerable this Christmas', *ITV News* (24 December 2017), www.itv.com/news/2017-12-24/jeremy-corbyn-think-of-the-lonely-and-vulnerable-this-christmas/.

Index